Nourishment for
the Spiritual Pilgrimage

Nourishment for the Spiritual Pilgrimage

Daily Devotions for Christian Disciples

VERNON T. JONES

RESOURCE *Publications* • Eugene, Oregon

NOURISHMENT FOR THE SPIRITUAL PILGRIMAGE
Daily Devotions for Christian Disciples

Copyright © 2017 Vernon T. Jones. All rights reserved. Except for brief quotations in critical publications or reviews, no part of this book may be reproduced in any manner without prior written permission from the publisher. Write: Permissions, Wipf and Stock Publishers, 199 W. 8th Ave., Suite 3, Eugene, OR 97401.

Resource Publications
An Imprint of Wipf and Stock Publishers
199 W. 8th Ave., Suite 3
Eugene, OR 97401

www.wipfandstock.com

PAPERBACK ISBN: 978-1-4982-3709-3
HARDCOVER ISBN: 978-1-4982-3711-6
EBOOK ISBN: 978-1-4982-3710-9

Manufactured in the U.S.A.   FEBRUARY 13, 2017

The Scripture quotations contained herein are from the New Revised Standard Version Bible, copyright © 1989 by the Division of Christian Education of the National Council of the Churches of Christ in the U.S.A. Used by permission. All Rights reserved.

This devotional book is dedicated to those who have helped, loved, encouraged, and supported me over the years. Their essence is still with me and an important part of whom I am today. Directly or indirectly you will read about how they helped shape my life and aided me on my pilgrimage. It is also for those who are now walking with me following the example left by Jesus Christ, and they are both close by and throughout the world.

This book is also for all of the former and current spiritual guides that have given all of us much upon which to meditate and ponder by how they daily walked and by what they had to say or by what was said about them. It is for those guides who will continue offering examples and writings for Christian disciples to follow.

In the morning, while it was still very dark, he got up and went out to a deserted place, and there he prayed.

—Mark 1:35

Contents

Acknowledgments | xvii
Introduction | xix

JANUARY

Striving for the Kingdom of God—
Repenting / Turning Around / Conversion | 1

1	The New Year	1
2	Striving First for God's Kingdom	2
3	Repenting	2
4	Turning Around	3
5	Good News	4
6	What if We Resolved to Be Like the Shepherds and the Magi?	4
7	Setting One's Mind on the Spirit	5
8	Listen to Him	6
9	God Restores Our Souls	6
10	A New Heart and a New Spirit	7
11	Born from Above	8
12	Kingdom Divided	9
13	The Heavenly Call of God	9
14	Broken Vessels	10
15	Old Self into a New Self	11
16	God's Kingdom in Our Daily Lives	12
17	God Is Light and Is Ready to Forgive Us	13
18	The Secret [Mystery] of the Kingdom of God	14
19	Praying for the Coming of the Kingdom	15
20	Turn, Then, and Live	16
21	Removing Oneself from Evil	16
22	God's Grace	17

23	Prophets Testify about Forgiveness	18
24	Peace with God	19
25	True Mercy Comes from God and Not Human Effort	20
26	Words of Repentance	21
27	Jesus Came to Save the World and Us	22
28	Jesus Lives to Make Intercession for Us	22
29	God Wants All to Come to Repentance	23
30	Humility	24
31	A New Creation	25

FEBRUARY

Striving for the Kingdom of God—Repenting/Turning Around/Conversion | 27

1	Turn Back	27
2	Forgive My Youthful Sins	28
3	Fruit Worthy of Repentance	29
4	God's Abundant Pardon	29
5	Freed by Truth to Be Jesus' Disciples	30
6	Confessing Our Sins to God Who Is Near	31
7	Jesus, the World's Atoning Sacrifice	32
8	Jesus Reproves Those He Loves	33
9	Being Freed, Delivered, and Redeemed	33
10	Seeking God's Mercy	35
11	Tested in the Furnace of Adversity	36
12	Clean Hands and Pure Hearts	36
13	God Is Our Salvation	37
14	The Lord Listens	38
15	We Have Turned to Our Own Way	39
16	Regarding Everything as Loss	40
17	Transgressions Swept Away	41
18	Justified by God's Grace	42
19	God Is with Us	43
20	Our Day of Salvation	44
21	Not Praying for Others	45
22	Turning to the Lord	45
23	Communicating	47
24	The Father Was Filled with Compassion	48
25	Purification	48
26	Humbling Ourselves	49
27	A Ransom for Many	50
28	Being Brought to God	51
29	Letting It Go	52

MARCH

Striving for the Kingdom of God—Where We Are Today | 53

1	Praise the Lord	53
2	Approval	54
3	Looking Back	54
4	Choose the Better Part	55
5	Setting One's Mind on Christ	55
6	God's Messenger	56
7	Dwelling in the House of the Lord	56
8	Day by Day	57
9	God's Kingdom	58
10	Seeing as God Sees	58
11	Letting God's Light Shine	59
12	What the Kingdom of God Isn't . . .	59
13	Jesus' Parables and the Kingdom of Heaven	60
14	Children and God's Kingdom	61
15	Riches and God's Kingdom	62
16	This Day	63
17	Scripture and Sleep	63
18	The Mind of Christ Jesus	64
19	Walking with God	65
20	God Is Near	66
21	Jesus Speaking about the Kingdom of God	67
22	God's Words Accomplishing God's Purpose	67
23	The World's Kingdom Becoming the Lord's Kingdom	68
24	Our Life's Lens	69
25	Keeping God's Word	70
26	Keep Awake	71
27	God's Kingdom Expressed in Our Present Day	72
28	Not Far from the Kingdom of God	73
29	Lessons Learned	74
30	Prayer Which Shakes the Ground	75
31	Becoming Effective and Fruitful in the Knowledge of Jesus Christ	76

APRIL

Striving for the Kingdom of God—Where We Are Today | 78

1	Christ Living in Me	78
2	The Lord Understands Every Plan and Thought	79
3	Open Minds	80
4	God's Countenance and Peace	81
5	One Body	82
6	In the World but Not of It	83

7	Teaching God's Commandments	84
8	Abiding in God	85
9	A Life Worthy of God	86
10	Great Grace	87
11	A New Heaven	88
12	Live to the Lord	89
13	God's Spirit Causes Growth	90
14	Exceeding the Righteousness of the Scribes and Pharisees	91
15	Draw Near to God	91
16	Praising God	92
17	God's Kingdom and Will	93
18	Daily Bread	94
19	Debts	95
20	Trials and Evil	96
21	Praising God—Where We Are Today	97
22	The Word of God Stands Forever	98
23	Set Your Mind on Divine Things	99
24	Jesus Appoints the Twelve to Be with Him	100
25	God's Kingdom Is Near	100
26	Human Glory versus God's Glory	101
27	The Kingdom of God Taken Away and Given to Others	102
28	The Kingdom Is Like Yeast	103
29	God's Word in Our Mouth and Heart	104
30	Walking Humbly with God	105

MAY

Prayer—How, What, and Why | 107

1	Quiet Places to Pray	107
2	Praying Always	108
3	Praising God with a Joyful Noise	108
4	The Lord's Prayer	109
5	Meditating Day and Night	109
6	The Lord Hears	110
7	Prayer of Deliverance	111
8	Calling for Help	111
9	Spiritual Food	112
10	Praying in Secret	112
11	A Time of Distress	113
12	Praying	114
13	The Prayer of the Righteous	114
14	God's Plans for Us	115
15	Rejoice, Pray, and Give Thanks	116
16	Seed Sown on Good Soil	117

17	God's Words Bring Joy and Delight	118
18	The Lord's Voice in the Sheer Silence	119
19	Praying Boldly	120
20	Meditating on God's Creation	120
21	God Does Not Reject My Prayer	121
22	Raised Arms in Prayer	122
23	Growth in Prayer	122
24	Morning Prayer	123
25	Waiting in Silence	124
26	Listening	125
27	Loud Prayers	126
28	Double-Minded, Unstable Prayers	127
29	Being Devoted to Prayer and Alert with Our Thanksgiving	128
30	Bold Asking	129
31	The Righteous Cry for Help	130

JUNE

Prayer—How, What, and Why | 131

1	Prayer—How, What, and Why	131
2	Finding Time to Pray	132
3	Prayer and Life's Decisions	133
4	Persevere in Prayer	134
5	Jesus Prays for His Disciples	135
6	God's Peace from Prayer	135
7	Praying for Space and Room in My Distress	136
8	My Waiting on the Lord Helps Others	137
9	Time Alone	138
10	Daniel Prayed Anyway	139
11	Prayer for the Really Tough Things of Life	140
12	Praying in the Spirit	141
13	The Lord Accepts My Prayer	142
14	Being Humble in Prayer	142
15	Hearing What the Lord Speaks	143
16	God's House of Prayer	144
17	God in the Quiet	145
18	Remaining Alert through Our Prayers	145
19	Prayer Answered in God's Time	146
20	Gathered in Prayer	147
21	Prayer and Persistence	148
22	Open the Door	149
23	Praying with a Companion	150
24	John the Baptist	151
25	Jesus Our Example Concerning Prayer	152

26	Praying Early in the Day	152
27	Proper Prayer	153
28	God Hears Us Before We Speak	154
29	A Road Less Traveled	155
30	Worshiping God in Spirit and Truth	156

JULY

The Holy Spirit | 157

1	God's Spirit Poured Out on Everyone	157
2	Baptized with the Holy Spirit and Fire	158
3	Spirit of God	158
4	Being Led by the Spirit	159
5	Spirit of Truth Promised	160
6	The Holy Spirit Teaches Us	161
7	Testifying	161
8	Truthful Words	162
9	Peace, the Holy Spirit, and the Great Commission	163
10	Power from the Holy Spirit	164
11	Praying Together	165
12	The Coming of the Holy Spirit	165
13	A Right Spirit	166
14	Trusting the Spirit	167
15	The Spirit Intercedes	167
16	Knowing the Spirit of God	168
17	Maintaining the Unity of the Spirit	169
18	Speaking with Boldness	170
19	Samaritans Receive the Holy Spirit	171
20	Spirit of Adoption	172
21	The Gifts of the Spirit	173
22	Spirit of Power, Love, and Self-Discipline	173
23	Being Transformed by the Spirit	174
24	Guided by the Spirit	175
25	Saul (Paul) Filled with the Holy Spirit	176
26	The Spirit Speaking through Us	177
27	Glorify God in Your Body	178
28	The Spirit Blows Where It Chooses	179
29	Renewal of Our Spiritual Minds	180
30	The Spirit Gives Life	181
31	Simeon and the Holy Spirit	181

AUGUST

Discernment | 183

1. Discerning the Will of God | 183
2. About Bible Verses | 184
3. Direction | 184
4. Wisdom and Understanding for Daily Life | 185
5. Laying Aside | 185
6. Cry for Help | 186
7. Daily Steps | 187
8. Change and New Paths | 187
9. Immediately | 188
10. God's Foolishness | 189
11. God Calling Us | 189
12. Be Strong and Courageous | 190
13. Our Plans | 191
14. Waiting for Direction/Deliverance/Discernment | 192
15. An Understanding and Discerning Mind | 193
16. A Wise Heart | 194
17. God's New Thing | 195
18. A Good Work Completed | 195
19. Called by Name | 196
20. God's Living and Active Word | 197
21. A Prayer for Discernment | 198
22. The Lord Gives Wisdom | 199
23. Asking | 200
24. Following Instructions | 201
25. Imitators | 202
26. Divinely Guided | 203
27. Jesus Taught and Continues to Teach with Authority | 204
28. A Balanced Life on This Pilgrimage | 205
29. God's Understanding | 206
30. God Called Abram, Jacob, Jeremiah, and Us | 207
31. God's Light and Truth Will Lead Us | 207

SEPTEMBER

Discernment | 209

1. Understanding God's Ways Requires Some Action on Our Part | 209
2. Following God's Will Versus the World's | 210
3. An Angel to Comfort and Lead | 211
4. What We Are to Be Is Unknown | 212
5. Compassion | 213
6. Discernment Is about Always Learning | 214

7	Following Jesus' Voice	215
8	What Am I to Do, Lord?	215
9	Going as Instructed	216
10	Human Wisdom and Divine Wisdom	217
11	Beginning of Wisdom	218
12	Making a Home Wherever We Are Sent	219
13	Strength and Understanding for the Pilgrimage	220
14	Dying to Bear Fruit	220
15	Jesus Christ Our Example	221
16	Remain True to Your Calling	222
17	Jesus Was Tempted and We Will Be Also	223
18	Jesus Our Help and Mentor	224
19	God's Temple	225
20	God Knows Everything about Us	226
21	Do Everything for the Glory of God	227
22	Put on the Whole Armor of God	228
23	Walk in the Truth	229
24	Jesus Walking with Us	230
25	Growing in Grace and Knowledge	230
26	Perseverance	231
27	Learning Is Part of the Pilgrimage	232
28	Speak for Your Servant Is Listening	233
29	We All Have Different Gifts	234
30	Doers of God's Word	235

OCTOBER

Hope | 236

1	Words of Comfort and Hope	236
2	Waiting for the Lord	237
3	Life's Miracles	237
4	Humans and Animals	238
5	The Lord's Steadfast Love	239
6	Bless the Lord	239
7	Love One Another	240
8	Hope in the Lord	240
9	God Is Our Refuge and Strength	241
10	New Birth	241
11	The Voice of God in a Great Storm	242
12	Complaining	243
13	Hope That Does Not Disappoint	243
14	Hope in the Steadfast Love of the Lord	244
15	Discipline Yourselves	245
16	Hope Is Not Seen	246

17	When I Cry to the Lord, My Hope Is That I Will Be Heard	246
18	A Lost Hope Is Now Reborn	247
19	Humble Yourselves	248
20	The Hope of Salvation	249
21	Hold on to Hope	250
22	Hope That Gives Us Great Boldness	251
23	God Working in Us	252
24	Called to a Life of Hope	253
25	Hope Even When We Are Cast Down	254
26	The Hope That Is in You	255
27	Hope in God's Good Gifts	255
28	No More Tears	256
29	Hope in God's Steadfast Love	257
30	Hope in the Gospel Message	258
31	Scriptures Give Us Hope	259

NOVEMBER

Faith Equals Trust | 260

1	Trust	260
2	The Lord's Help	260
3	By Faith	261
4	God's Faithfulness	261
5	Trust in the Lord	262
6	God's Spirit of Faith	263
7	New Adventure	263
8	Unafraid	264
9	Faith to Believe in the Unseen	265
10	Our Faith and Hope Are Set on God	266
11	God Has Not Left Us Alone	267
12	Peace from Trusting in the Lord	267
13	A Faith That Conuers the World	268
14	Faith to Trust in the Promise of God	269
15	The Lord Is the Stronghold of My Life	270
16	Entrusted	271
17	Faith to Forget What Is Behind	272
18	Deliverance	273
19	My Heart Trusts in the Lord	273
20	Faith through God's Grace	274
21	Christ Dwelling in Our Hearts through Faith	275
22	Faithful Service	276
23	Not Tested Beyond Our Ability	277
24	Have No Fear	279
25	Faith Based on the Power of God	280

26	Who Will Roll Away the Stone for Us?	281
27	Spiritual Eyes	282
28	Nothing Can Separate Us from the Love of God	283
29	Walking by Faith and Not by Sight	284
30	Saved through Faith	285

DECEMBER

Discipleship | 287

1	Called	287
2	God Disciplines Us	288
3	The Parable of the Rich Fool	289
4	Daily Discipline	289
5	God Wants to Dwell with Us	290
6	A Vision for the Appointed Time	290
7	The Lord Surrounds Us	291
8	Rejoice and Pray	292
9	Discipleship and Learning	293
10	Children of Light	293
11	Making Disciples	294
12	Abounding in Hope	295
13	Being Purified	295
14	Faith Community	296
15	Written on Our Hearts	297
16	Here Is Your God	298
17	God Walking Among Us	299
18	Growing in the Knowledge of God	300
19	Advent Anxiety	301
20	Our Cross / Our Calling	301
21	Bearing Fruit	302
22	The Cost of Discipleship	303
23	Joseph and Change	304
24	Christmas Eve	304
25	Christmas Day	305
26	Jesus Presented to the Lord	306
27	Bonding Time	306
28	Discipleship and Stewardship	307
29	Strengthened and Encouraged	308
30	Living a Worthy Life	309
31	Beginnings and Endings	310

SOME FINAL WORDS FROM JESUS ABOUT BECOMING HIS DISCIPLE! | 311

Acknowledgments

All of us on this spiritual pilgrimage are heading in the same general direction as we become a lifelong disciple of Jesus Christ; we are just using different methods to get there. However, we aren't by ourselves in this endeavor. I have certainly not come to this point solely by my own efforts. In addition to God's infinite mercy, love, and grace, together with the guidance of the Holy Spirit, many people and events have also influenced my life, thoughts, and emotions and thus are part of what has been written here, even if they didn't directly write these words.

My marriages, family, friends, coworkers in many organizations, the many faith communities of which I have been a member are all part of my current spiritual, mental, and emotional makeup. Even those whom I no longer have contact with or who have passed away are still in my core and a part of the person I am right now. This isn't something new or insightful, all of us are made up of those who have been part of our lives; however, it is important for me to acknowledge this fact.

My life experiences and the many people who have helped me are more than can be mentioned here and I am grateful for them all. Over the years I have been fortunate enough to be involved in a number of congregations, including the Baptist, Catholic, and Lutheran (ELCA) faith traditions. Besides my church involvement, I worked for a number of businesses and held a wide range of positions. During the time that I was in the business world moving around the country and later being married to a Lutheran pastor, the faith communities that I was connected to were in nine cities over six states. Thus, these groups offered me many different ways of looking at the positives and negatives of belonging to a worshiping body, doing ministry, and growing in my spiritual pilgrimage.

Over the years I have had an active role in a number of church functions and positions, all of which have added to my life and faith journey experiences. One of the main areas of growth for me was my own personal daily spiritual practice which has changed and evolved during my lifetime. After going to Trinity Lutheran Seminary I was a small group director, spiritual consultant, and a supply preacher for a number of different churches.

A really powerful influence on my journey has been my two marriages. During my marriage to my late wife, Judy, I was able to be involved in several Roman Catholic congregations. I took part in many of the activities of the churches to which we belonged, but I never officially joined; however, they did impact my spiritual growth. At one point Judy was the religious education coordinator for a large Catholic church in Ohio; I helped her by teaching classes. She was a woman of strong faith, and being with her during our marriage and over the final years of her life helped my faith to grow as well.

Shirley and I met at Trinity Lutheran Seminary and that experience at Trinity changed me in more ways than I can count. The time there prepared me to write my first book and now this one. Shirley and I were married after I finished my master's degree. She finished her MDiv, received her first call, became an ordained Lutheran (ELCA) pastor and we moved to Louisville, Kentucky. She served there for eight years before taking another call to serve a church in Michigan. She is also a person of strong faith and being married to her has strengthened my faith as well. Additionally, being involved in the community life of the churches she served has impacted who I am now. Shirley has also graciously agreed to read and help edit this book, for which I am so very thankful.

None of us is an island; we all need the support, encouragement, love, and prayers of many people. In this section, I have listed but a few who influenced the person I am today. I would suggest at some point that you reflect on and think of all of those people, communities, and events that have helped shape who you are. Thank them if possible, but most importantly acknowledge that we all need others in this life and on our spiritual pilgrimage.

I am thankful for and indebted to all of the experiences and people that have been part of my life. This book that you now hold in your hands reflects all of it in some fashion.

Introduction

HOW THIS BOOK CAME ABOUT

The purpose of this devotional book is to provide an aid for those who want to participate in the spiritual pilgrimage of becoming a lifelong disciple of Jesus Christ. It offers insight and support for those who daily want to turn their hearts, souls, and minds to God's will in their lives, as they strive to help in bringing about God's kingdom in this present time. There are countless other daily devotionals of one fashion or another, but my hope and prayer are that this one can offer something that the others may not, a specific focus on the concept of discipleship.

My first book, *Discipleship—A Lifelong Spiritual Pilgrimage,* was written for the same purpose. In that book certain aspects of becoming a disciple on the spiritual pilgrimage were outlined and discussed. It was written to offer encouragement and new ideas for those who are actively involved in some spiritual practices and also to give suggestions to those who want to begin this journey and need help in starting. The material for that book came from my experiences in working with churches on a discipleship and small group basis.

Generally those who have read the *Discipleship* book have found it to be helpful because it presented them with some new aspects about this walk or gave them a different viewpoint of how to approach this topic. A main focus is the importance of getting involved in the spiritual practices of prayer, Bible study, and reflection. It can be extremely challenging to deepen one's relationship with God, and along the way become a lifelong disciple of Jesus Christ, without investing one's emotional and physical energy, time, and effort into these spiritual habits.

Just prior to the *Discipleship* book being published I was encouraged to design a web site as a way to publicize the upcoming book and my ministry services. I set up a web site and a Facebook page outlining my services along with giving updates about when the book would be published. The web provider suggested doing a blog to periodically give the audience something fresh to read. I started doing scripture reflections in order to minister to those who viewed it. I didn't know it at the time but those early reflections were to become the foundation for this devotional book.

After writing a number of reflections I felt the Holy Spirit leading me to begin writing a devotional book. It seems essential that every day as we take part in our spiritual pilgrimage we should turn our hearts and souls to the Lord, and a devotional book is a helpful tool to assist in that. As noted this book is somewhat different from many devotional books because its principal focus is on the reader becoming a lifelong disciple of Jesus Christ.

Jesus taught by his words and actions. He gave us guidance about what to pray, how to pray, and why to pray. He also was very familiar with the Hebrew Scriptures. Thus, if we want to become a lifelong disciple of Jesus Christ, we should follow the model of his life and teachings.

THE WORLD'S RELIGIONS

The use of prayer, study, and reflection are found in all of the world's major religions. All of them in some form stress the importance of taking the time and energy to pray and reflect on their faith's teachings. In addition to Christianity, four of the largest world religions are Islam, Hinduism, Buddhism, and Judaism.

The followers of Islam are referred to as Muslims and they face toward Mecca when they pray five times a day. Prayer is the main method of worship in the Islamic faith. The basis of their faith is the Qur'an, the holy word of God.

For those who practice Hinduism, the home is where many families pray daily. Their hope is that the study of the texts of Hinduism, together with prayer, and meditation will bring peace to the faithful.

Buddhism teaches that enlightenment comes while one is meditating. Worship includes giving honor to the Buddha and reading sacred prayers.

In Judaism the Hebrew Bible is the foundation of faith. Prayer is an important part of daily life, and some Jews pray three times a day. Prayer is seen as a way to talk with God.[1]

These four religions are just some of the faiths and practices in the world today. If one were to study the other world's religions, prayer and worship would most likely be a part of their rituals as well. They all are

---

1. See Philip Wilkinson, *Illustrated Dictionary of Religions* (London: Dorling Kindersley, 1999).

based upon sacred writings, prayer, and contemplation as a way to enrich the spiritual lives of their followers.

Christianity, as one of the major world religions, also has many forms of prayer and worship. Like those who practice Judaism, prayer is communicating with and building up a relationship with God. As with the other religions, many Christians also use prayer in the home today in addition to communal worship. The Holy Bible is the text that is the foundation of the Christian faith and the Lord's Prayer is prayed throughout the world.

I have been fortunate enough to attend overnight retreats at several Christian retreat centers. In one case the religious community worshiped seven times a day, besides having other times of personal prayer. Thus, various Christian denominations, as well as many of the desert mothers and fathers, have expressed the need to pray and worship throughout the day or at least several times during the day.

The enduring aspect of the prayer life of faithful Christians, Muslims, Hindus, Buddhists, Jews, and others is that it helps individuals, families, communities, and nations cope with the many challenges that are facing humankind today. Prayer doesn't exempt one from the trials of the day, but it aids in centering people and opening them to the divine will. I believe that whenever people of any religion or faith hear about natural disasters, war, violence, disease, poverty, or the inhumane treatment of other humans, the first thing they frequently do is to pray to God for those who are suffering. The United States has a Judeo-Christian foundation. However, many of the non-Christian religions are being practiced throughout America and in fact are growing in number.

Some of the practices of the Christian spiritual pilgrimage are also demonstrated in these other world religions. What is being expressed here is universal and has been practiced in one form or another for thousands of years. These rituals are both ancient and become new every day when used faithfully.

THE BOOK'S FORMAT

This book has a devotion written for every day of the year and the overall subject matter concerns the disciple's spiritual pilgrimage and all that it entails. The months of the year are broken down into the same chapter topics as my *Discipleship* book. Thus if you have read the *Discipleship* book you may be familiar with the themes used for each month; however, if you haven't read it, this book can still be used as a daily devotional for each reflection stands on it's own and, hopefully, will encourage readers on their spiritual journey.

INTRODUCTION

Nourishment for the Spiritual Pilgrimage: Daily Devotions for Christian Disciples is heavily based on the word of God. The daily meditations are written from my viewpoint, my life experience in both the joyful times and the times of challenge, and reflect how I have felt the guidance of the Holy Spirit during this entire process. If you were to ask ten people what they glean from the scriptures cited, you would likely get ten very different answers. Those responses wouldn't necessarily be right or wrong, just the viewpoints of those reading them. Thus, you may disagree with some of these reflections, but my prayer is that many of them will aid you in your spiritual pilgrimage.

HOW TO USE THIS BOOK

Please read and meditate on the daily reflections and allow the Holy Spirit to guide your contemplation and your spiritual practices, and if you only use this book for your daily devotions that would be a good start. However, if you haven't already begun some additional daily spiritual practices I would encourage you to continue and this book would then become one of the additional resources you use.

Before reading a selection consider praying for guidance regarding what you are about to reflect on. Starting your mediation time with prayer is a good habit to get into for it opens your inner being to be receptive to what comes next. You could start your prayer with something like, "Gracious Lord, please guide my study of your word and this reflection and help me to be open to where the Holy Spirit may be leading me. . . . " Be creative and develop some type of introductory prayer that is comfortable for you.

Most of the meditations in this book have a short scripture at the beginning. One way to use the daily selection is to read the verses preceding and following the biblical passage selected, so that you can get a sense of what the writers were trying to say overall. Also read any footnotes or study notes pertaining to the verses, so that you can obtain some understanding of the background and context on the passage. If you don't already have one, consider purchasing a good study Bible that gives additional insights on the various books.

Meditate on the devotional entry and the scripture passage, and see if it touches some aspect of your life, someone you know, or some situation of which you are aware. Be open to what the Holy Spirit may be saying to you through these words. Are you being given a new way to approach certain aspects of your life; are you being asked to step out in faith in some manner; or are there some areas in your life that need to be resolved or forgiven? Allow the Holy Spirit to enter deeply into your spirit to direct, change, support, and bring you closer to becoming the person that God created you to be.

At the end of each reflection is a prayer; think of using this prayer as a springboard to pray for other aspects of your life, your family, vocation, career, community, or issues in the nation or world. Let prayer become a habit that can be done at any time or place. Also try to get into the routine of praying the Lord's Prayer daily, as this is the one prayer given to us by Jesus. When you use this prayer you are joining countless others who have come before you, and many throughout the world are saying it even as you are praying it. It has been called the perfect prayer in that it covers so many areas of our daily lives. Additionally remember that many different peoples and religions around the world practice a prayerful and reflective life just as you are attempting to do.

Occasionally in this book, the practices and/or wisdom of the "desert mothers and fathers" are mentioned. These individuals were searchers who, in the second and third centuries, moved away from the established Christian church and the cities in which they were previously connected. They believed that society and the church had created too many barriers to living the Christian life to which Jesus had called his followers. They wanted a space and environment where they would be able to grow into a closer relationship with God.

These pilgrims felt they were following the guidance of the Holy Spirit and the Holy Scriptures in order to have lives of solitude and prayer. They would often go far out into the desert areas to practice a more prayerful life and thus acquired the name of desert mothers and fathers. Often, they wouldn't see other humans for years. However, they were well known for their wisdom, love of God and neighbor, and for their highly-disciplined and prayer-centered lives.

If you would like to know about this movement, there have been many books written about that time in the church's history. Here are three books I have read that would be a good starting point to learn more about this period: *In God's Holy Light: Wisdom from the Desert Monastics*, by Joan Chittister; *The Wisdom of the Desert Fathers and Mothers*, translated by Henry L. Carrigan Jr.; and *Journeying into God: Seven Early Monastic Lives*, translated by Tim Vivian.

During the year my hope and prayer are that this book can support you through every phase of your life and that it helps you to trust in the promises of our gracious and loving God, who will be with you no matter what you are going through at the moment. May you experience God's love all around you as you strive to become a lifelong disciple of Jesus Christ!

January

Striving for the Kingdom of God— Repenting / Turning Around / Conversion

JANUARY 1

The New Year

One of my favorite spiritual writers is the late Henri Nouwen, who was a Catholic priest, and a very important writer in the last century. In his book *Bread for the Journey* he writes about having light for the next step. As we begin a New Year, we can become concerned about what this year holds for us. He notes that generally we only have enough light for the coming hour or the following day.

He writes, "The art of living is to enjoy what we can see and not complain about what remains in the dark."[1] He goes on to say that when we can take the next step with faith, our life can be filled with joy. May you be able to trust the Lord about the future and live today with that faith. Blessings on your spiritual pilgrimage throughout the New Year!

God of light, help me to trust the next step in my life to you, and take it knowing that it is all that is needed for the moment! Amen.

---

1. Henri J. M. Nouwen, *Bread for the Journey: A Daybook of Wisdom and Faith* (New York: HarperCollins, 1985), entry for January 8.

JANUARY 2

Striving First for God's Kingdom

> But strive first for the kingdom of God and his righteousness, and all these things will be given to you as well. So do not worry about tomorrow, for tomorrow will bring worries of its own. Today's trouble is enough for today.
>
> MATTHEW 6:33–34

This passage is part of what has become known as the *Sermon on the Mount*. Jesus is teaching those close to him about how he wants them to live. This message wasn't for everyone, but only for those who were willing to follow him and risk going against the culture at that time.

This message offers all of us who are attempting to become a disciple of Jesus Christ guidance about where our focus should be. By stating that we are to strive first for the kingdom of God, it reminds us that our daily decisions should be made through the lens of God's kingdom and not the lens of the world or on long-term plans. That is hard to do especially when there are so many worldly voices crying out for our attention. May the Holy Spirit assist you in striving first for the kingdom of God before anything else!

Lord of all creation, please give me the focus to daily strive first for your kingdom, versus the many competing worldly voices that are all around me! Amen.

JANUARY 3

Repenting

> Repent, for the kingdom of heaven has come near.
>
> MATTHEW 3:2

In this passage John the Baptist is in the wilderness near Judea announcing that because God's kingdom was near the time for the people to repent was upon them. People from the Jerusalem and Judea areas were attracted to his message and were baptized in the Jordan River as they confessed their sins. John the Baptist may have seemed strange to those around him, but his message was what he was guided to give, and people listened and repented. This message is reported to have come before Jesus started his public ministry.

This aspect of repenting on the spiritual pilgrimage is sometimes overlooked as something that is not needed. However, it is essential and repenting is not just a once in a lifetime event, but could be looked at as a daily one. Each day asking for God's forgiveness acknowledges the fact that we are all imperfect human beings with shortcomings and faults. John's message continues to speak to us today, and hopefully we are able to listen and repent!

Forgiving Lord, help me to daily repent of those things in my life that prevent me from becoming the person that you want me to be! Amen.

JANUARY 4

Turning Around

> Therefore say to the house of Israel, Thus says the Lord God: Repent and turn away from your idols, and turn away your faces from all your abominations.
>
> Ezekiel 14:6

In this verse the Lord God wants the prophet Ezekiel to tell the Israelites to not just repent from their past sins, but to actually turn away from the idols and abominations that they had been facing. Repentance is the attitude of the heart and is the first step in seeking God daily, but turning around is the next step. God knew that they were worshiping idols and not the Lord, and things needed to be changed. We repent with our hearts, but some physical action is needed as well.

On our spiritual pilgrimage doing things differently, forming new spiritual habits and practices, staying away from aspects of our lives that once caused us harm, and turning away from idols in our lives and facing toward God's will for us are all action things. May you be able to understand the importance of this aspect of your spiritual walk!

Today Lord, help me to take some action to turn away from those aspects of my life that are a barrier to my spiritual growth and relationship with you, and turn toward your loving arms! Amen.

JANUARY 5

Good News

> Now after John was arrested, Jesus came to Galilee, proclaiming the good news of God, and saying, "The time is fulfilled, and the kingdom of God has come near; repent, and believe in the good news."
>
> MARK 1:14–15

This is apparently Jesus' first public message, and he is basically saying the same thing that John the Baptist and some of the Old Testament prophets declared, that it was now time to repent. Jesus went on to talk about how the *good news*, or the *gospel* had to be proclaimed and also noted that the kingdom of God had come near. John also talked about God's kingdom being near. In these two short verses a lot is being announced for the people in Jesus' time and of course for us.

Today no matter how you say it, repenting, turning around, or conversion, are important aspects of this spiritual pilgrimage. All three terms involve letting go of the things that may keep us from having a closer relationship with God. As all aspects of the spiritual walk, it requires self-disciple, struggle, and change. Believing in the *good news* or *gospel* means that Jesus Christ is Lord of our lives, and we look to his life for direction in ours. Today may you believe in this *good news* and that God's kingdom is near, which allows you to daily repent, turn around, and become his disciple!

Holy Spirit, guide me today to believe in this good news and believe that God's kingdom has come near to me, which will encourage me to repent of everything that is a barrier to my spiritual growth! Amen.

JANUARY 6

What if We Resolved to Be Like the Shepherds and the Magi?

> When the angels had left them and gone into heaven, the shepherds said to one another, "Let us go now to Bethlehem and see this thing that has taken place, which the Lord has made know to us."
>
> LUKE 2:15

May the spirit and peace of God be truly with you during the New Year! As we tell the birth story of the baby Jesus, the shepherds and Magi often get forgotten. Following Jesus' birth, they were never mentioned again in

Scripture. However, they were chosen by God to become the living birth announcements to Mary and Joseph.

Now, what if we resolved to be like the shepherds and the Magi? Would we be willing to follow directions given to us by God? Would we be willing to venture out in haste not knowing where or why we are going, but going anyway because of the guidance given to us? Blessings on your spiritual pilgrimage throughout the New Year!

May I be open to following God's guidance in small and large ways on a daily basis throughout this New Year! Amen.

JANUARY 7

Setting One's Mind on the Spirit

> ... to set the mind on the Spirit is life and peace, ... for all who are led by the Spirit of God are children of God.
>
> ROMANS 8:6B, 14

The book of Romans is a powerful letter written by the Apostle Paul to the Christians in Rome. This chapter has a number of verses that are frequently quoted for many different reasons. The basis for these passages is a life lived in the Spirit. Paul wants his readers to set their mind on the things of the Spirit, which provides life and peace, versus having their mind be on things of the flesh that lead to death.

For those on this spiritual pilgrimage it is so important to keep our minds and hearts on the things of the Spirit, on the love of God for the world, on the life that Jesus lived for us, and on the things that allow each of us to become the persons that God wants us to be. Read all of Romans 8 and reflect on the many words of wisdom that are there. May these words and lessons support and enrich your spiritual practices!

Lord of the Spirit, give me the courage and strength to set my mind on the things of your Spirit, and allow that Spirit to comfort and guide me and give me your peace! Amen.

JANUARY 8

Listen to Him

> This is my Son, the Beloved, with him I am well pleased; listen to him!
>
> MATTHEW 17:5B

In this story from Matthew, Jesus is with three of his closest disciples, Peter, James, and John, on a mountaintop experience, which is normally called the *transfiguration*. At this time, Jesus' face shone like the sun, and his clothes became dazzling white. However, with all of this excitement, God wants the three disciples to just *listen* to Jesus.

Listening is an important step on our spiritual journey. After we listen—really listen and focus on what we have to learn—this knowledge may cause us to change. This change will continue as long as we are on this path, and will allow us to see life differently. Blessings on your spiritual pilgrimage as you try to listen!

During this walk, may I be open to listening for the voice of God through the Holy Spirit in many and varied ways and in the process, be prepared to change! Amen.

JANUARY 9

God Restores Our Souls

> The LORD is my shepherd, I shall not want.
> He makes me lie down in green pastures; he leads me beside still waters; he restores my soul. He leads me in right paths for his name's sake. Even though I walk through the darkest valley, I fear no evil; for you are with me; your rod and your staff—they comfort me. You prepare a table before me in the presence of my enemies; you anoint my head with oil; my cup overflows. Surely goodness and mercy shall follow me all the days of my life, and I shall dwell in the house of the LORD my whole life long.
>
> PSALM 23

This is one of the most loved and quoted psalms, used for many different occasions. Take time to read and reflect on it. It can help us through many stages of our earthly journey. The image of God being our shepherd could help us to realize how God loves and cares for us and how the Lord is interested in every detail of our lives. Just as the shepherd looks out for the sheep, God looks out for us.

Looking at the verse where God restores us is especially powerful for those on a spiritual pilgrimage. If we want to be restored and led into right paths, we have to do our part, to be in a position to listen to God's voice and hear the instructions that are given. On this walk we can position ourselves to be restored by the Lord when we engage in spiritual practices, in that manner we can condition our hearts and souls to be made into the persons that God wants us to be. While on your spiritual journey, may you be restored in your heart and soul!

Good shepherd, help me to be open to your voice and guidance so that I may be restored in heart and soul! Amen.

JANUARY 10

A New Heart and a New Spirit

> A new heart I [the Lord God] will give you, and a new spirit I will put within you; and I will remove from your body the heart of stone and give you a heart of flesh. I will put my spirit within you.
>
> EZEKIEL 36:26–27A

In this Old Testament book, we have the priest and prophet Ezekiel outlining what the Lord God directed him to tell the Israelite nation. Their hearts that were like stone would be turned into hearts of flesh. In Ezekiel 37 we have the story of the "Valley of Dry Bones" and how God puts a new life into something that was dry and dead. This is an excellent story for those who want to engage in spiritual practices, for it gives us all hope about what can come from it, a new heart and new spirit.

However, some of us may feel that obtaining a new heart and spirit is an extremely difficult thing to do, depending on what is going on in our lives. One such time for me was when my late wife, Judy, died in late January 1999. After her funeral and all of the related activity calmed down, I can remember how depressed, lonely, and sad I was. Up until her death, I had been busily caring for her at home, and then life suddenly slowed down. During that time of the year the days were short and having to be alone during those winter evenings was especially challenging for me. There were many stressful moments for me then. It took a long time, but spring did come, and by July my energy level began to improve. My heart and spirit were renewed over time.

Think about reflecting on these chapters from Ezekiel as an example of how we can also be reborn. Being on our spiritual pilgrimage isn't always a bed of roses, but we can daily be given a new heart and spirit when we are open to God's love, grace, and mercy. Blessings on your spiritual travels!

Lord of new life, guide me to be open to receiving a new heart and new spirit that can then be shared with those I will be meet today! Amen.

JANUARY 11

Born from Above

> Jesus answered him, "Very truly, I tell you, no one can see the kingdom of God without being born from above." Nicodemus said to him, "How can anyone be born after having grown old? Can one enter a second time into the mother's womb and be born?" Jesus answered, "Very truly, I tell you, no one can enter the kingdom of God without being born of water and Spirit. What is born of the flesh is flesh, and what is born of the Spirit is spirit."
>
> JOHN 3:3–6

In this passage a Pharisee leader, Nicodemus, visits Jesus and Jesus tells him about having to be reborn from above in order to see God's kingdom. This of course confused Nicodemus and Jesus had to repeat himself, and Nicodemus still didn't get it. Being born from above, or born anew (as some translations read) was a hard concept to grasp for this religious leader. Nicodemus probably thought that he knew all of Moses' written law and how it was interpreted, but he failed to envision what Jesus was talking about.

It appears, however, that what Jesus is talking about centers on the repenting / turning around / conversion discussion. That is, changing one's life in order to become part of God's kingdom. In this passage, being born from above suggests being baptized (water) and having the Holy Spirit (spirit) become part of one's spiritual essence.

This concept may be challenging to comprehend today, however, as you strive for God's kingdom in your daily life, and become involved with spiritual practices, may you see the importance of being born from above or being born anew!

Lord of the Spirit, please give me the insight and guidance to be able to seek your kingdom on a daily basis by being born anew, and may I bring that understanding to those that I come in contact with today! Amen.

JANUARY 12

Kingdom Divided

> But if it is by the Spirit of God that I [Jesus] cast out demons, then the kingdom of God has come to you.
>
> Matthew 12:28

In the section from Matthew 12, the Pharisees had been saying that Jesus could only cast out demons because the ruler of demons, Beelzebul, allowed him to do it. Jesus goes on to tell them that if a kingdom, house, or city is divided against itself it can't stand, also Satan can't cast out Satan. Additionally, if what Jesus was doing was by God's Spirit, then the kingdom of God had come upon them.

This is another case where Jesus teaches that God's kingdom had come near to them because of his life and actions. This is also a valuable lesson for us today, for when we are following Jesus' teaching we are also taking part in bringing God's kingdom into this time and place.

Maybe we can't cast out demons as Jesus did, but we can love others, and walk this spiritual pilgrimage by the power of the Holy Spirit to bring God's kingdom here today. For us personally, this is also done when we take part in the spiritual practices of prayer, Bible study, and reflection!

May I strive for God's kingdom every day, and look to God's Spirit for guidance, support, and encouragement! Amen.

JANUARY 13

The Heavenly Call of God

> Not that I have already obtained this or have already reached the goal; but I press on to make it my own, because Christ Jesus has made me his own. Beloved, I do not consider that I have made it my own, but this one thing I do: forgetting what lies behind and straining forward to what lies ahead, I press on toward the goal for the prize of the heavenly call of God in Christ Jesus.
>
> Philippians 2:12–14

This passage is often quoted and has a lot of powerful messages in these three short verses. The Apostle Paul is writing to the Christians in the city of Philippi and in this passage, wants them to keep pressing toward the goal of their heavenly call. Paul acknowledges that his spiritual race isn't finished, he wants the goal to be his own like it was for Jesus. He wants to stay focused on just one thing—to let go of the things of the past and focus on what is ahead, as he moves on toward the prize of the heavenly call of God in Christ Jesus.

As we talk about striving for God's kingdom on this spiritual pilgrimage, Paul gives us guidance for our walk. In our spiritual practices, we too should try to let go of the things of our past that hold us back from becoming the person that God wants to be. We ought to attempt to stay focused on just one thing and that is God's kingdom and this heavenly call. Our spiritual travels can move us on toward this goal. Blessings on your journey as you let go of the past and reach forward toward this prize!

Today may I be like Paul and forget what is behind that is holding me back, and reach forward to what lies ahead, and stay focused on this heavenly call of God in Christ Jesus! Amen.

JANUARY 14

Broken Vessels

> Be gracious to me, O Lord, for I am in distress; my eye wastes away from grief, my soul and body also. For my life is spent with sorrow, and my years with sighing; my strength fails because of my misery, and my bones waste away.... I have passed out of mind like one who is dead; I have become like a broken vessel.... But I trust in you, O Lord; I say, "You are my God." My times are in your hand; deliver me from the hand of my enemies and persecutors.
>
> Psalm 31:9–10, 12, 14–15

Many of us have had times when we have felt like what was expressed in verses 9–10. These verses outline a life that is filled with distress, grief, sorrow, declining strength, and a body that is worn down. For those of us who have gone through periods like this one, it is extremely difficult to function or to maintain any hope.

The writer goes on to note about having a body that has died, and feeling like a "broken vessel." A broken vessel can't do what it was made to do, that is to hold something liquid, thus the owner has no use for the vessel any longer. For it to be of any use it must be repaired or it will have to be thrown away.

This relates to the spiritual pilgrimage in that as imperfect human beings, we too are broken and need to be repaired. One way that this can be done is by asking God for the forgiveness of our sins and trespasses. As we attempt to strive for the kingdom of God, an important daily step is the act of repentance, turning around, or conversion, however you state it.

Those on this spiritual journey can often overlook this because it can be viewed as a once-in-a-lifetime action, rather than a daily one. When this is done, we can then repeat the words in verse 14 that we can trust in the Lord whose hands we are in!

God of repaired vessels and humans, help me to daily repent and to be made whole again, so that my new life can be shared with those I meet today! Amen.

JANUARY 15

Old Self into a New Self

> . . . seeing that you have stripped off the old self with its practices and have clothed yourselves with the new self, which is being renewed in knowledge according to the image of its creator.
>
> Colossians 3:9b–10

Two months after my high school graduation, I started working in a steel mill's open-hearth department. I continued to work full time for nearly nine years until I earned my undergraduate degree. I had many different jobs during my time there, and some of the jobs required me to either get really dirty, or be around a lot of heat causing me to perspire quite a bit.

Thus, I normally had to take off the work clothes and shower before putting on my street clothes. It was a wonderful feeling to remove the dirty and smelly work clothes after my shift was over. After the shower and putting on the clean clothes I felt almost like a new person.

In this passage from Colossians we have the image of being stripped of the old self (old clothes) and being renewed into a new self (new clothes). We are encouraged to leave behind the old practices that we were once involved in, and to be renewed with the knowledge of a new life in Christ.

As we take part in the spiritual pilgrimage, the practices of the old self (old clothes) may become something we don't feel like wearing any longer. Somewhat like when I couldn't wait to get off my dirty clothes after my shift was over. While striving to become a lifelong disciple of Jesus Christ, may you leave behind those old things that prevent you from being renewed. May you be clothed with your new self (new clothes) in the image of Christ!

Lord of new life, please clothe me with a new self in Christ, and may that new self be a witness of the good news to those I meet today! Amen.

JANUARY 16

God's Kingdom in Our Daily Lives

> And do not keep striving for what you are to eat and what you are to drink, and do not keep worrying. For it is the nations of the world that strive after all these things, and your Father knows that you need them. Instead, strive for his [God's] kingdom, and these things will be given to you as well. Do not be afraid, little flock, for it is your Father's good pleasure to give you the kingdom.
>
> Luke 12:29–32

The beginning of this passage begins with the words, "He said to his disciples." Thus, it is implied that the message that followed was for those who were his closest followers and not specifically for the crowds who were mainly interested in following Jesus because of the miracles he performed, or the religious leaders who wanted to be there when Jesus did something wrong in their eyes.

As he tells his disciples, they were to strive first for the kingdom of God in their daily lives and trust that the Lord God would provide for whatever else was needed. This is a very challenging concept in our modern world that places a lot of emphasis on being overly concerned about one's stock earnings, retirement nest egg, status in society, etc. Striving first for God's kingdom before anything else is not for the faint of heart.

This is a lesson that I have had to learn over and over again in my life, and it continues to be a challenge for me. One of the first major times that I encountered this was when I was working full time in a steel mill and going to college part time. Twice during that time, I was forced to sit out a term because my grade point average was too low compared to the number of hours I was taking. I kept thinking that I could do more than I was capable of and couldn't pull up my grades fast enough, and thus was forced to sit out and think about what was going on.

I was able to get off probation for a number of reasons, but the major one was that I consciously tried to strive for God's kingdom while taking my classes. I had to try to put God's will and kingdom first in my life, versus anything else. This focus didn't happen overnight, but slowly my heart and mind tried to strive for God's kingdom in my life on a daily basis and it impacted how I prepared for my class work, and how I saw my college experience.

Throughout your spiritual pilgrimage, may you recognize the importance of striving first for God's kingdom on a daily basis, versus anything else that you may encounter on your earthly journey!

Lord of life, please help me to focus on your kingdom and will in my life before anything else, and allow me to share this understanding with those whom I meet today! Amen.

JANUARY 17

God Is Light and Is Ready to Forgive Us

> This is the message we have heard from him and proclaim to you, that God is light and in him there is no darkness at all. . . . If we say that we have no sin, we deceive ourselves, and the truth is not in us. If we confess our sins, he who is faithful and just will forgive us our sins and cleanse us from all unrighteousness.
>
> 1 John 1:5, 8–9

For most of us, admitting our sins or shortcomings is tough to do. We generally don't want other people to know where we have failed or come up short. We may even attempt to put up a facade which prevents those around us from knowing what is actually going on with us. The ironic part about this is that very often we will feel better once we are able to let go of what we have done, and are then able to move forward being freed of our past thoughts and actions.

The other issue about this is that God already knows what has happened. Once we come to believe the Lord is truly light and that there is no darkness at all and that light will shine on everything we have done. We can't hide from God those things that we may try to hide from other humans. When we can just trust that the Lord loves us no matter what situation we are in and wants us to come and seek forgiveness, we may be more inclined to do so.

On your spiritual pilgrimage, may you daily ask for forgiveness for those things in your life that are keeping you from becoming the person that you were created to be. God is faithful and will forgive our sins and shortcomings, and in the process, cleanse us from all unrighteousness!

Lord of all love, help me to have the faith and confidence to come before you with everything that I have done, and give me the trust to believe in your grace, love, and mercy! Amen.

JANUARY 18

The Secret [Mystery] of the Kingdom of God

> When he [Jesus] was alone, those who were around him along with the twelve asked him about the parables. And he said to them, "To you has been given the secret [mystery] of the kingdom of God, but for those outside, everything comes in parables."
>
> MARK 4:10–11

Jesus talked about the kingdom of God more than any other topic during his earthy ministry. He proclaimed that God's kingdom was now near, and that it was the time to repent and to proclaim the good news. However, the secret or mystery about the kingdom seemed to be for those who were closest to him, or those who were willing to become his disciples. Here he says that those who were outside, which evidently means those who weren't around him all the time or one of the twelve, would receive his message as a parable.

Apparently, the parables were very difficult to grasp, for even Jesus' closest followers had a hard time understanding them. In Mark 4 Jesus goes on to explain to his followers what they actually meant, which is done when he is alone with them, and not with the crowds.

Being able today to read a printed account of the parables and Jesus' explanation allow us to have a better perspective of what they mean versus the people around him at that time. However, unless we are willing to take part in the spiritual practices of prayer, Bible study, and reflection on a regular basis, it is more difficult for Jesus' words to become part of our inner being and impact our spiritual pilgrimage. As we change from year to year, so does the meaning of Scripture for our lives and for the situations and the environment around us. Time and study are needed on an ongoing basis to continue receiving the new messages that Scripture has for us.

May you be given the emotional and physical energy needed, so that you can better comprehend God's kingdom, and be able to apply its meaning to your spiritual walk in your efforts to become a lifelong disciple of Jesus Christ!

Lord Jesus, may your words about God's kingdom become part of my very being and may that presence encourage me to share this message with those whom I meet today! Amen.

JANUARY 19

Praying for the Coming of the Kingdom

> Your kingdom come. Your will be done, on earth as it is in heaven.
>
> MATTHEW 6:10

This passage is from what has come to be called the "Sermon on the Mount" where Jesus talks to his disciples about a variety of topics. In the beginning of chapter 6 Jesus gave instructions about how and what to pray. He gives the words to what is known as the Lord's Prayer. This passage gives those wanting to take part in a spiritual pilgrimage quite a bit of direction about prayer, while chapters 5–7 of Matthew give us so many important points about how to live as a disciple of Jesus Christ.

The Lord's Prayer is often thought of as a perfect prayer because it covers so many areas that we should be concerned about in our prayer life. I would encourage you to include the Lord's Prayer at some point in your daily prayer time, and if you can't do anything else during the day, at least take some quiet time to pray this prayer.

Some of the first words that Jesus spoke as he began his public ministry was that the kingdom of God had come near. In the Lord's Prayer Jesus wants us to pray that God's kingdom comes to us today, and that God's will be done on earth as in heaven. When we sincerely pray for that in the Lord's Prayer, it becomes part of our essence and helps direct how we daily live. We bring the kingdom of God about when we strive to do God's will in our lives, and the lives of those around us.

When we attempt this, it isn't something that brings glory or fame to us, but our lives become a reflection of the love of God shining through us to those around us. The kingdom of God coming into our lives is often something that can't be seen with the human eye. However, in most cases it can be witnessed best with a spiritual eye and soul that can see and feel the Holy Spirit flowing through and around situations in our lives. As you daily pray the Lord's Prayer, may you be open to the Holy Spirit showing you how to bring about God's kingdom into your life and the lives around you!

Holy Spirit, today please guide me about how to seek God's kingdom in my life, and then help me to do my part in bringing it to those around me! Amen.

JANUARY 20

Turn, Then, and Live

> Cast away from you all the transgressions that you have committed against me, and get yourselves a new heart and a new spirit! Why will you die, O House of Israel? For I have no pleasure in the death of anyone, says the Lord God. Turn, then, and live.
>
> Ezekiel 18:31–32

In this chapter from Ezekiel, God is the hope of justice for all individuals. God is saying that everyone will be accountable for their own actions, and will live or die based on what they do versus the deeds of their parents.

The instructions are fairly modest: "Turn, then, and live." They are simple words but so very demanding for most of us on a daily basis. Each day we have to decide whom we are to follow, our own self-created gods or the Lord of all creation. The gods we create are made in the image of things that we are comfortable with, and allow us to grow in the eyes of the world. However, the God of the universe may cause us to turn away from our need to be praised by the world—seeking its approval, and instead strive for God's kingdom in this time and place.

Turning toward God's kingdom and will may require us to leave beyond aspects of our lives that we may not want to give up. However, in the process, God knows that we will be richer and fuller as it relates to becoming a lifelong disciple of Jesus Christ. May you be willing to turn from yourself, and turn toward God, to become the person that God wants you to be!

Lord of new creation, help me to know that each day I must turn from myself and the world toward you, and then live and embrace this new life that has been given to me! Amen.

JANUARY 21

Removing Oneself from Evil

> Wash yourselves; make yourselves clean; remove the evil of your doings from before my eyes; cease to do evil, learn to do good; seek justice, rescue the oppressed, defend the orphan, plead for the widow.
>
> Isaiah 1:16–17

Please read this entire passage, especially starting with verse 10. The Lord God doesn't want a lot of ritual offerings without a real change in one's behavior. This section is letting us know that God wants to forgive us, but we should also ask God to help us in removing ourselves from the evil that is all around us. We are to cease from doing evil and to learn to do good, seek justice and help the oppressed, orphans, and widows.

This is an aspect of any walk of life that is always a challenge to improve upon. Old habits die hard, especially those that are ingrained in us for many years. Some of us may have things in our lives that probably control us more than we care to acknowledge. I don't have the time or space to note many of the personal aspects about me that I have had to struggle with over my life. Needless to say, I still struggle daily with doing God's will. That will always be the case because all of us are imperfect humans.

But, the Lord wants us to continue to sincerely strive to ask for help and guidance to remove ourselves from the evil that is all around us and, in fact also inside of us. When we do this, we are in a better position to cease from doing the evil that we do, and seek to learn to do good and justice for those who are less fortunate than we are. Please remember that God is always willing to grant forgiveness when we come with a humble and contrite heart!

Lord of all love, help me to strive for your will in my life, and in the process, help me to turn away from the evil that so easily comes my way. May I be a reflection of your infinite grace, love, and mercy! Amen.

JANUARY 22

God's Grace

> But by the grace of God I am what I am, and his grace toward me has not been in vain. On the contrary, I worked harder than any of them—though it was not I, but the grace of God that is with me. Whether then it was I or they, so we proclaim and so you have come to believe.
>
> 1 CORINTHIANS 15:10–11

Think for a moment about events in your life when you have been given something that you didn't expect, or been given time to complete a project or assignment that you didn't think you would be granted, or allowed to move ahead with something that you didn't think you would be permitted to finish. All of these examples and many more that you can probably think of, are all forms of grace in one way or the other. Grace is about getting something unexpected or undeserved.

In my own life, I have been shown grace countless times for various reasons, and hopefully I was aware of this and able to acknowledge how fortunate I was then. I remember when I was going to college part time and working full time that I was shown my share of grace. Several times I took more classes than I should have taken and had a very hard time keeping up with all of the course work.

At the same time my grade point average was lower than it should have been and I was about to be put on probation. At one point one of my professors showed me tremendous grace by working with me to keep my grade point average high enough to continue in school. However, I didn't learn my lesson then and later on was put on probation. Over time I realized that I had to slow down and deal with what I could handle. I did get off of probation and completed my course work to earn my degree. But a lot of people helped me and grace was shown to me in many different ways.

Please be encouraged that the grace that was described in this passage is still very much available to us today, when we come before the Lord with a sincere and contrite heart. May you, like the Apostle Paul, be able to state that the grace from our Lord was not given in vain!

God of love, help me to come before you asking for forgiveness for all my shortcomings, knowing that your infinite grace will be given me and that your love will surround me! Amen.

JANUARY 23

Prophets Testify about Forgiveness

> All the prophets testify about him that everyone who believes in him receives forgiveness of sins through his name.
>
> ACTS 10:43

In this chapter from Acts, Peter is talking to a man named Cornelius and others in the city of Caesarea. This passage indicates that the mission of the early church community was now extended to the Gentiles. Peter was telling them about the life of Jesus and about the good news of his ministry. This group then received the Holy Spirt and was baptized after hearing this message.

One of the key points that Peter declared was that the prophets had told about Jesus' coming and that those who believed in him would receive forgiveness of their sins. Jesus' purpose for coming to earth was foretold long before he came and his life was expected by those who were aware of what was written.

Those of us who live in this present time don't have to rely on a prophet's message to learn of the Messiah's coming. Because of Jesus' life, death, and resurrection, we are able to come to God through Jesus for the forgiveness of our sins and trespasses. We have scriptures like this one that informs and enlightens us about how Jesus still interacts with us today. On this spiritual pilgrimage know that when we come asking for forgiveness with a contrite and sincere heart we will be heard and forgiven!

Lord of all time, help me to understand the importance of daily repentance, and may I faithfully believe that my pleas are heard and accepted! Amen.

JANUARY 24

Peace with God

> Therefore, since we are justified by faith, we have peace with God through our Lord Jesus Christ, through whom we have obtained access to this grace in which we stand; and we boast in our hope of sharing the glory of God.
>
> ROMANS 5:1–2

Peace can mean various things to different people depending on the circumstance. It could be the end of friction between parties who were once at odds. The peace could be temporary or permanent, a period when everyone takes time to communicate without any strife. There can be peace between warring nations and countries, between communities, between family members or between friends.

There can also be peace in a person's mind, heart, and spirit depending upon where their focus happens to be at the moment. When our inner being is filled with hate, doubt, and fears, peace is probably impossible. By being hung up with things that can easily stop us from being the person that God wants us to be, it can be more challenging to receive the peace and hope that are ours through Jesus Christ.

Once we can truly believe that we are justified by faith, and that when we come before the Lord and ask for forgiveness God will indeed accept our pleas of repentance, then we can have peace about whatever comes our way. When we have hope that no matter what happens in this life or the next, that God's grace and love will surround us and comfort us, we can have peace in our mind, heart, and spirit. May you be able to embrace this inner peace in your daily spiritual pilgrimage!

Grace-filled Lord, help me to be open to the peace that you have for me when I come before you with my prayers of repentance, and may the peace that is in me reflect God's love to those that I meet today! Amen.

JANUARY 25

True Mercy Comes from God and Not Human Effort

> What then are we to say? Is there injustice on God's part? By no means! For he says to Moses, "I will have mercy on whom I have mercy, and I will have compassion on whom I have compassion." So it depends not on human will or exertion, but on God who shows mercy.
>
> ROMANS 9:14–16

There are so many aspects of this spiritual pilgrimage that run against the dominating thought in today's modern culture. Becoming a lifelong disciple of Jesus Christ carries a mind-set and motivation with it that at times may seem to be the direct opposite of worldly intentions. The Lord wants us to strive first for God's kingdom in our lives before anything else. In our society, we are encouraged before anything else to seek and work for those things that will made us more successful, better looking, able to live longer and better, and to improve our overall life with our own efforts and careful planning.

However, being forgiven of our sins and trespasses and looking for God's mercy comes about not so much because of what we do, but rather through God's infinite mercy and love. We do have to come seeking this mercy with a humble and contrite heart, but after that the forgiveness comes from the Lord and not because of our own will.

This may be hard for some of us to understand or grasp because of the many and varied signs that are all around us and coming to us through mass media stating just the opposite. That is where our spiritual practices of prayer, Bible study, and reflection may help us. With the comfort and guidance that we can get when we are involved in these rituals, we may be in a better position to accept the mercy from God versus believing that we have to do more to be forgiven. On this journey, may you have the faith to trust in these promises about God's mercy and love!

Lord of infinite love, help me to come before you knowing that your mercy and compassion are freely given to those who are open to receiving them! Amen.

JANUARY 26

Words of Repentance

> Return, O Israel, to the Lord your God, for you have stumbled because of your iniquity. Take words with you and return to the Lord; say to him, "Take away all guilt; accept that which is good, and we will offer the fruit of our lips."
>
> Hosea 14:1–2

The prophet Hosea is encouraging the nation of Israel to return to the Lord and to ask for forgiveness for the things that they have done. The implied message is that God doesn't want their sacrifice, but, rather for them to express their need of repentance in words and actions. In my life, I have found that unless I could share my feelings with someone, and then show them how I felt, nothing else seemed to matter in trying to renew or build up a relationship with them.

During the first few years of my marriage to my late wife, Judy, one of the really hard things that I had to learn was that of sharing my feelings and thoughts, versus keeping them inside of me. Judy had a very outgoing personality and found it easy to express what she was thinking and how she felt about most anything. I, on the other hand, was more reserved and had not learned how to share my emotions with others. This was an area where we struggled quite a bit in those early years.

Thankfully she was patient with me, loved me, and was willing to walk with me through that period, as I slowly became comfortable in sharing with her and then over time with others. It took a lot of prayers, love, and persistent effort but things did improve. Today, I am still somewhat reserved, however, I am better than I used to be, but it is something at which I have to constantly work.

No matter what your personality is, according to Hosea, God wants to hear the words from our lips about how we see ourselves, about our shortcomings, and where we need to ask for forgiveness. Part of our spiritual pilgrimage is to daily talk to God. Today return to God and strive to share all areas of your life, your prayer requests, and your shortcomings!

Lord of grace, may your Holy Spirit give me the courage and confidence to share all of my feelings with you that are on my lips and in my heart and soul! Amen.

JANUARY 27

Jesus Came to Save the World and Us

> For God so loved the world that he gave his only Son, so that everyone who believes in him may not perish but have eternal life. Indeed, God did not send the Son into the world to condemn the world, but in order that the world might be saved through him.
>
> JOHN 3:16–17

God sent Jesus into the world not to condemn it, but in order to save it. Think about that for a moment, Jesus came not as a condemning/punishing force but a saving one for the world. God is love and can't help but love all of creation including all of us fallible/sinful humans. On this side of the kingdom no matter how many times we fail, when we repent, God's love through Jesus Christ is there with open arms to embrace us again and again. No matter how far we think we may have fallen or messed up, it's not too far for God's loving reach to pull us back.

Regardless of how good we are with our spiritual practices, or how long we have been on our spiritual pilgrimage, or how prayerful or humble we have become, or how involved we are with a faith community, we have a need for daily repentance. All of us have occasions where we need to repent of our sins, to turn around from facing our will toward facing God's will, and to convert and live our life in a new way.

Jesus came *not* to condemn the world but to save it, and that means you and me. May that fact daily impact how you live, think, and act in all aspects of your life!

Saving Lord, may your Holy Spirit give me the courage to boldly live as your disciple, knowing that your Son came to save me. May my life be a reflection of your saving grace, love, and mercy! Amen.

JANUARY 28

Jesus Lives to Make Intercession for Us

> Consequently he is able for all time to save those who approach God through him, since he always lives to make intercession for them.
>
> HEBREWS 7:25

This is a well-known passage that indicates that because of Jesus' life, death, and resurrection, priests would no longer be needed to offer sacrifices on a daily basis for the sins of the people. Jesus has taken that role of a high priest forever and is able to save those who approach God through him. Additionally, he is living forever and is able to make intercession for those who come to him.

Thus, when we come asking for God's mercy and forgiveness we will be heard and Jesus is praying for us and making intercession for us. Many of us pray for others doing our meditation time, we pray for our family, friends, work situations, faith community, and issues around us or in the world. However, knowing when we come to God that Jesus is praying for us can encourage us to strive for God's kingdom in a faithful and persistent manner.

In my life when someone says that they will pray for me, it helps me realize that I am not alone in my journey, and that others care about what I am going through. Likewise, when I hear of someone needing prayers, and where it is possible and appropriate, I let them know that they are in my prayers, and often their lives are lifted up when they hear this. In the same manner on our spiritual pilgrimage when we approach the Lord in prayer, knowing that we are being prayed for as well by Jesus can also elevate and brighten up our souls!

Lord Jesus, thank you for life and for your prayers and intercession for me, and help me to pray for those around me who are in need! Amen.

JANUARY 29

God Wants All to Come to Repentance

> But do not ignore this one fact, beloved, that with the Lord one day is like a thousand years, and a thousand years are like one day. The Lord is not slow about his promise, as some think of slowness, but is patient with you, not wanting any to perish, but all to come to repentance. But the day of the Lord will come like a thief, and then the heavens will pass away with a loud noise, and the elements will be dissolved with fire, and the earth and everything that is done on it will be disclosed.
>
> 2 Peter 3:8–10

Many wise people have written about the point that God's timing is not ours. When we look at life through our human lens we are always limited because our knowledge and insights can only see things so far ahead. Generally, the best we can do is to know what is happening at this very moment, and what can and may occur later on is hard to determine. Apparently, this passage was trying to address those who felt that God's future kingdom wasn't coming fast enough for them. Does that sound like many of us today who live in a world of instant everything, we would probably be saying the same thing, why does God appear to take so long in doing something?

This writer is noting that as mortals we can't begin to understand how God sees time. Just trying to express this topic in human terms probably shouldn't be done, because our finite words can't fully describe God. However, we continue to try to do this because words are how we communicate. Thus, noting that for the Lord one day is like a thousand years and a thousand years is like one day is the best we can do.

However, one of the main points of this passage is that the future kingdom is coming in God's timing versus human's timing. God doesn't want any to perish, but *all* to come to repentance. God is love and can't help but love all of creation. All of the creation means those who are like me and those who are different, all of what God has made. There will come a point when the next kingdom will come as noted in verse 10. But until then, the Lord is allowing the time for all to come to repentance. On your spiritual pilgrimage, while you are striving for God's kingdom today may you ask the Lord to forgive you of your trespasses, knowing that because of God's grace and love it will be granted you!

Lord of all time, help me to trust in your timing in all things, and may I always seek your forgiveness knowing that I will be heard and loved! Amen.

JANUARY 30

Humility

> Do nothing from selfish ambition or conceit, but in humility regard others as better than yourselves.
>
> PHILIPPIANS 2:3

Being humble is a trait that doesn't come easily. Most humans want to be liked and cared about and thus may try to push themselves into situations where they are looked upon favorably. Like things in life having a healthy balance is the key, so that we don't go too far in either extreme. However, on this spiritual pilgrimage when we are attempting to become a lifelong disciple of Jesus Christ, we have to look toward how Jesus lived, and use his life as our model. Verse 8 in this passage notes that Jesus humbled himself.

Even though Jesus came in the form of God, he emptied himself and became obedient to what he was called to do.

The peculiar thing about being humble is that if we tried to be humble we would be missing the point. Some spiritual writers have noted that when we pray and open ourselves to what God wants for us in our lives, we are on the way to living as Jesus lived, a humble and obedient life. As we take part in our spiritual practices we come to realize over time that whatever we become, and whatever we do, comes from God as a gift. Our practices merely put us in a position to receive this gift, but it doesn't come because of these practices. What comes is because of God's grace and not our own efforts. Humility is not something that is sought after, but comes to us while we are on our spiritual pilgrimage.

Striving for God's kingdom in this time and place and becoming the person that God wants us to be is both a concrete and mysterious situation. It is concrete because by taking part in the spiritual practices of prayer, Bible study, and reflection we are doing our part for our own personal growth, and for bringing God's kingdom into this present time. It is mysterious because we don't know what will come out of it, nor do we know the timing of anything.

The part that keeps us on the path of humility is that we continue with our spiritual practices not knowing what will come out of them, only that we have been called to continue. Our trust is in the Lord and not our own efforts. Jesus humbled himself by emptying himself and being obedient to his heavenly Father. Our humility comes from seeking to be obedient to God's will each day.

Loving Lord, in my spiritual practices help me to be open to where you are guiding me, and leading me to become the person that you want me to be, and in the process, may I help others to do the same thing! Amen.

JANUARY 31

A New Creation

> So if anyone is in Christ, there is a new creation: everything old has passed away; see, everything has become new! All this is from God, who reconciled us to himself through Christ, and has given us the ministry of reconciliation.
>
> 2 CORINTHIANS 5:17–18

This is one of my favorite Bible verses, because it establishes that if anyone is in Christ, there is a new creation, everything old has passed away. On this spiritual pilgrimage, situations from our past can sometimes weigh us down and prevent us from becoming the person that God wants us to be. Because we are reconciled to God through Jesus Christ, we are a new creation, a new person, and those things that once held us back are gone. Becoming a new creation happens because of our relationship with God, and it can come in large and small ways; it can also come about when we go through some milestones in our lives.

This has occurred in my life on a number of occasions, and one of the more significant times was after earning my bachelor's degree. I had been working full time in the open-hearth department of a steel mill while going to college part time. The job at the mill could be very hot and dirty at times, and thus required me to change out of my work clothes and clean up after my shift. After going to college part time for eight years I graduated and was able to obtain a job in the insurance industry. At that point I felt that my life was a new creation.

I went from working forty hours a week in a mill and going to school part time, to just working forty hours a week as a trainee with the insurance company. I also went from wearing work clothes and working shift hours to wearing shirts and ties and only working during the daytime. The mill was in my hometown of Youngstown, Ohio, and the insurance company moved my family to Denver, Colorado. I felt both very fortunate and very humbled about this new role. This new created life was a joy-filled experience for me and my family.

Think of times in your life when you have been part of a new creation, which also can happen in little ways every day as you take part in the spiritual practices of this journey. God can make us into a new creation daily as we open ourselves up to the love that God has to offer, and to the guidance that the Holy Spirit has for us!

Creating Lord, please help me to realize that in Christ I am a new creation and that everything old has passed away, indeed, everything has become new! Amen.

February

Striving for the Kingdom of God— Repenting/Turning Around/Conversion

FEBRUARY 1

Turn Back

> Therefore thus says the Lord: If you turn back, I will take you back, and you shall stand before me. If you utter what is precious, and not what is worthless, you shall serve as my mouth.
>
> JEREMIAH 15:19

The prophet Jeremiah indicates that the Lord is willing to take the Israelite people back if they turn back and stand before the Lord; this verse supports the concept of striving for the kingdom of God as it relates to repentance, turning around, and conversion. As we take part in our spiritual pilgrimage, we have to keep in mind that each day we have to make life choices. Do we seek the things of the world and in ourselves that prevent us from striving first for God's kingdom in our lives, or is our focus on God's kingdom and will before anything else?

Repenting, turning around, or converting is something that happens in our hearts, minds, and souls. However, that inner action impacts how we live each day. It can be described in physical terms, "If you turn back, I will take you back." This action can be thought of as a physical one because it can guide our daily direction and choices. How we function each day and how we deal with issues in life are determined by this turning back to God who will always take us back.

During your journey may you understand the importance of turning away from the things that keep you from becoming a lifelong disciple of Jesus Christ, and as you turn around be assured that God will take you back and love you with an everlasting love!

Loving Lord, please give me the courage to turn back from the things of life that keep me from doing your will, and in the process, may I be a witness to those around me of your infinite grace, love, and mercy! Amen.

FEBRUARY 2

Forgive My Youthful Sins

> Do not remember the sins of my youth or my transgressions; according to your steadfast love remember me, for your goodness' sake, O Lord! . . . For your name's sake, O Lord, pardon my guilt, for it is great.
>
> PSALM 25:7, 11

This psalm is asking God for guidance and deliverance, and verse 7 is specifically asking for the Lord to not remember the transgressions of one's youth. Most of us can probably think of any number of things we did when we were young about which we now look back and say, *"What was I thinking?"* No matter how we were raised or what the environment was, we can all look back and wonder what caused us to do some of the things that we did.

Of course, we all know people who seem to have never grown up. Just because we get older doesn't mean that we don't still make mistakes, but hopefully as we age we learn from our past.

This psalm is asking that the Lord forgive the transgressions of one's youth, and to be honest, this isn't something that I normally think of doing, even though I made my share of youthful errors. As you take part in your spiritual practices today think about things from your past that may be weighing you down and ask God for forgiveness. The Lord's love is steadfast and always there to embrace you and pardon you and to remove any of your past guilt!

Lord of everlasting love, through your grace and mercy please forgive me for all of my past and present transgressions! Amen.

FEBRUARY 3

Fruit Worthy of Repentance

> But when he [John the Baptist] saw many Pharisees and Sadducees coming for baptism, he said to them, "You brood of vipers! Who warned you to flee from the wrath to come? Bear fruit worthy of repentance."
>
> MATTHEW 3:7–8

John the Baptist was very bold and blunt. He always said what he was thinking, and he didn't care whom he might have offended in the process. He definitely wasn't out to win any popularity contest. When he saw the Pharisees and Sadducees coming to be baptized, he knew that their lives didn't match their desire for baptism.

John knew that even though they wanted to be baptized their lives weren't bearing fruit worthy of the repentance that could go along with the desire to be baptized. When we talk about repenting, turning around, or conversion on this spiritual pilgrimage these acts might cause some change of direction, or purpose in our lives. Striving for God's kingdom and will in our lives could change how we live, and what we might do versus what we did last week, last year, or twenty years ago. Our actions are now directed by the Holy Spirit.

Bearing fruit worthy of repentance could mean among other things simply asking God for guidance for today, and being ready to follow the Holy Spirit. Be open to where this journey may be taking you and may your walk with Christ reflect your spirit of repentance!

God of everlasting forgiveness, today help me to strive for your will in my life, and in the process, may my life be a witness to your steadfast love! Amen.

FEBRUARY 4

God's Abundant Pardon

> Seek the Lord while he may be found, call upon him while he is near; let the wicked forsake their way, and the unrighteous their thoughts; let them return to the Lord, that he may have mercy on them, and to our God, for he will abundantly pardon.
>
> ISAIAH 55:6–7

The prophet Isaiah was telling the nation of Israel about the need to seek and to call upon the Lord, forsake their evil ways and thoughts, return to God, and then the Lord would have mercy on them and abundantly pardon them.

One could ask why should we worry about doing this when we know that God is love and can't help but love us? Why should we take the time to acknowledge our shortcomings and sins? We do this because as disciples of Jesus Christ, we follow his life and teachings. When he gave directions about how to pray, he gave us what has come to be called the Lord's Prayer. In that prayer, we ask God to forgive us our debts, sins, or trespasses, as we forgive others for the way they have wronged us.

The Lord wanted the nation of Israel, and Jesus wanted those who would be his followers, to turn away from the things that would hold them back from becoming the nation and persons that God wanted them to be. We do this when we turn toward the Lord, ask for mercy, and then expect to receive a pardon for what has been done. On this side of God's kingdom, because we are imperfect human beings, asking for forgiveness of our shortcomings is an ongoing occurrence.

On your spiritual pilgrimage, may you find the time and energy to daily turn toward God, asking for God's mercy!

God of love, help me to seek your forgiveness each day and then forgive others as you have forgiven me! Amen.

FEBRUARY 5

Freed by Truth to Be Jesus' Disciples

> Then Jesus said to the Jews who had believed in him, "If you continue in my word, you are truly my disciples; and you will know the truth, and the truth will make you free."
>
> JOHN 8:31–32

As Jesus was talking to the Jews who believed in him, he wanted them to know a couple of things. That as they followed his word, his teaching, they would be his disciples, and they would become free.

When we take part in the spiritual practices of prayer, Bible study, and reflection we learn about Jesus' words and our faith grows and matures in the process. When we repent of our shortcomings or turn around from the things of the world toward God's kingdom and will in our lives, we grow in the knowledge of the truth that Jesus taught and lived.

This truth, which comes from the saving power of God through Jesus Christ, can set us free of the worry and concern about what lies ahead, and gives us the ability to live today for God's kingdom. We are freed to walk the path of becoming a lifelong disciple of Jesus Christ. We are freed to be open to where the Holy Spirit may be asking us to go next on our journey, and hopefully this freedom will give us the courage and strength to follow the guidance given.

May you be willing to step out in faith to believe in the promises of God about your spiritual pilgrimage!

Lord of all truth, help me to trust and believe in you and in the process, be receptive to where you may be asking me to go today!

FEBRUARY 6

Confessing Our Sins to God Who Is Near

> I confess my iniquity; I am sorry for my sin. . . . Do not forsake me,
> O Lord; O my God, do not be far from me; make haste to help me,
> O Lord, my salvation.
>
> PSALM 38:18, 21–22

This entire passage (vv. 11–22) describes how we are left to deal with suffering alone, it outlines how we may have people who stand far off while we are going through a tough period. It may seem that those around us don't understand nor comprehend what we may be going through at the moment. When we do have people who can lovingly walk with us during our rough patches, we realize that we are very fortunate indeed to have life companions such as these.

This psalmist however, after acknowledging that those around them may not care about what they are going through, confesses their sin and asks that the Lord not forsake them. They realize that God is the one constant for them in their lives and is not far from them and becomes their help and salvation.

In some ways, this may be a hard concept to understand as we take part in this spiritual pilgrimage, that the people we see every day in some cases may be actually further away from our lives and what we may be going through at the moment, than the Lord that we can't see with our physical eyes, but just with our spiritual ones. On this journey, may you be open to confessing your sins, repenting of them and then asking God to be close and to help you through whatever you may be going through at the moment!

Loving Lord, please forgive me all of my sin and trespasses and remain close to me, help me and daily become my salvation! Amen.

FEBRUARY 7

Jesus, the World's Atoning Sacrifice

> My little children, I am writing these things to you so that you may not sin. But if anyone does sin, we have an advocate with the Father, Jesus Christ the righteous; and he is the atoning sacrifice for our sins, and not for ours only but also for the sins of the whole world.
>
> 1 JOHN 2:1–3

The last insurance company that I worked for, before leaving that industry to enter Trinity Lutheran Seminary, took their management team to an outdoor bonding experience to improve the working relationships between the staff and the many departments of the company. There were many events and projects that required groups to depend on each other in order to achieve the task at hand. These assignments forced many of us completely out of our comfort zone, and caused us to think and act in ways that took us much further than we ever thought we could be stretched. We did things that we never thought of doing before going there.

One of the terms that was used during that event that has stayed with me is "Fallible Human Being." The point was that all of us were fallible human beings with just as many hang-ups and shortcomings as the next person. The exercises stressed that no matter how we looked at each other, everyone had issues, old baggage, warts, etc., that had to be acknowledged and dealt with before moving on to accomplish some task or project. Thus, part of this event for us was telling others what things were preventing us from accomplishing the project or task.

All of us have things that we need to express, let go of, and for which we seek forgiveness. We know that Jesus Christ is the atoning sacrifice for our sins and for the sins of the whole world. On your spiritual pilgrimage, may you become increasingly more aware that all of us are fallible human beings in need of forgiveness!

God of life, help me to be open to the thought that we all have shortcomings and issues that need addressing, but we do have an advocate for these in Jesus Christ! Amen.

FEBRUARY 8

Jesus Reproves Those He Loves

> I reprove and discipline those whom I love. Be earnest, therefore, and repent.
>
> REVELATION 3:19

This passage was written to the church in Laodicea, which was roughly one hundred miles east of Ephesus. The preceding verses tell us what was thought about this church. Their faith was lukewarm, neither hot nor cold; they prospered and apparently thought too much of their riches. They were encouraged to seek the gold that was refined by fire and to accept the discipline of Jesus for those he loved. They were to be earnest and honorable in their behavior and to repent of their sins.

There is quite a bit that we could take from this passage that applies to our spiritual pilgrimage. One of the main points will be the importance of seeking those things that have been refined by the fires or challenges of life, and to know that we need to repent for our sins and trespasses. We have never been promised that this journey would always be perfect without the normal issues that come the way of anyone living in this time and place. However, such times do refine our faith by removing the impurities so that we can continue on our life's spiritual walk, becoming the person that God wants us to be.

Please be open to where the Holy Spirit may be leading you, it may take you to a point where things that were once important to you become less vital. The Spirit may be asking you to let go of objects that might be holding you back in this journey. Be ready to let go, repent, and move toward God's kingdom in your daily life. You are loved, and with this love may come guidance about a change in your spiritual walk!

Lord of everlasting grace, help me to turn from myself and to let go of the earthly riches in my life, daily repent, and then move toward you in all I do! Amen.

FEBRUARY 9

Being Freed, Delivered, and Redeemed

> Say therefore to the Israelites, "I am the Lord, and I will free you from the burdens of the Egyptians and deliver you from slavery to them.

> I will redeem you with an outstretched arm and with mighty acts of Judgment."
>
> Exodus 6:6

The Lord is telling Moses about what he is to say to the Israelites. Even though they wouldn't listen, God wants Moses to deliver the message anyway. There are many messages that we could get from this verse. There are three words that are key to this passage: *free*, *deliver*, and *redeem*. God wants to free the people from their heavy burdens, deliver them from slavery, and redeem them to be God's people.

Down through the years in many cultures, enslaved peoples or those at the very bottom of society have used the messages given to the Israelites as a sign for them that they also can be freed, delivered, and redeemed. When you are born in a time or place that has little to offer in the way of hope, or when you are constantly told in word and deed that you don't matter, or when you are put down by the society you live in because of your skin color, your religion, or your background, or when you have made tremendous mistakes in your life and pulling yourself away from your past is extremely difficult, you need someone to give you hope about a promised new day.

When we come to the Lord and ask for the love and forgiveness that are offered, even if our situation hasn't changed, nonetheless, we have been freed, delivered, and redeemed from the spiritual forces that may have pulled us down. Knowing this allows us over time to come to know that whatever condition we are now in is only temporary, and that we do have the gift of eternal life now and in the time to come because of Jesus' life, death, and resurrection. This knowledge can and should affect how we think about where we are today, even when the physical surroundings are the same.

No matter where you are at the moment please be encouraged to continue with your spiritual pilgrimage with the knowledge that when we ask the Lord for help, it will be given to us!

Loving God, help me to come to you regardless of what is going on with me, you understand and love me, and are always willing to free, deliver, and redeem me! Amen.

FEBRUARY 10

Seeking God's Mercy

> Have mercy on me, O God, according to your steadfast love; according to your abundant mercy blot out my transgressions. Wash me thoroughly from my iniquity, and cleanse me from my sin.
>
> PSALM 51:1–2

This entire psalm is a sincere cry to God by the writer to be forgiven of the sins that have been committed. The writer is asking for mercy according to the steadfast love of the Lord which can blot out all transgressions. The words used for this process are about the washing and cleansing of one's sins. What is described is similar to a physical washing and cleaning of one's own body.

I grew up in a family of all boys, and needless to say we often came home from being out and about with enough dirt on us to leave our marks all around our house. However, my mom was the clean police and was around to be sure we did what was expected of us. She made sure that our bodies and clothes were clean when we went to school, church, or anyplace else. One of the habits that we got into when we were young was polishing our church shoes on Saturday night, so that they would look nice for Sunday worship. Thus, washing up and being clean became something my brothers and I got used to doing. This is a routine that many of us have and this can be carried over to the habit of seeking forgiveness from our Lord.

The writer of this psalm knows the importance of washing up and being clean as it pertains to the sins and shortcomings in their life, and asks the Lord to wash and cleanse them from their sins. On our spiritual pilgrimage, we should think about doing something similar. As humans with many faults and warts we can never be totally free of shortcomings on this side of the kingdom and will always have a need for God's forgiveness. God is faithful and will hear our pleas and grant us mercy and forgiveness. In this way, we will be washed thoroughly of our iniquities and be cleansed of our sins!

Lord of steadfast love and mercy, hear my cry for your forgiveness, and blot out all of my transgressions, so that I am washed and cleansed! Amen.

FEBRUARY 11

Tested in the Furnace of Adversity

> See, I have refined you, but not like silver; I have tested you in the furnace of adversity.
>
> ISAIAH 48:10

A wise person once said that the only people without problems were those buried in the cemeteries. The thought being that as long as we were still alive there would be challenges, struggles, and everyday issues to deal with. That is surely the case for the people of Israel at the time of this writing, they would have things to deal with and adversity would test them. However, out of that the Lord would refine them.

If you are like me, you would rather not go through any furnace of adversity where we are being refined through our testing. However, on this spiritual and physical pilgrimage there will come periods when we have to go through trying times, but it is part of life as we grow and mature into the person God created us to be. The main thing to remember is that just as the Lord was with the nation of Israel, God's love and comfort will be with us as well.

We always need to acknowledge our need for forgiveness and ask for God's mercy. Additionally, remember that when we go through the really painful moments of our journey, that may be when we are being refined. God doesn't want any of us to suffer, but God knows that our refining is part of the process in becoming the people that God wants us to be!

Lord of life, help me to look toward you in all times of my life, both the good and not so good, and help me to grow and be refined no matter what stage of life I am in! Amen.

FEBRUARY 12

Clean Hands and Pure Hearts

> Who shall ascend the hill of the Lord? And who shall stand in his holy place? Those who have clean hands and pure hearts, who do not lift up their souls to what is false, and do not swear deceitfully. They will receive blessing from the Lord, and vindication from the God of their salvation.
>
> PSALM 24:3–5

This passage is describing who is able to enter the holy sanctuary. The sanctuary is noted as the hill of God and a holy place. The writer mentions that those who have clean hands and pure hearts, and whose words are true are able to enter in. Why do you think this is?

There are many different reasons that could be given as to why this was written. One thought could be that if we come into God's presence harboring negative or hateful feelings toward others, if we are unable to leave behind the worries of the world, we may have erected barriers between us and God. If our hands have been a part of things that we are ashamed of, and if our hearts are full of sinful feelings, or we have been untruthful in our words and actions, then our attempts to focus on God and worship can be extremely challenging.

Of course, as fallible humans we may find it difficult to totally get rid all of the issues in our hearts and souls that may keep us from entering in, however, that is where repentance comes in. Asking the Lord to forgive us of our sins and trespasses on a daily basis puts us into a better place to worship and praise the Lord. No matter where we happen to be at the moment, because God is love, and can't help but love us, God will welcome us, at any point in our lives. But, from our standpoint, we can better focus on worshiping God when we are able to do so with clean hands, a pure heart, and honest words.

Approach the sacred space in your life with the assurance that the Lord wants and welcomes our sincere songs of praise, and will always hear our requests when we ask for forgiveness!

Gracious Lord, give me the guidance and courage to come to you with all the issues in my life, knowing that you love me and only want the best for me, including giving me clean hands and a pure heart! Amen.

FEBRUARY 13

God Is Our Salvation

> Surely God is my salvation; I will trust, and will not be afraid, for the Lord God is my strength and my might; he has become my salvation.
>
> ISAIAH 12:2

Every new day carries with it unknowns, no matter our stage of life. We may hope and pray that everything will go well, and we most certainly will do our part to make sure that it does. However, sometimes things occur in our lives that we have no control of, that could affect our lives in small or large ways. Accidents, sicknesses, acts of violence, or weather-related events, you name it, can come our way unexpectedly. It is up to us to not let these things paralyze us from living as normal a life as possible, and handle whatever is coming at that moment.

One way to do this is to take to heart verses such as this one. To firmly reflect upon and take into our inner being these words of comfort. The Lord is our salvation, and thus we can trust and not be afraid, for God is our strength and might. When we can truly believe that our salvation in this life and the next life comes from our Lord, and not from anything in this world that is here today and gone tomorrow, we can have a peace that is not offered anywhere else.

There are many voices in the world that state that they have the answer for happiness, well-being, and a so-called successful life, by buying their product, or following their program, or believing in their message. Anything that they promise will only last for a short period until the next best thing is out, and thus will fade away. However, as you come to the Lord in prayer and with pleas of forgiveness may you experience this strength and might, which can help you to trust and not be afraid, knowing that the Lord God is your salvation, today, tomorrow, and for all circumstances and is unlike anything that is offered by the world!

Lord, help me to turn toward you for my salvation and not to anything that is temporal. May I feel your strength helping me to deal with whatever comes my way today! Amen.

FEBRUARY 14

The Lord Listens

> For you, O Lord, are good and forgiving, abounding in steadfast love to all who call on you. Give ear, O Lord, to my prayer; listen to my cry of supplication. In the day of my trouble I call on you, for you will answer me.
>
> Psalm 86:5–7

This short passage places a real importance on the point that what is being said will be heard by God. Words like call, ear, listen, cry, and answer indicate that the writer is confident that what they will be saying will be heard by the one being addressed and that their pleas will be answered. I have often said that a person with good listening skills was well on their way to having good relationships with others.

Before going to Trinity Lutheran Seminary, for more than twenty-seven years, I worked in the insurance industry, primarily in marketing. One of my main tasks was visiting the agencies that sold insurance for the companies that I represented. For me to be effective in what I did I had to be fully aware of what was being said. On those calls I had to be a good listener to the concerns and issues that were raised so that I could correct any misinformation, help to solve any service problems, uncover why our products were not being sold, or deal with any number of assorted things. If I couldn't clearly understand what was being communicated I wouldn't be able to do what needed to be done.

Of course, good communication is vital in any relationship, in a marriage, in family situations, in communities, in work environments, in governments, among nations, etc. This passage lets us know that God is also a good listener besides being forgiving and abounding in steadfast love. When we come before the Lord with our prayers and supplications they will be heard, and we can be assured that we will be answered especially in our day of trouble. May you be bold in speaking to God about anything that you need forgiveness for or help with, knowing that when you call you will be heard!

Lord of steadfast love, help me to come to you knowing that you are the everlasting listener of love, and you welcome and hear my prayers and will answer them in your own time and fashion! Amen.

FEBRUARY 15

We Have Turned to Our Own Way

> But he was wounded for our transgressions, crushed for our iniquities; upon him was the punishment that made us whole, and by his bruises we are healed. All we like sheep have gone astray; we have all turned to our own way, and the Lord has laid on him the iniquity of us all.
>
> ISAIAH 53:5–6

There are countless passages in the Bible that refer to direction and movement. There are references to people on a journey, the nation of Israel going to the promised land, Jesus and his followers on their way to Jerusalem, and individuals moving toward God's will in their lives rather than their own way. This latter reference has more to do with where a person's focus is and for whom and what they are living.

This passage refers to those who have gone astray and have a need of turning around. The idea is that in this case the persons involved are more interested in going on their own way rather than daily striving for God's kingdom. Repenting, turning around, and conversion as it relates to striving for God's kingdom is something that those of us on this spiritual pilgrimage should attempt to frequently do.

Each day we have to decide which direction we will follow. Will we listen to our own voice or the voices all around us that encourage us to do things our way instead of following the guidance of the Holy Spirit and move toward God's kingdom and will in our lives? Turning around from listening to our own voice rather the Holy Spirit's direction isn't a one-time event, but a daily, maybe even moment-by-moment choice that we have to make. On your journey, may you remain open to the wisdom and comfort offered by God's Spirit, and may that give you the courage to turn from your own voice, and to turn toward the things of God's kingdom!

Loving Lord, help me to turn from my own way toward your will in my life, and may the Holy Spirit provide what I need today to take the necessary steps in your direction! Amen.

FEBRUARY 16

Regarding Everything as Loss

> Yet whatever gains I had, these I have come to regard as loss because of Christ. More than that, I regard everything as loss because of the surpassing value of knowing Christ Jesus my Lord. For his sake I have suffered the loss of all things, and I regard them as rubbish, in order that I may gain Christ.
>
> PHILIPPIANS 3:7–8

In this passage the Apostle Paul is stressing how important Jesus is to him and that everything else is regarded as loss and rubbish. He was always very strong in expressing his thoughts and feelings and he didn't seem to be shy when letting others know how he felt about his faith. Philippians is a short book but so powerful for those on this spiritual pilgrimage for it holds much wisdom and insight about becoming a lifelong disciple of Jesus Christ. However, Paul could be viewed for being too far out there by some people living in today's modern, fast-paced world.

In reading these words through our current life lens we could easily say that those thoughts were okay for Paul's time, however with so many other things that could become number one in our lives, they don't hold water for us today. Because of the abundance of mass media information and the 24/7 technology connections that are available to us, we are always being offered something else to buy or be a part of to make our lives better or to become more informed. It could be said that this is something that Paul didn't have to deal with, that life was simpler back then. Basically, why do I need to worry about knowing Christ Jesus our Lord, when I like my life just the way it is and I have so many wonderful things to occupy my time with?

Each day that we wake up we have to decide who is the most important person, facet, or god in our lives. Even if we don't believe in the Lord, whatever becomes the most important thing in our life is our god. A god could be you, your spouse, a special friend, your children, your career or job, your material possessions, almost anything can become one's god. However, all of the things on this earth will in time pass away except for the love of God given to us in Jesus Christ. That is why Paul said what he did, he knew that everything else would pass away, only Christ lasts.

On your journey, may you daily think about Paul's words and reflect on them. Everything we can gain in this life is rubbish except for our belief *in* and our knowledge *of* Jesus Christ!

Lord of life, help me to realize that compared to your love everything is considered as loss, and may my daily pilgrimage reflect that awareness! Amen.

FEBRUARY 17

Transgressions Swept Away

> I [the Lord God] have swept away your transgressions like a cloud, and your sins like mist; return to me, for I have redeemed you.
>
> Isaiah 44:22

This passage from Isaiah is letting the people of Israel know that the Lord God who formed and redeemed them has not forgotten them. Their transgressions will be swept away like a cloud, and their sins cleared away like the mist from the morning sun—every wrong will be forgotten and wiped away.

Many of us, including myself, carry with us things that we have done in the past, that we wish had been done differently. We may have made the best decision that we could have made at that time based on the facts at hand. However, what happened was not what we had hoped for, and in hindsight we may have wished that another choice had been made. As I look back in my life, there are several choices made where I wish I'd taken another path, e.g., a certain job relocation; decisions around certain family issues; and some decisions made at the time of my late wife's illness, to name a few.

If I could do some of these things over again, I like to think that I'd take different steps. But as most of us know, given the facts at that time, and who we were at that time, probably the same choice would have been made; we just like to think it would have been different.

Thus, we just have to acknowledge what was done and then ask the Lord to forgive what we have done or failed to do. The hard part for us as fallible humans is to accept this forgiveness and to let go of what is behind us, focusing instead on seeking God's mercy each day, and trying to envision our sins and transgressions being swept away as the sun melts away the morning mist!

Redeeming Lord, help me to come to you for your infinite grace, love, and mercy, and help me to accept your forgiveness and be able to live this day free of any past shortcomings! Amen.

FEBRUARY 18

Justified by God's Grace

> Since all have sinned and fall short of the glory of God; they are now justified by his grace as a gift, through the redemption that is in Christ Jesus.
>
> ROMANS 3:23–24

One of the more challenging aspects of human life is the ability to forgive oneself when we commit some wrong. We may hold our emotions and have a hard time seeking forgiveness and over time letting them go in order to move on. We also may struggle with forgiving others who may have hurt us. I know that this is an area that has caused me more stress and pain than it should. Often when I hold onto the hurts caused by others, it actually causes the hurt to grow and take on a life of its own, which causes me more pain. I mentally realize that it is better to forgive after a certain point and move on, however, my emotional side will not let it go very easily.

However, in this letter to the Romans, Paul is letting them know that all have sinned and come short. But God's grace through the redemption of Jesus Christ saves us from our sin. May this verse allow you the courage to believe in this promise of grace, and in the process free you from any guilt about past shortcomings and give you the faith to continue on your spiritual pilgrimage. God's grace comes to us because of God's love for us, and when we experience this grace and love we can live out our calling freed of our past!

Lord of love, help me to trust your promise of grace and seek forgiveness from those I may have harmed, and also be willing to offer this same pardon for those who may have hurt me! Amen.

FEBRUARY 19

God Is with Us

> She will bear a son, and you are to name him Jesus, for he will save his people from their sins. All this took place to fulfill what had been spoken by the Lord through the prophet: "Look, the virgin shall conceive and bear a son, and they shall name him Emmanuel," which means "God is with us."
>
> MATTHEW 1:21–23

This is a well-known passage that is usually read during the Advent/Christmas season in many Christian communities, for it talks about the birth of Jesus Christ. Joseph was told in a dream that he shouldn't be afraid to take Mary as his wife when she was expecting, because the child was conceived by the Holy Spirit. What was happening was to fulfill the prophecy that Jesus was to save his people from their sins, and he would be "God is with us."

Jesus' birth changed the entire world, for he did in fact save his people from their sins and he became God with us. Additionally, Jesus wouldn't be a far-off figure that was apart from the people whom he came to save. This savior would be with and among the people. Jesus walked the earth, was part of a family, had all of the emotions of those around him, he ate, cried, got angry, went off to be alone when the pressures of his ministry got to be too much, and *oh yes*, he saved his people from their sins. He became a comfort to those around him, and he continues to do the same for us today through the gift of the Holy Spirit.

On your spiritual pilgrimage while you strive for God's kingdom and God's will in your life, know that repenting / turning around / conversion is part of the journey as well. Also, know that this same Jesus who came to be with and among humans came to save us as we repent of our shortcomings. We can ask for forgiveness knowing that we will be heard and forgiven. Today may you feel the presence of Jesus in your life and may this free you to become a lifelong disciple of Jesus Christ!

Loving Lord, thank you for your Son who came to be God with us, and to save us from our sins, and may this help me to share your infinite grace, love, and mercy with all those whom I meet today! Amen.

FEBRUARY 20

Our Day of Salvation

> As we work together with him, we urge you also not to accept the grace of God in vain. For he says, "At an acceptable time I have listened to you, and on a day of salvation I have helped you." See, now is the acceptable time; see, now is the day of salvation!
>
> 2 CORINTHIANS 6:1–2

As humans on this earthly journey we share together a number of common traits and functions. We all have to eat, drink, take care of our bodies, and get some rest and exercise. Normally we have to do these things and many others on a daily basis. Something that a number of us do more often than we care to admit is to put things off until later on, or until we are forced to do them, and sometimes things just don't get done. A word defining this condition is procrastination! When we delay a task, we are taking part in procrastination.

Sometimes it's a good idea to do this when an action needs more research or information, or when the time isn't right to do it, or for any number of good, sound reasons. However, often we throw roadblocks up that don't need to be there when we are unwilling to move forward with something.

But when it comes to asking for forgiveness from our Lord and then accepting God's grace for our shortcomings, today is that day, we shouldn't take part in procrastination when it comes to this! Today is the day of our salvation, and each and every day thereafter. As noted by many spiritual writers, asking for repentance, turning around, or conversion can be a daily event.

As fallible humans, we are always in need of this salvation, however, the wonderful part is that God's infinite grace, love, and mercy are always there waiting to absorb any and all of our sins and trespasses. Continue to be open to this aspect of your spiritual pilgrimage so that no matter what stage you are in, or regardless of how far your spiritual practices have been developed, you know that today is your day of salvation!

Eternal Lord, help me to daily come to you seeking forgiveness, knowing that today is my day of salvation as well as all of my future days! Amen.

FEBRUARY 21

Not Praying for Others

> Moreover as for me, far be it from me that I should sin against the Lord by ceasing to pray for you; and I will instruct you in the good and the right way.
>
> 1 Samuel 12:23

In this passage the prophet Samuel promises to pray for the people of Israel and tells them that he would instruct them in the proper way to live. His offer to continue to pray is centered upon the fact that, in his mind, it would be a sin against the Lord if he stopped praying for them. From our standpoint, reading this many years after it was written, Samuel's reasoning may seem a bit strange or extreme. We may never think of our ceasing to pray for someone as a sin against God, but that is what Samuel believed.

There are countless things that we can ask forgiveness for because as fallible humans we are always in need of repentance. But thinking about not praying for others as a sin may be new to many of us as it certainly is for me. Daily I pray for many people and situations, as I am sure you do as well. Please be encouraged to continue to do so, even when others may not be aware that you are praying for them.

Obviously, prayer for Samuel was a necessity, causing him to believe that it would be a sin to stop praying for the people. With your prayers on your spiritual pilgrimage, always be open to changing how you pray, whom or what you pray for, and how often you pray. Additionally, be aware of your daily need for God's forgiveness, because as long as we are on this side of God's kingdom we will sin and come short of how we are expected to live!

Loving Lord, may my prayers become a central part of my essence and may my life be a witness to others of your forgiving grace! Amen.

FEBRUARY 22

Turning to the Lord

> Then I turned to the Lord God, to seek an answer by prayer and supplication with fasting and sackcloth and ashes. I prayed to the Lord my God and made confession.
>
> Daniel 9:3–4

My sense of direction is quite good, and normally I can find my way around in most places. However, many years ago, I got used to getting maps of any city I lived or worked in to help in getting around. This started after I finished my insurance training in Denver, Colorado, with St. Paul Insurance Company and was moved to the Bay Area of Northern California to work with my first territory as a marketing representative.

The agencies that were assigned to me were spread all over the East Bay in a number of cities, including Oakland, Berkeley, and San Leandro. Because I hated getting lost, and didn't want to be late for my appointments, I acquired maps of all the cities and of the general area. Until I learned my way around the region, those maps were a life saver for me in so many ways. Now remember this was before we had smart devices that provided directions or computer-generated maps at our fingertips.

Since then I continue to use maps, even when computers can be used to help get directions. Those maps helped me get to the right places and kept me going in the right direction. On our spiritual pilgrimage, daily we should attempt to do the same thing, that is to find out where the Holy Spirit wants us to go, and then head in that direction.

In this passage, Daniel got it right when he turned to the Lord and sought an answer through prayer and supplication. Note the title for this month's devotions, "Striving for the Kingdom of God—Repenting / Turning Around / Conversion." Turning around is part of this process of seeking the Lord's mercy and forgiveness. When we move away from the things of the world and from our own agenda and desires toward the Lord and what God wants for us in our lives we are engaged in becoming the persons that we are called to be.

On your spiritual pilgrimage, may you daily strive to turn from yourself and face God with your prayers and supplications, knowing that you will be heard and will have the Holy Spirit to comfort and guide you!

Dear Lord, help me to listen to your voice and then face you instead of whatever else is around me, so that my entire being is focused on you and your will for me in this time and place! Amen.

FEBRUARY 23

Communicating

> But afterward, David was stricken to the heart because he had numbered the people. David said to the Lord, "I have sinned greatly in what I have done. But now, O Lord, I pray you, take away the guilt of your servant; for I have done very foolishly."
>
> 2 Samuel 24:10

Having to acknowledge that we have done something wrong or communicating our feelings of guilt to someone takes courage and a willingness to correct some past wrong or to improve on one's relationship. King David admitted to God that he had done wrong in numbering his people. He was sorry for what he had done and asked for forgiveness. He was heard by the Lord, however, some of the people suffered because of what he had done.

From my standpoint having the courage to share one's shortcomings or feelings is not a small feat. My late wife, Judy, was a very outgoing person and willingly shared her thoughts and feelings with me and those she loved. I on the other hand was very reserved and guarded with sharing my thoughts and feelings. In my own family, I knew I was loved, however, we generally didn't talk much about feelings, so that wasn't something that I was comfortable in doing. I was not as outgoing as Judy was and I wasn't inclined to being very open.

This was a really challenging part of our relationship during the first few years of our marriage. Because of this I knew at times that Judy was very frustrated with me. However, over time I improved, and we were able to communicate much better.

This may be the case for some of you on this spiritual pilgrimage. You may have a difficult time admitting to God or others in your life your shortcomings or sharing your feelings. From what I have read and experienced God welcomes any communication from us, no matter if asking for pardon, giving thanks, or just the day-to-day sharing of our thoughts and feelings. May you be open to coming to the Lord as King David did, knowing that you will be heard!

Listening Lord, may I have the courage and faith to come before you with all of my concerns, sorrows, joys, and requests of forgiveness, knowing that all of it is welcomed and received! Amen.

FEBRUARY 24

The Father Was Filled with Compassion

> So he set off and went to his father. But while he was still far off, his father saw him and was filled with compassion; he ran and put his arms around him and kissed him.
>
> LUKE 15:20

This passage is taken from a parable that Jesus told in Luke and it is surrounded by several parables. This parable is commonly called the parable of "The Prodigal Son and His Brother." Some of us know the story well: the younger brother asks for his share of the family property, goes off and squanders it, and ends up coming back to his family and father asking for forgiveness. However, while he is far off his father is filled with compassion and welcomes him back into the family and gives a feast in his honor.

Most often what is focused on in this story are the drama and conflict between the two brothers. But, the bigger issue is about how the father was so willing to forgive and welcome his son home. He wants to rejoice because his son was once dead to the family and had now returned. What was once lost had now been found. Jesus was making a point with this parable and in some of his others that when we return to God, there is great cause for a celebration.

When we ask for forgiveness or return to worshiping the Lord after time away, God welcomes us and is full of compassion, as the father in this story. During your spiritual practices may you come with a sincere and contrite heart to the Lord, and know that God will receive you with outstretched arms of grace and love!

Lord of compassion, may your Holy Spirit direct and lead me to return again and again to you seeking your forgiveness, knowing that your love and compassion will welcome and embrace me! Amen.

FEBRUARY 25

Purification

> I came to bring fire to the earth, and how I wish it were already kindled! I have a baptism with which to be baptized, and what stress I am under until it is completed!
>
> LUKE 12:49–50

In this passage, Jesus is talking about how he came to bring division on earth and about the end times. In that culture fire was a sign of purification or judgment, for it was used to remove impurities from metals. Jesus came to dwell among us for many reasons and one of the things that could easily get overlooked is that he came to purify, that is to burn off those issues in our lives that need to be removed.

In our spiritual pilgrimage letting go of things in our lives that hold us back from becoming the person that God wants us to be is part of the process. This of course can happen to individuals as well as faith communities and occurs on a daily basis. How we do things, how we think, and where our focus is, will change over time as we take part in our spiritual practices. The change will not be one that comes from aging, but because we are moving along on our spiritual journey.

The purification can be large or small, can happen over time or suddenly, but it will come. This process is an important part of our spiritual pilgrimage. On this walk we need to welcome this change that will come and be willing to let go of those aspects of our life that need to be removed and left behind!

Loving Lord, may your Holy Spirit burn off the impurities in my life that need to be removed to allow me to become a lifelong disciple of Jesus Christ! Amen.

FEBRUARY 26

Humbling Ourselves

> If my people who are called by my name humble themselves, pray, seek my face, and turn from their wicked ways, then I will hear from heaven, and will forgive their sin and heal their land. Now my eyes will be open and my ears attentive to the prayer that is made in this place.
>
> 2 Chronicles 7:14–15

In this passage, God is responding to Solomon's prayer. God outlines what is expected from Solomon and the people regarding the temple. These words can also apply to any of us who want to be forgiven and who desire to become the person that God wants us to be.

Humbling oneself, praying, seeking the Lord's face, and turning from our wicked ways in order to be heard and forgiven sounds very hard to do in our current society. This entire thought of repenting so runs against what we see and hear in our media-crazed world that informs us to get and acquire as much as we can and don't worry about how it impacts God's creation and those around us.

Yet this is what God expected of the people in Solomon's day and what is expected of us today. If we think that through our own efforts and wisdom we can save ourselves, if we think that we can have a relationship with our Lord without communicating with God, if we think we can strive for God's kingdom by turning away from God and turning toward our own ways, we are wrong! The Lord alone saves and heals us.

On your spiritual pilgrimage, daily attempt to prayerfully come to the Lord with a humble and contrite heart, turning toward God's will in your lives, and the Lord will welcome you with open arms, hear you, and forgive your sins!

Lord of all compassion, help me to humbly come to you in my prayers, turn toward you and your will on a daily basis, so that I may become a lifelong disciple of Jesus Christ! Amen.

FEBRUARY 27

A Ransom for Many

> For the Son of Man came not to be served but to serve, and to give his life a ransom for many.
>
> MARK 10:45

A lot has been written about how Jesus' followers had a hard time understanding what he was trying to tell them and what his life was all about. In this passage, we have James and John asking Jesus if they could sit on Jesus' right and left hands when he came into his glory. Of course, he tells them why that wasn't his decision to make, for he came to serve and not to be served and to offer his life as a ransom for many.

He came to offer his life for the sins of humankind and to give those who believe in him the gift of eternal life now and in the time to come. He was the sacrifice for all time and all people, the sacrifice that ended the need for temple sacrifices.

Part of the challenge for some of us on this spiritual pilgrimage is the question of why once we come to believe in Jesus Christ, we still need to acknowledge our sins on a daily basis. We are all fallible human beings who constantly fall short in one fashion or the other. Just as we pray for daily bread in the Lord's Prayer, we also daily ask for forgiveness of our sins and trespasses, knowing that Jesus gave his life as a ransom for all of us!

Forgiving God, help me to come before you with a sincere heart asking for your grace, knowing that my ransom has already been paid by your Son! Amen.

FEBRUARY 28

Being Brought to God

> For Christ also suffered for sins once for all, the righteous for the unrighteous, in order to bring you to God. He was put to death in the flesh, but made alive in the spirit.
>
> 1 PETER 3:18

I grew up in Jerusalem Baptist Church, which was on the east side of Youngstown, Ohio. It was a church full of people that worked in or around the steel mills that were throughout the area. Many in that community moved from other parts of the country, mostly from the southern states, to find employment in these mills. They brought a strong work ethic and a commitment and loyalty with them to the church community to which they belonged. Thus, my mother brought my three brothers and me to church and Sunday School every Sunday. She did this because her mother brought her to church as well.

When we are young, the things we often do become habits that we carry on throughout our lifetime. In my case worshiping in a faith community is something that I still faithfully do each week.

This verse tells us that Jesus Christ suffered for our sins once for all in order to bring all believers into a relationship with God. Because of Jesus' sacrifice we have a pathway to God knowing that all of our sins have been forgiven. Our role is to daily acknowledge our sinful nature and ask for forgiveness, knowing that Jesus has made all of this possible.

On your spiritual pilgrimage, realize that because we are fallible humans, we will fail and fall short, however our saving grace is through Jesus' actions and the steadfast grace and love of God. Today may you repent of these things that need it, knowing you are forgiven, and just as my mother brought us to church faithfully each week, Jesus faithfully brings you to God!

God of life, help me to come before you repenting of my sins, aware that Jesus has brought me to be with you and into your loving arms of grace and mercy! Amen.

FEBRUARY 29

Letting It Go

Repent therefore, and turn to God so that your sins may be wiped out.

ACTS 3:19

One of the best bits of wisdom that I received when I was very young came from a deacon in my home congregation, Jerusalem Baptist Church in Youngstown, Ohio. During my youth, I was really involved in this small community in many ways and one of them was my participation in Sunday School. After we had our classes, someone would give a brief overview of the lesson for that day.

During one of these times in which we studied about forgiveness the deacon said something that went like this: whenever we hate someone or hold negative feelings about others, it is like acid inside of us and those feelings will actually hurt us more than the person with whom we are upset. His point was about letting these feelings go, asking the person for their forgiveness, and then of course going to God in repentance.

It appears that God does indeed want us to repent for things we have done to ourselves and to those around us. In the long run our lives will be better, for we have removed these acid-like feelings from inside us, and we can attempt to live free without them weighing us down or causing us more emotional harm. I know from personal experience that can be extremely hard to do during certain times of our lives. However, be encouraged to strive to repent, asking forgiveness from God and for those who have hurt us!

God of all love, help me to open my heart and soul to receive your forgiveness, so that I can be renewed in body and mind! Amen.

March

Striving for the Kingdom of God— Where We Are Today

MARCH 1

Praise the Lord

O sing to the Lord a new song; sing to the Lord, all the earth.... For great is the Lord, and greatly to be praised.

Psalm 96:1, 4a

A number of the psalms encourages us to praise the Lord. These verses note that all the earth should do this. On sunny mornings birds are often loudly chirping, singing to the new day, and some could say they are praising the Lord of Creation in the only way they're able to. Despite all of the environmental challenges there are nevertheless countless examples of beauty and miracles of nature all around us that cause all the earth and us to sing praises to God in gratitude for what we've been given to enjoy!

Creative God, today may I be able to see some of nature's beauty and take a moment to sing praises for the joy that it brings! Amen.

MARCH 2

Approval

> Am I now seeking human approval, or God's approval? Or am I trying to please people? If I were still pleasing people, I would not be a servant of Christ.
>
> GALATIANS 1:10

The Apostle Paul established the churches of Galatia and he was concerned that they were beginning to follow messages other than the one given them about the gospel of Jesus Christ. He wanted them to know that they couldn't seek human approval and God's at the same time.

On this spiritual pilgrimage, *daily* we decide who is leading us. Are we facing toward God's kingdom and will in our lives or are we seeking human approval more than God's? This is a decision that we have to make each and every day!

Holy Lord, may your Holy Spirit guide my daily choices to follow you and not the ways of the world! Amen.

MARCH 3

Looking Back

> Jesus said to him, "No one who puts a hand to the plow and looks back is fit for the kingdom of God."
>
> LUKE 9:62

In Luke 9:57–62 we have a few people who want to follow Jesus because of the miracles he had performed. He told them what was needed in order to follow him. Jesus taught that following him meant that the disciple would be required to turn away from their previous life and circumstances looking only to Jesus and the kingdom of God.

Such is the case with anything we might want to achieve in our life; we may have to give up something from the past in order to attain our goal. May you be open to looking ahead toward God's kingdom in your life instead of the things that may be holding you back from becoming the person that God wants you to be!

Gracious Lord, please give me strength to let go of the things in my past that prevent me from striving for your kingdom! Amen.

MARCH 4

Choose the Better Part

> But the Lord [Jesus] answered her, "Martha, Martha, you are worried and distracted by many things; there is need of only one thing, Mary has chosen the better part, which will not be taken away from her."
>
> Luke 10:41–42

Most of us are familiar with the story of Martha and Mary. Martha was concerned about getting all of her tasks done, while Mary only wanted to sit at Jesus' feet. Looking back at this scripture with our modern lens, it is easy to pick on Martha and what she was doing while in the presence of Jesus.

However, even though we don't have Jesus right in front of us, we, too, may have many other issues that cause us to be distracted from becoming the person God wants us to be. Whenever we put our total focus on something other than God and God's kingdom, that becomes our god. On our spiritual pilgrimage, we are encouraged to choose the better part and to daily strive for God's kingdom!

Heavenly Lord, help me to choose the better part and not be distracted by the things of the world versus God's kingdom! Amen.

MARCH 5

Setting One's Mind on Christ

> So if you have been raised with Christ, seek the things that are above, where Christ is, seated at the right hand of God. Set your minds on things that are above, not on things that are on earth, for you have died, and your life is hidden with Christ in God.
>
> Colossians 3:1–3

When I was younger I read a lot of self-help positive-thinking books. These books encouraged one to constantly think of their goals and how to achieve them. If a person's goal was to sell so many products over a certain period of time, then one needed to focus on those targets and visualize what was needed to accomplish the goal.

What the writer of Colossians is encouraging the audience to do is somewhat similar. Our life and actions should reflect a focus of things connected to Christ and his kingdom versus earthly things. At times this can be very challenging when we have so many distractions in our society that can prevent us from doing this. That's why having a daily habit of spiritual practices is so important, as it can aid in keeping one's focus on things above versus things on the earth!

God of light, please give me the focus needed to seek those things above where is Christ is seated versus the things on earth! Amen.

MARCH 6

God's Messenger

The seventy returned in joy.

LUKE 10:17A

Jesus sent his disciples out as messengers to proclaim that the kingdom of God had come near. The disciples came back from their travels with joy, for they were amazed about how well things had gone. In the same way, when we go out as Jesus instructs us, we, like the disciples, are often filled with joy and thanksgiving for the wonderful things that are done in Jesus' name.

We can rejoice when we are acting as God's hands and feet in spreading God's love to those whom we meet. May we be ready to act as God's messengers in our daily walk and may we be open to receiving God's Holy Spirit through our daily prayer, Bible study, and reflection, which supplies the strength and guidance needed for this journey!

May I have the courage to spread the joy within me that comes from my relationship with Jesus Christ to those that I will be meet today! Amen.

MARCH 7

Dwelling in the House of the Lord

How lovely is your dwelling place, O Lord of hosts! . . . Happy are those who live in your house, ever singing your praise.

PSALM 84:1, 4

In our society today there are many challenges/barriers to attending worship regularly within a specific faith community. There are also many options for one to choose other than attending a worship service. From sporting events, to coffeehouses, to people being too stressed out, to having been hurt in the past by a church community, etc., many things seem to keep people away from participating in community worship.

Contrary to today's practices, the writer of this psalm rejoices in being able to be in the house of the Lord. The writer goes so far as to indicate that a person is happy when able to be in the Lord's house, singing God's praises. Many spiritual mothers and fathers throughout the centuries have expressed the belief that worshiping in community is vitally important for this spiritual pilgrimage. On your spiritual walk, may you find the time and a community to help you grow as you worship and praise the Lord!

Today Lord, give me the guidance and discipline to set aside time and space to worship in some spiritual community! Amen.

MARCH 8

Day by Day

> They devoted themselves to the apostles' teaching and fellowship, to the breaking of bread and the prayers. Awe came upon everyone, because many wonders and signs were being done by the apostles.... Day by day, as they spent much time together in the temple, they broke bread at home and ate their food with glad and generous hearts, praising God and having the goodwill of all the people. And day by day the Lord added to their number those who were being saved.
>
> Acts 2:42–43, 46–47

This passage shows how the early church community functioned in the time right after Jesus' ascension and the coming of the Holy Spirit. The first few chapters of Acts give us a picture of a community that seemed to get along, for the most part, and attempted to follow Jesus' teaching.

They were open to being taught, they joined together in prayer, they shared their material possessions, and they broke bread together. They sought the will of God and looked out for each other and because their actions many joined the community. They also lived *day by day*!

They didn't seem to be overly concerned about the future for they trusted that the Lord would take care of them. Living day by day is also a good way to live on this spiritual pilgrimage. Trying to figure out where God may be leading you in the future can be very challenging. Most of the time all we can see is the next step on our journey. Attempting to look too far ahead may only confuse and overwhelm us. May you be open to living day by day as the early church lived and trust that the Holy Spirit will show you the long-range spiritual steps!

O God may your Holy Spirit guide me day by day and help me to trust that my future is in your loving hands! Amen.

MARCH 9

God's Kingdom

> Once Jesus was asked by the Pharisees when the kingdom of God was coming and he answered, "The kingdom of God is not coming with things that can be observed; nor will they say, Look, here it is! or There it is! For, in fact, the kingdom of God is among [or within] you."
>
> LUKE 17:20–21

Much has been written about God's future kingdom. It is our human nature to always look for what is to come, versus living in the moment. Granted there are times in our lives when we must plan and think about what is to come in our lives, in the lives of those around us, and in society as a whole. However, we may frequently miss those things around us that are part of God's kingdom.

Jesus notes that the kingdom of God is among us and within us. When we do something for someone without them knowing it, or when we help those less fortunate, when all these things are done out of love, we are bringing God's kingdom among us. There are many other examples of how God's kingdom is among and within us. May your spiritual pilgrimage allow you to experience and see God's kingdom in this moment, right now!

Great Lord, help me to strive for your kingdom in my life daily and to bring that kingdom to those around me! Amen.

MARCH 10

Seeing as God Sees

> But the Lord said to Samuel, "Do not look on his appearance or on the height of his stature, . . . for the Lord does not see as mortals see; they look on the outward appearance, but the Lord looks on the heart."
>
> 1 SAMUEL 16:7

This passage from 1 Samuel concerns the anointing of David as king of Israel, and how the Lord looked at his appearance. In our culture we spend a lot of time, money, and effort on how we look and how we think others should look. For some of us the importance of looking good overshadows many other aspects of life. We of course all need to spend some time on our personal appearance, but how much is enough?

This passage tells us that God looks on our heart and not on our outward appearance. As we spend time with our appearance, may we also find time to strengthen our heart with our spiritual practices of prayer, Bible study, and reflection, for that is what God is looking at!

Today, may I find time to strengthen my heart through my spiritual practices! Amen.

MARCH 11

Letting God's Light Shine

> You are the light of the world. A city built on a hill cannot be hid....
> Let your light shine before others, so that they may see your good works and give glory to your Father in heaven.
>
> MATTHEW 5:14, 16

One time I was fortunate enough to preach at all three services at a former church of mine and at the same time was able to do a book signing after each service. I preached on this verse about allowing one's light to shine instead of keeping it hidden.

I used the concept that all of the experiences that I had at that church and other former churches were still with me. Their light was a part of who I am today and would always be a part of me. We are made up of all of the experiences and people that have impacted our lives. Reflect on those experiences that you have had, that have given you a light to share. May you be willing to let God's light, which is in you, shine so that others may see that light!

May my past experiences give me the courage to let the light of Christ that is in me shine to those that I meet today! Amen.

MARCH 12

What the Kingdom of God Isn't...

> For the kingdom of God is not food and drink but righteousness and peace and joy in the Holy Spirit. The one who thus serves Christ is acceptable to God and has human approval. Let us then pursue what makes for peace and for mutual upbuilding.
>
> ROMANS 14:17–19

The Apostle Paul is letting the Christians in Rome know what the kingdom of God isn't. It isn't all about food and drink. He doesn't want those who are strong in the faith to eat or drink something that may cause others to stumble because they may see what has been consumed as unclean. Paul declared that in Jesus nothing is unclean in itself; however, when people think that something is unclean then it is unclean to them. He didn't want food that was eaten to cause some to fall back in their faith.

Paul states that the kingdom of God is righteousness, peace, and joy in the Holy Spirit. The human eye cannot see these traits, as it is able to perceive physical elements such as food and drink. Paul wanted the Christians in Rome to do those things that allowed people to become a part of God's kingdom, rather than being excluded from it. He wanted the early church to strive for peace and those aspects of the spiritual walk that builds a mutual understanding between each other.

Today, as we reach for God's kingdom on our spiritual pilgrimage, may we also seek the righteousness, peace, and joy of the Holy Spirit through our spiritual practices and then minister to those to whom we are called!

God of righteousness, joy, and peace, may your Holy Spirit help me to spread your grace, love, and mercy to those I meet today! Amen.

MARCH 13

Jesus' Parables and the Kingdom of Heaven

In Matthew 13 Jesus' parables are teaching his followers about what the kingdom of heaven is like. Jesus' disciples and the crowds who followed him seemed to have a hard time understanding what Jesus was trying to express in these stories.

Jesus' disciples asked him why he spoke in parables and in Matthew 13:11 Jesus answered them by saying, "To you it has been given to know the secrets of the kingdom of heaven, but to them it has not been given." The parables explained the mysteries of the kingdom and Jesus took extra effort to fully explain them to his disciples. By verse 51 his disciples finally acknowledged that they understood them.

In this chapter, Jesus gives us the parable of:

> The Sower
> Weeds among the Wheat
> The Mustard Seed
> The Yeast
> The Treasure Hidden in a Field

A Merchant in Search of Fine Pearls
A Net Used for Fishing

Jesus concludes his teaching on the parables in verse 52: "Therefore every scribe who has been trained for the kingdom of heaven is like the master of a household who brings out of his treasure what is new and what is old."

Read and reflect on these parables and see how their messages can influence your view God's kingdom and how this can impact your own personal walk. As Jesus taught, combine things of your past with your new understanding of these parables and then you can include this new awareness in your spiritual pilgrimage!

All-knowing Lord, give me the guidance to understand the mysteries of your kingdom, and then integrate this knowledge into my spiritual walk! Amen.

MARCH 14

Children and God's Kingdom

> At that time the disciples came to Jesus and asked, "Who is the greatest in the kingdom of heaven?" He called a child, whom he put among them, and said, "Truly I tell you, unless you change and become like children, you will never enter the kingdom of heaven. Whoever becomes humble like this child is the greatest in the kingdom of heaven."
>
> MATTHEW 18:1–4

In the culture in which Jesus lived, women and children had a very low status as compared to men. Thus, for Jesus to place a child among them was a really big deal, and then to say that in order to enter God's kingdom one had to be like a child was an even more momentous statement. Two key points especially apply to those of us on this spiritual pilgrimage: that of being changed and becoming humble as a little child.

As you grow through your spiritual practices there may be times when you will be changed and led to do things that could take you out of your comfort zone. These spiritual habits might also bring you into a deeper awareness that all of life is a gift from God and that fact could cause you to become humble as a little child.

Later on, in Matthew 19:13–15, little children were brought to Jesus. He rebuked his disciples for trying to stop the children from reaching him. Jesus blessed the children and said that the kingdom belongs to such as those. By his actions and words, he demonstrated that being like a child was an important aspect of striving for God's kingdom. On your spiritual walk, may you be willing to be changed and humbled!

Lord of life, give me the humility to see your kingdom through the eyes of a little child! Amen.

MARCH 15

Riches and God's Kingdom

> Then Jesus said to his disciples, "Truly I tell you, it will be hard for a rich person to enter the kingdom of heaven. Again I tell you, it is easier for a camel to go through the eye of a needle than for someone who is rich to enter the kingdom of God." When the disciples heard this, they were greatly astounded and said, "Then who can be saved?" But Jesus looked at them and said, "For mortals it is impossible, but for God all things are possible."
>
> MATTHEW 19:23–26

You may be familiar with this story about the rich man and Jesus. This unnamed man asked Jesus what good deed must be done for him to have eternal life. The man told Jesus that he had kept all of the commandments to which Jesus told him that there was just one more thing to do. He should sell everything he had and give the money to the poor so that he would have treasure in heaven. However, the man left and was very sad for he owned many things.

This person's focus was on his riches and possessions instead of God's kingdom and God's will in his life. He thought that it was enough to just keep the commandments, but Jesus thought otherwise. Jesus' words in verses 23–26 remind us that it is very difficult for a rich person to enter the kingdom.

Our focus determines how we look at material things. Is it through the lens of our spiritual pilgrimage and the fact that all we have comes from God and we are then asked to be good stewards of what we have, or do we look at them through the lens of our modern society where what we have comes from our hard work, drive, and wisdom and therefore can be used as we see fit?

May our spiritual practices give us the view that who we are is not dependent on what we have, or what others think about us, but rather on whose we are, a beloved child of God through whom all things are possible!

Lord of all creation, may I acknowledge that all that I have, and all I am is from you, and all of that is meant to be shared with those I meet today! Amen.

MARCH 16

This Day

> This is the day that the Lord has made; let us rejoice and be glad in it.
>
> PSALM 118:24

One of the more challenging lessons in my life that I have had to learn over and over is to not think too much about what is coming down the road. On this spiritual pilgrimage, most often we are only given enough light for the current step; the steps that come after the existing moment may still be out there in the clouds and fog somewhere. However, our trust is in the Lord God who will be with us in those steps when they are taken.

Many spiritual writers have noted that the spiritual pilgrimage is a one day/step at a time scenario. This verse from the Psalms encourages us to rejoice in today, to enjoy what God has made for us today. It reminds us to bask today in all of the beauty and wonder around us, in God's creation, and in each other. This of course can be very challenging in our very fast-paced society, which always seems to be looking forward to what is coming next.

However, we should rejoice in each day, and savor the moment that you have right now. It is okay to plan when you need to, but don't forget, that the present moment is all that is guaranteed!

Lord of the new day, help me to rejoice in this moment, in this day that you have made, and help me to realize that I can't enjoy the next moment until I get there! Amen.

MARCH 17

Scripture and Sleep

> The Lord God helps me; therefore I have not been disgraced; therefore I have set my face like flint, and I know that I shall not be put to shame; he who vindicates me is near.
>
> ISAIAH 50:7–8A

For many years, I read a number of positive-thinking books, to help me cope with my low self-esteem. One thing I learned from them was to try and not let things in the evening affect my sleeping patterns. I have always had challenges turning my mind off at night, and when something happens late in the day I tend to rehash it into the nighttime. I know some people can fall soundly asleep as soon as their head hits the pillow; however, I have never been able to do that.

Because of this, I don't like watching the late news or hearing things that I don't have enough time to process before going to bed. I do keep up with what is going on in the world; however, the information generally is taken in when I have enough time to absorb it. I started repeating positive mantras to help me go to sleep.

Over the years, I have replaced the positive mantras with more spiritual-related ones, additionally I have repeated scripture during this time. This passage from Isaiah is one that I have used to help me relax and hopefully fall asleep. I pray that you don't have any sleeping issues, but if you do, I would encourage you to use prayers or scriptures like this one to try to help in this. Remember, memorizing Bible verses can be an important aspect of your spiritual pilgrimage!

Holy God, help me to believe that you can indeed help me, and that I don't have to be worried, for your presence is always near me! Amen.

MARCH 18

The Mind of Christ Jesus

> If then there is any encouragement in Christ, any consolation from love, any sharing in the Spirit, any compassion and sympathy, make my joy complete: be of the same mind, having the same love, being in full accord and of one mind. . . . Let the same mind be in you that was in Christ Jesus.
>
> PHILIPPIANS 2:1–2, 5

St. Paul's letter was written to the Christians living in the city of Philippi as a form of encouragement. This passage conveyed the importance of having the same mind that Jesus had, which expressed itself in love, compassion, sympathy, and in sharing the Spirit. The followers there were urged to live in unity, being of one accord.

It seems easy to read in our Bibles about how we should have the mind of Christ Jesus, but very challenging, to say the least, to express this and then live that out in our modern cynical society. There are so many strong forces, systems, and barriers around us every day that make even attempting to live this way difficult at best. No matter how long we have been on our spiritual pilgrimage and taking part in our spiritual practices, trying to have the mind of Jesus can at times be overwhelming.

However, seeking to have the mind of Jesus, that is one of love, compassion, sympathy, and being led by the Spirit, shouldn't be thought of as an impossible task. From my own experience and from the writings of many spiritual authors, being faithful is far more important than being successful. Once we acknowledge that any results of spiritual practices belong to God and not to us, that might help us to better understand our role as disciples of Jesus. If we are faithful to our calling of striving to have the mind of Christ Jesus, we have done our part, and what happens after that and around us is in God's hands. Blessings on your spiritual journey as you seek to have the mind of Jesus!

God of love, may your Holy Spirit open my mind and soul so that it can be the same as Christ Jesus, as I share your love with those I meet today! Amen.

MARCH 19

Walking with God

> Noah was a righteous man, blameless in his generation; Noah walked with God. . . . Noah did this; he did all that God commanded him.
>
> GENESIS 6:9B, 22

The story of Noah and the great flood is one that we probably all learned while we were young and is one that many from all walks of life know well. We remember God talking to Noah, God's displeasure with the human race, the directions about making the ark, the flood coming, and what happened afterward. Sometimes we miss the fact that Noah was righteousness, walked with God, and did what God commanded him to do.

God chose Noah and his family to be the ones who would start the earth's recreation after the flood because of how he lived his life, and because of the kind of person he was. Other than these verses, the Scriptures don't give us a lot of details about Noah, except for the critical fact that "Noah found favor in the sight of the Lord" (v. 8).

We, however, can learn from what is noted about Noah and we can apply it to our spiritual pilgrimage. Being a righteous person, walking with God, and doing what God asks us to do can evolve from our spiritual rituals of prayer, Bible study, and reflection. When we take part in these practices, we open ourselves to the guidance of the Holy Spirit. This Spirit has been sent to guide, to comfort, to help us along our pilgrimage, and to show us how to walk with God as Noah did. May you be open to the Spirit's direction in your life so that through the highs and lows of this earthy journey, you are able to trust God's presence in your life, no matter what you may be dealing with at the moment!

Holy Spirit, help me to walk with God and follow the direction given, so that I may be an example to others whom I meet today of God's desire to walk with all of us! Amen.

MARCH 20

God Is Near

> So that they would search for God and perhaps grope for him and find him—though indeed he is nor far from each one of us. For "In him we live and move and have our being"; as even some of your poets have said, "For we too are his offspring."
>
> Acts 17:27–28

For many years, I have tried to learn and memorize Bible verses. I started doing this to help with my low self-esteem after reading positive-thinking books that encouraged practices such as this. I found this practice to be helpful for me and I've continued it.

The following has been especially helpful for me: "In him we live and move and have our being." I think this says so much to anyone who is struggling with life's challenges. The fact that in God we can live a renewed life daily, we can take steps knowing that the Lord will walk with us, and in God we have our very being and existence and thus can make it through whatever comes our way.

Think of using Scripture as a way to reinforce your spiritual practices, try memorizing Scripture as a way of coping with life's ups and downs. It will not keep you from having problems in life, but it may help you get through them. This verse would be a good one to start with, and you could even personalize it. "In God, I live, move, and have my being!"

Loving Lord, help me to feel you near me, and may your presence give me the courage and wisdom to boldly live today knowing that you are with me! Amen.

MARCH 21

Jesus Speaking about the Kingdom of God

> After his suffering he presented himself alive to them by many convincing proofs, appearing to them during forty days, and speaking about the kingdom of God.
>
> ACTS 1:3

After Jesus' resurrection and before his ascension he wanted his disciples to know that he was really alive. Because he would soon be ascending to heaven, he felt that they had to continue to learn about the importance of God's kingdom in their daily lives.

Jesus was always trying to educate and give his disciples knowledge that they would need in order to carry out their mission. The kingdom of God was a topic Jesus talked about more than any other to those closest to him. Therefore, right before he is taken up, he is teaching about the kingdom.

If Jesus believed that speaking on and teaching about God's kingdom was so essential, as modern-day disciples of Jesus Christ, shouldn't that be our focus as well? May your spiritual practices of prayer, Bible study, and reflection help you to daily strive for the kingdom of God!

Gracious Holy Spirit, guide my spiritual pilgrimage so that I may strive for God's kingdom in my daily walk and may this focus be a witness to those whom I meet today! Amen.

MARCH 22

God's Words Accomplishing God's Purpose

> For as the rain and the snow come down from heaven, and do not return there until they have watered the earth, making it bring forth and sprout, giving seed to the sower and bread to the eater, so shall my word be that goes out from my mouth; it shall not return to me empty, but it shall accomplish that which I purpose, and succeed in the thing for which I sent it.
>
> ISAIAH 55:10–11

This passage speaks of the power of God's word to accomplish God's purpose. Just as the water and snow give new life and growth to the earth, so also the promises of God will give new life and growth to Israel. The message for us is that God's words are still doing the same thing today.

There are many competing voices in our modern society that vie for our attention, time, money, and emotional energy, it seems that these voices are constantly changing and often cause confusion in us about what is really important in our lives and in the world around us. God's words are so very different, for when we take them to heart, they can help us determine what is essential for the long haul and into eternity. God's words will accomplish God's purpose and will not return empty, and in the process will bring new life and growth into our lives.

Our call as spiritual pilgrims is to take these words into our hearts and souls and then let them direct how we live to bring about God's kingdom into this time and place. God's word becomes embedded in our hearts and souls when we spend time reading and reflecting on it. That is why taking part in the spiritual practices of prayer, Bible study, and reflection is so crucial to this journey.

Please be encouraged to continue these routines, believing in God's promises that what comes out of God's month will succeed. May you feel God's presence all around you today!

Lord of all creation, help me to take your words into my inner being and may these words direct my steps, as I do my part to bring your kingdom into the world today! Amen.

MARCH 23

The World's Kingdom Becoming the Lord's Kingdom

> Then the seventh angel blew his trumpet, and there were loud voices in heaven, saying, "The kingdom of the world has become the kingdom of our Lord and of his Messiah [Christ], and he will reign forever and ever."
>
> REVELATION 11:15

The heading for the month of March in this devotional is "Striving for the Kingdom of God—Where We Are Today." As we engage in our spiritual pilgrimage we are, in fact, fulfilling our role in bringing about God's kingdom into this time and place. The kingdom of God is something that can spring up in the present time when God's will is being done, and it will fully arrive in the kingdom that is to come later. This is commonly referred to as the "already" and "not yet" times.

The book of Revelation is one that is often misread and misquoted as people sometimes look for signs, symbols, hidden messages, and numerical calculations. In each generation, a segment of believers predicts that the world is in the end times. However, no matter who reads it or when it is read, it can best be viewed in that there is something for everyone about one's present time and what is to come.

This verse assures us that the kingdom of the world becomes the Lord's and his Messiah's (Jesus Christ's). Thus, for us today, we should be aware that the things of the world will pass away and God's kingdom will come in the fullness of time. However, we can trust that everything is in God's hands, therefore, as we stay focused on our spiritual practices, we'll be better able to bring about God's kingdom here and now.

Lord of life, help me to strive for your kingdom today in all that I do, and may this seeking reflect your saving grace and love to others! Amen.

MARCH 24

Our Life's Lens

We all have a life lens that determines how we look at every aspect of our life. Our life lenses are influenced by the spiritual practices that we take apart in while striving for God's kingdom in this present time. The focus of our lens is also developed by our life experiences; all of the things that we have been a part of, all of the people that have come into our lives, and all of the events that have happened around us, impact who we are and how we see life.

For me, my life lens has been developed by my upbringing by a single mother growing up on the east side of Youngstown, Ohio. My first church community was Jerusalem Baptist Church, which was made up of people who had come to Youngstown from the southern states to make a new and better life in the north.

My life lens was later influenced as I worked in a steel mill, went to college part time for eight years in order to earn my bachelor's degree, and married Judy, who was of the Catholic faith, which also affected my spiritual growth. Her death years later, after a long battle with cancer, caused my life lens to change radically. My many moves around the country as I worked for different insurance companies gave me more experiences. Joining a Lutheran church and eventually graduating from a Lutheran seminary and then being married to a Lutheran pastor continues to change my life lens.

I've recounted my life experiences to encourage each of you to think about all of the events, both large and small, and all of the people that have come and gone in your lives as you reflect upon how all of these people and situations have gotten you to where you are today. We are who we are today because of what has happened to us in the past and how we look at life through our life lenses has been formed by these experiences. How we look at things that occur on a daily basis, how we spend our time and money, and how we react to the events that confront us are determined by our life lens.

Please be encouraged to either begin or continue to enhance taking part in the practices of prayer, Bible study, and reflection. These habits will give you the ability to see things from a spiritual perspective versus a worldly one. This may help you to better deal with the many and varied issues of life!

Lord of my life, help me to look at every aspect of my life through the spiritual lens of your kingdom versus the things of the world! Amen.

MARCH 25

Keeping God's Word

> Jesus answered him, "Those who love me will keep my word, and my Father will love them, and we will come to them and make our home with them."
>
> JOHN 14:23

Keeping God's word in our hearts can come out of our spiritual practices. When we refer to striving for the kingdom of God where we are today, we acknowledge that this spiritual pilgrimage isn't a one-time event but an everyday one over a person's lifetime. Jesus said that when we keep his word he and the Father will make their home with us. This is a very powerful and comforting thought for us.

When my late wife, Judy, and I got married we really needed God's presence with us. In addition to the normal issues that confront young married couples, we were faced with several added ones. When we got married, I was still working full time in the steel mill and both of us were taking college courses. A significant challenge that we faced was that we were from different faith traditions and ethnic backgrounds. She was raised in a Roman Catholic home and both her parents were Italian. I grew up in an American Baptist Church and my heritage was mostly African American. We got married at a time when interfaith and interracial marriages weren't as accepted as today.

Despite these differences, we both were very involved in our church traditions and our faith that we were beloved children of God continued to grow and provided a strong bond between us. We had faith that God was with us and would dwell with us and this helped us through many difficult periods in our married life. Our life was far from perfect, but our faith in

God strengthened our love and faith in each other. Looking back over what we faced when we began our lives together makes me realize that without the Lord dwelling with us, I'm not sure that we would have made it. When Judy passed away we had been married for more than twenty-eight years.

All of us have times in our lives when we aren't sure if we can make it another day. Please be encouraged to keep the word of God in your heart through taking part in your spiritual practices. This will not eliminate all of the problems in your life, however, knowing that you are loved and that you will not be alone makes it easier to take it one day at a time!

Lord of life, help me to keep your word in my heart and soul and may that presence help me to see that you are making your home with me right now! Amen.

MARCH 26

Keep Awake

And what I say to you I say to all: Keep awake.

MARK 13:37

In this verse Jesus is telling his disciples about the need to keep awake for no one knows when the coming age will take place. From verses 32–37 of the passage he is quoted as telling his followers three different times to keep awake/alert! He seems to want to make the point that they are to keep their focus on what he has taught them and continue upon the path that he has walked with them.

One of the ways that we can keep awake or alert is to continue with our spiritual practices on a regular basis and follow Jesus' example of taking time to maintain a life of prayer. Waiting for something when we don't know when it will happen or exactly how it will occur takes faith to believe in and trust the one who made the promises. On our own strength and understanding it would be very easy to follow every so-called modern prophet or new prophecy that comes along, which could prevent us from striving for God's kingdom on a daily basis. Through our prayer life, the Holy Spirit will give us what is needed to follow Jesus' instructions to stay alert for the promised future.

May your spiritual practices of prayer, Bible study, and reflection provide what you need to live, wait, and remain awake for the daily coming of Jesus into our lives as well as for his future coming!

Lord of the present, past, and future, while I maintain a life of prayer, help me to stay alert for your promises coming today and every day! Amen.

MARCH 27

God's Kingdom Expressed in Our Present Day

One of the first public messages that was recorded at the beginning of Jesus' ministry was his statement, "The kingdom of God has come near." Thus, when Jesus came he established the kingdom of God here on earth in that time and place. When Jesus gave us the words to what has been called the Lord's Prayer, he told us to pray "your kingdom come, your will be done, on earth as it is in heaven." Additionally, we are also to pray for and do our part to continue to bring about God's kingdom into our present day. We take part in doing this when we strive for God's kingdom and guided by the Holy Spirit do what we think is God's will.

There are times in life when it is really apparent that God's kingdom is present. Shirley and I have been fortunate to be a part of something special when she was called to be the pastor of St. Paul Lutheran Church in Alpena, Michigan. In this town, there is a group of churches that have lived out a little bit of how God's kingdom can look in this present age as they join together to take part in various activities. This ecumenical group was formed and working together long before we arrived in Alpena and have a history of organizing and leading functions throughout the year. However, the most involved event is the midweek Lenten worship service.

Each Wednesday during Lent the services are rotated from church to church, and begin with a simple soup and bread supper, which is followed by a worship service with a different clergy person preaching each week. It is truly neat and wonderful to have so many faith traditions coming together to break bread and worship together.

The community is able to visit the churches, hear different speakers, and take part in a variety of worship styles. Even though each week the format is unlike the previous week, the worship is centered around praising God and being in fellowship with other believers. Each year a specific Lenten theme is used for all of the services and the sermons delivered are based on that theme. In my mind this is a real example of bringing God's kingdom into a particular time and space.

The churches that are involved in the movement here are from the United Methodist, Presbyterian, United Church of Christ, Episcopal, Lutheran (ELCA) and Roman Catholic faith traditions. I realize that Alpena isn't the only place where this is happening and in fact there are probably many other places where there is greater diversity than the churches mentioned here. Ecumenism in today's world should involve a wide range of faiths and religions.

On your spiritual pilgrimage look for places and events where you can sense that God's kingdom is present, and where God's will is being done, and where persons from many faiths, cultures, and ethnic backgrounds are coming together for a common purpose. Then rejoice and praise God for being able to witness and take part in those wonderful movements!

Lord of all creation, help me to be open to those events around me that show the presence of your kingdom and your will being done, and guide me to share this experience with those I meet today! Amen.

MARCH 28

Not Far from the Kingdom of God

> When Jesus saw that he answered wisely, he said to him, "You are not far from the kingdom of God." After that no one dared to ask him any question.
>
> MARK 12:34

This passage involves a dialogue between Jesus and an unnamed scribe about the commandments and which were the most significant. Jesus stated that the first and most important commandment was about loving God with all one's might, and the second commandment involved loving one's neighbor. The scribe agreed with this and added that doing these were more vital than offerings or sacrifices. Jesus then told the scribe that he wasn't far from the kingdom of God.

In the first chapter of Mark, Jesus is proclaiming that the kingdom of God has come near and that it was time to repent and believe in the good news. Jesus brought the kingdom to earth and it was spreading. This scribe knew that loving God with all one's heart, soul, mind, and strength and our neighbor as ourselves was at the heart of the Jewish law. When we, too, keep these two commandments we aren't far from the kingdom of God and, in fact, are doing our part to bring it into this time and space.

Loving God and our neighbor are the right things to do from an emotional/spiritual standpoint. However, because we are fallible humans with all the warts and hang-ups that come with being human, doing either of these can be challenging, depending upon what is going on in our lives. We, of course, might have issues with God or our neighbor which could prevent us from truly loving either based on our thinking/perspective. God is love and can't help but love us no matter what may be happening with us at the moment. However, loving our neighbor, at times, can be extremely difficult for us to do.

On this spiritual pilgrimage, may your practices open your heart, soul, and mind to receive the wisdom and courage you need from the Holy Spirit to love God and your neighbor, no matter what you or your neighbor may be going through at the moment. May you be like the scribe and realize that you are taking part in God's kingdom when you, with the Spirit's help, love God and others!

Lord of life, guide me to daily pray that your kingdom come and your will be done on earth, and when I love you and my neighbor may I know that your kingdom is near to me! Amen.

MARCH 29

Lessons Learned

> You shall love the Lord your God, therefore, and keep his charge, his decrees, his ordinances, and his commandments always. Remember today that it was not your children (who have not known or seen the discipline of the Lord your God), but it is you who must acknowledge his greatness, his mighty hand and his outstretched arm.
>
> DEUTERONOMY 11:1–2

As humans, we start learning as soon as we are born. Normally a healthy newborn, who is in a loving, caring environment, begins crying when they are hungry or needs their diaper changed. As they grow they learn that crying gets attention. This discovery and the entire learning process continue in some form throughout one's earthly life. Each person goes through this developmental process.

In this passage the Lord's commandments and directions are given to the people. However, each generation must learn them and live by them. It didn't matter what people did, who came before or who would come after this group, each had to assimilate and absorb these lessons and have them become a part of their daily lives. Just as each newborn must learn the lessons of life to live and survive, the people of Israel at that time had to learn to follow God's instructions.

On this spiritual pilgrimage, I can't learn lessons for you, neither can you learn them for me. We can help each other on the journey and we can be aided by other people or communities along the way. But at some point my mind and heart have to be open and willing vessels to learn, grow, and become enlightened. The Holy Spirit becomes our guide and can help and support us; however, it is up to us individually to learn what has been set before us!

Lord of all knowledge, as I strive for God's kingdom each day, give me what I need to learn the lessons that you have for me and in the process, help me be an encouragement to others on their pilgrimage! Amen.

MARCH 30

Prayer Which Shakes the Ground

> When they had prayed, the place in which they were gathered together was shaken; and they were all filled with the Holy Spirit and spoke the word of God with boldness.
>
> ACTS 4:31

The period to which this passage refers was a unique time in the history of the early Christian community. This community was bold in their witness of the life and resurrection of Jesus Christ and in the manner in which they lived as a group of believers. The way in which they were able to function, hold everything in common, worship, and do their ministry became a wonderful model that so many others, through the centuries, have tried to follow. This early community helped bring God's kingdom into the place they were at that time. We may not be called to totally live as they did but we can follow several of their practices.

Prayer and worship were central to their existence and a strong aspect of their life. It's amazing that their ability to pray so fervently actually shook the place in which they were gathered! That must have been some really powerful prayer. When we pray, we open ourselves to be changed and then directed by the Holy Spirit we may be asked individually or as a community to take risks and do something that may take us out of our comfort zone. Certainly, the early church was asked to do something that most of those followers had never done before.

On our spiritual pilgrimage, sincere daily prayer is one of the rituals that may help us fulfill our role in bringing God's kingdom into where we are today. The ground may not shake all around us, but we may be able to be changed ourselves, affect those near us, or alter some aspect of the world around us to more closely reflect God's presence in this time and space. May this early community be an example for you to follow and give you hope that when prayers are offered up they are heard, and over time change may indeed come!

Lord of all creation, help and guide me in my prayer life to be open to what may come next, knowing that I am doing my part to bring your kingdom into this present time! Amen.

MARCH 31

Becoming Effective and Fruitful in the Knowledge of Jesus Christ

> For this very reason, you must make every effort to support your faith with goodness, and goodness with knowledge, and knowledge with self-control, and self-control with endurance, and endurance with godliness, and godliness with mutual affection, and mutual affection with love. For if these are yours and are increasing among you, they keep you from being ineffective and unfruitful in the knowledge of our Lord Jesus Christ.
>
> 2 PETER 1:5–8

During my career in the property and casualty insurance industry I was able to work for a number of companies in a variety of cities. The first company that I worked for put me through a training period that lasted over a year. During that time, I learned about the insurance business and how that particular company operated. When I left that first company and moved to another the learning curve was much less steep because I had acquired both basic insurance knowledge and valuable experience, also many of the products were the same. However, what I did have to learn was how the new company was dissimilar to the last one. Each company had their unique ways of operating, marketing, and each had a few products that were specific to them which had to be learned in order to work for them. Thus, no matter what one does in this world there are always things to learn as we encounter new situation.

The spiritual pilgrimage brings with it some aspects that maybe different from other areas of life. For example, the language in this passage is different from that of a company policy and procedures manual. Words such as faith, goodness, knowledge, self-control, endurance, godliness, mutual affection, and love are placed here to show how one matures in their spiritual journey. In this text the author is indicating that our faith can help us embrace all of these characteristics. When these aspects become part of our inner being, we grow into being more effective and fruitful in our knowledge of Jesus Christ.

This knowledge doesn't come overnight, rather, it is a process that becomes part of our striving for God's kingdom here and now. Just like I had to learn about the companies I worked for, we have to learn about the life of Jesus through our spiritual practices. When we open ourselves with prayer, Bible study, and reflection, the Holy Spirit will guide us. However, don't be overwhelmed by all of these qualities, but remember that you're not walking alone, for many have come before you and many are presently involved in the same journey that you are on! Each day carries with it something new to learn or to experience and the Holy Spirit is your constant guide and strength!

Dear Lord, help me to daily learn about Jesus and may that knowledge and insight guide me always and may it be reflected to those whom I meet today! Amen.

April

Striving for the Kingdom of God—Where We Are Today

APRIL 1

Christ Living in Me

> And it is no longer I who live, but it is Christ who lives in me. And the life I now live in the flesh I live by faith in the Son of God, who loved me and gave himself for me.
>
> GALATIANS 2:20

Many spiritual writers as well as the desert mothers and fathers down through the ages have written about or have left us examples to follow regarding the idea of Christ becoming part of their very being and living within them. Many of those individuals felt that their spiritual pilgrimage was about their relationship with Jesus Christ which grew stronger each day of their lives and impacted everything they did. This is one of the more challenging aspects of this journey to understand, that Jesus lives in us and we live by our faith in him.

As we strive for the kingdom of God each day, we're attempting to put God's kingdom first in our lives before anything else. Our spiritual practices daily pull us toward this kingdom in all that we do. Over time we are changed and this continues throughout our earthly walk. We are converted to becoming a lifelong disciple of Jesus Christ and Jesus' presence in our lives grows and grows. Therefore, we're able to state that it is no longer I who live, but it is Christ who lives in me.

Once you sincerely begin your spiritual journey you are opening yourself for the Holy Spirit to mold you into a new and different person. Be encouraged to pray and reflect on where God maybe asking you to go and who and what you are being asked to become. In the process, embrace the growing presence of Jesus Christ in your life!

Living Lord, while I am striving for your kingdom today help me to welcome the indwelling of Jesus Christ in my life and may my life reflect to others the One who is living in me! Amen.

APRIL 2

The Lord Understands Every Plan and Thought

> And you, my son Solomon, know the God of your father, and serve him with single mind and willing heart; for the Lord searches every mind, and understands every plan and thought. If you seek him, he will be found by you; but if you forsake him, he will abandon you forever.
>
> 1 CHRONICLES 28:9

Think about the middle part of this verse for a moment: the Lord searches every mind. That means that no one is beyond God's reach. The Lord additionally understands every plan and thought; therefore, no matter what we may think about doing, or what we may believe about others, or how we rationalize our past or future actions, God is aware of them.

My mind sometimes goes quickly from one topic to another and back again, covering everything from world events, to things going on around me, family situations, work stuff, or what will I eat or wear today. At times, I tend to judge people by how they look, what they wear, or how they are behaving. I know that I shouldn't be doing this for I wouldn't want someone else to do that to me. Even though the other person may not know what I am thinking, God does.

Since all of us are fallible humans with many faults and warts, I realize that it is very challenging to constantly control our thoughts, but maybe by thinking about this verse it'll cause us to pause for a minute before we go down those paths. Being on this spiritual pilgrimage doesn't take us to a perfect place where we never do or think anything that we might later regret. However, taking part in spiritual practices while striving for God's kingdom may give us some tools and habits that could help us on our journey.

Regular times of prayer can get us in the habit of praying at all times, even when our minds want to take us places we'd be better off not going.

Asking the Holy Spirit for guidance on a daily basis doesn't necessarily keep us from making mistakes; however, we know that we aren't alone and that the Spirit's support helps us get through whatever we are facing. When we study the Bible, we read and learn about how Jesus lived as a human and what God expects of us on this earthly walk. Reflecting on our pilgrimage and reading about how the desert mothers and fathers lived can also help us deal with the day to day events of our lives.

Hopefully, when we realize that God knows our minds and what our plans and thoughts are, this knowledge will help influence our dominant thinking each day!

Lord of all knowing, may your Holy Spirit guide my thoughts and actions so that I can become the person that you want me to be today! Amen.

APRIL 3

Open Minds

> Then he said to them, "These are my words that I spoke to you while I was still with you—that everything written about me in the law of Moses, the prophets, and the psalms must be fulfilled." Then he opened their minds to understand the scriptures.
>
> LUKE 24:44–45

Jesus appeared to his followers and many others for some forty days after his resurrection until he ascended. His presence gave his disciples encouragement and support during that challenging time. His followers always seemed to have difficulty understanding his parables and many of the lessons that Jesus tried to relate to them while he was doing his public ministry. However, during this period they appeared to grasp what his life was all about. In this passage, Jesus opened their minds to better understand the Scriptures and how he fulfilled the Old Testament writings.

You can probably think of times in your life where you just couldn't comprehend what was presented to you in a class, or info given you from a doctor's visit, or when you tried to learn some new technological device. Sometimes things just take time and energy before we can begin to understand what has been presented. This has certainty been the case for me; I don't have enough space to detail all the times that I have struggled with some new data or project that gave me pain and discomfort as I wrestled with it.

As we strive for God's kingdom we will probably be confronted with many areas where we'll need to have the Spirit open our minds as well.

APRIL: STRIVING FOR THE KINGDOM OF GOD

Having doubts on this journey is not something to be avoided, because the doubts can be a way to continue learning and growing. Often things in life and on this spiritual pilgrimage require much hard work and persistence by us before our minds are able to know and understand what the Holy Spirit wants us to learn. Be faithful to your spiritual practices of prayer, Bible study, and reflection and may they allow your mind to receive whatever is next as you seek to become a lifelong disciple of Jesus Christ!

Gracious God, let my mind and soul be opened to your Holy Spirit, and in the process, help me to grow in my understanding and awareness of your presence in my life and in the world around me! Amen.

APRIL 4

God's Countenance and Peace

> The Lord spoke to Moses, saying: Speak to Aaron and his sons, saying, Thus you shall bless the Israelites: You shall say to them, the Lord bless you and keep you; the Lord make his face to shine upon you, and be gracious to you; the Lord lift up his countenance upon you, and give you peace.
>
> NUMBERS 6:22–26

This passage is often used as a benediction at the end of a worship service or gathering of believers. It is a wonderful passage that offers reassurance to those who hear it. Sometimes hearing these words before going out into the world lets one know that they are not alone, because the Lord is with them and will walk with them.

Reflect for a moment on these words, the Lord will bless and keep you, the Lord's face will shine on you and be gracious to you, and the Lord's countenance will be upon you, and you will be given peace. Any of these phrases can give us encouragement as we take part in our spiritual pilgrimage, while striving for God's kingdom in our daily life! These words can also offer comfort for those who are going through a rough period in their lives.

God's countenance being on us could mean many things, but one thought is that God approves of what we are about, or God's favor is on us, or that God is gazing at us in love. Knowing that God approves of us can help us to be bold in our willingness to follow the lead of the Holy Spirit on our spiritual walk. We can have confidence to trust that no matter what happens on this side of the kingdom that the Lord will be with us. That when we daily strive to do God's will, God finds delight in us.

Similarly, knowing that we will be given peace on our walk can also support us in our spiritual practices and what daily occurs in our lives. The peace that we receive from our Lord God is much more unique than any peace that we can receive from our own efforts or from anything that can be given to us from other humans or from the world. God's peace is a deep-down awareness that nothing on this earth can separate us from God's love in this present period or in the future time.

May you be open to receiving God's countenance and peace in all the moments of your pilgrimage, and may these gifts of God's love help you to become the person that God wants you to be!

Loving Lord, may your grace-filled arms surround me today, to support, comfort, and guide my journey, and may your presence be reflected to all those that I meet today! Amen.

APRIL 5

One Body

> For just as the body is one and has many members, and all the members of the body, though many, are one body, so it is with Christ. For in the one Spirit we were all baptized into one body—Jews or Greeks, slaves or free—and we were all made to drink of one Spirit. Indeed, the body does not consist of one member but of many.... Now you are the body of Christ and individually members of it.
>
> 1 Corinthians 12:12–14, 27

The Apostle Paul would have been great in whatever field he would have chosen to take part in. In today's world, he would probably have been a good sports coach. He seems to have had the ability to describe how different units work best together. Part of a good coach's role is getting everyone to buy into the concept that all team members have to put aside their egos and do things for the greater good of the team. That everyone's function is vital, as long as it contributes to the overall goal of the team. This is sometimes challenging because most of us would rather be the one up front getting all of the praise and glory. However, under a true team concept, what's good for the team comes first and everyone's individual needs are secondary.

In this passage, Paul is noting how the body of Christ is to function. The body has many members; however, they come together to form one body in Christ. Like the parts of the human body, Christ's body has many different parts that do a variety of things and have separate roles to fulfill. Thus, it doesn't matter if we're male or female, young or old, rich or poor, or where we were born, or who our ancestors were, we have something that we are called to do for Christ's body, his community.

This function or role can change over time, depending on where you are in your spiritual pilgrimage. The main thing is that it contributes to bringing the kingdom of God into this present time, while at the same time helping you to become a lifelong disciple of Jesus Christ. May you be open to where the Holy Spirit may be leading you in this regard. Be willing to accept your part with a humble heart not looking for praise for what you do, but being content just knowing that you are doing what you have been called to do on this journey. Any glory belongs to the Lord!

Lord of all creation, may your Holy Spirit guide, comfort, and support me in what I have been called to do for Christ's body in this present time and in the process, help me to become the person that God wants me to be! Amen.

APRIL 6

In the World but Not of It

> I have given them your word, and the world has hated them because they do not belong to the world, just as I do not belong to the world. I am not asking you to take them out of the world, but I ask you to protect them from the evil one. They do not belong to the world, just as I do not belong to the world. Sanctify them in the truth; your word is truth.
>
> JOHN 17:14–17

In this chapter from John, Jesus prays for his disciples just before he was arrested. He wants the Lord to protect them and be with them. One of the more challenging aspects to his prayer is that he doesn't want them taken out of the world, even though they didn't belong to it. His followers would be left in the world even when they weren't a part of it. They were left so that they could carry on the ministry that Jesus had started, and they were to spread the gospel message to the ends of the world, and to continue to bring God's kingdom into their time and place, the very ministry that Jesus had begun.

This message is for us as well. As we strive for God's kingdom where we are today and seek to become lifelong disciples of Jesus Christ, we are still in the world, although our focus is on God's kingdom versus the things of the world. This can be frustrating at times for some of us on this spiritual pilgrimage because the language we use as it pertains to God's kingdom is so different from the temporal world. Jesus wants the Lord to protect his followers from the evil one. This evil can easily come into us, or come around us in many different forms or people to distract us away from our spiritual journey.

May you heed the prayer of Jesus to be in the world and not of it, and may this truth give you the courage to take part in the spiritual practices of prayer, Bible study, and reflection which can help place you in a better position to live as Jesus prayed that you would. Know that Jesus continues to pray for each one of us so that we can be protected from the evil one and become a lifelong disciple of Jesus Christ!

Holy Spirit, please guide, comfort, and protect me, and keep me from the evil one! Amen.

APRIL 7

Teaching God's Commandments

> You shall put these words of mine in your heart and soul, and you shall bind them as a sign on your hand, and fix them as an emblem on your forehead. Teach them to your children, talking about them when you are at home and when you are away, when you lie down and when you rise. Write them on the doorposts of your house and on your gates.
>
> Deuteronomy 11:18–20

Something that took me a long time to realize was that in this life most of us never stop learning. It may be in small or large ways or it could be in a formal setting or just by reading a book alone. The learning could be about a new hobby, about the new gadgets we buy, or learning a foreign language. Each day can bring an opportunity to learn something new about faith, about life, about discernment, about most anything in which we are involved.

My own life always bought new challenges from a learning standpoint, some formal and some otherwise. After high school I went to college part time for eight years while working full time in a steel mill. After getting my degree and going to work for an insurance company, I spent nearly eighteen months in a training program learning the insurance business. After that was completed, I began taking industry-based courses, beyond that of my company training that took a number of years to complete, earning me several insurance designations. While in the insurance industry I continued to take various insurance courses, and at the same time I began some training others.

Then in 2000 I left the insurance industry and went to Trinity Lutheran Seminary full time while earning my master's degree. Since that time, I have continued to read and learn more and more about the ministry to which I feel called—that of being a spiritual consultant to groups regarding their discipleship journey. Like many people, I'll probably continue to read and learn in some form or another for the rest of my life.

This passage encourages the reader to take God's words in their heart and soul, binding them into one's very life and being. God's followers were to teach the commandments to their children and talk about and think about them all the time. Thus, the word would be so close to them that it would become part of their being and would have influence on every aspect of their life. On your spiritual pilgrimage realize that part of your spiritual practice is learning, reading, and reflecting on God's word and commandments. May this practice become part of your daily striving for God's kingdom!

Lord of life, may I realize that just as you continue to create and recreate all of your creation, you are making my life new each day as I read and relearn the lessons that you have for me in this time and place! Amen.

APRIL 8

Abiding in God

> So we have known and believe the love that God has for us. God is love, and those who abide in love abide in God, and God abides in them.
>
> 1 JOHN 4:16

Please take a moment to read this entire passage from verse 7 to 21. There is much to reflect on in this section, and it is one of my favorites and one which I frequently use. I starting reading it around the time my late wife was under hospice care, for I needed the comfort and assurance of knowing that God was love and that love was still available to me even as I was losing Judy.

One of the messages from this passage is that if we love others we are born of and know the Lord and God lives or abides in us and us in the Lord. This interaction is part of the kingdom of God being brought into this present time and space. By loving and being open to God's love we are doing our part to help bring the kingdom here now. On the other hand, when we do not love we fail to know God. We are told to love those around us, for if we can't love those around us whom we can see, how can we love the God whom we cannot see.

God is love and can't but help love humankind and all creation; however, it is up to us to have a willing spirit to receive this love. We aren't forced to love others or love the Lord, it is a choice that we make every day. Our basic nature is such that we make decisions based on what is the most important thing in our lives at that moment. Are we more interested in following our own selfish motives or more intent in striving for God's kingdom where we are today and having God's presence abiding in us in love? On your spiritual pilgrimage, may you be receptive to God's ever-present love being in your life to help, comfort, and guide you!

Loving Lord, help me to receive the love that you have for me and guide me to make time and give you the space to abide in and around me today! Amen.

APRIL 9

A Life Worthy of God

> Urging and encouraging you and pleading that you lead a life worthy of God; who calls you into his kingdom and glory.
>
> 1 Thessalonians 2:10

This passage is urging, encouraging, and pleading with the reader to lead a life worthy of God who has called them into God's kingdom and glory. These words imply a loving, gentle request to do so, instead of being asked in a demanding, harsh tone. When we are called to take part in God's kingdom in this time and space we do so as fallible humans with all of the faults and warts that all humans, and in fact, all of the creation has. On this side of the kingdom we often fail, fall, come up short, disappoint ourselves and others, and are continually in need of forgiveness. Yet and still we are asked to be part of God's kingdom and glory where we are despite all of our shortcomings.

Therefore, regardless of how human we all are, we are still gently asked and called to lead a life worthy of God. It is safe to say that we'll never be perfect on this side of the kingdom, but we can always continue to strive first for God's kingdom before anything else in our lives. How do we seek to live a life that is worthy of God? There are many methods to do this based on our own preferences and personal rituals.

Some of the ways that this can be done depend on our daily focus; is it on us and what we want or on God's kingdom and will in our lives? Do we spend quality time with our spiritual practices or do our everyday events rob us of all of our time and energy with little or nothing left for communicating with our Lord? Are we too busy running around from place to place to ask the Holy Spirit to go with us to comfort and guide us? Life is a gift from God who wants all of us to enjoy a life worthy of the gift we're been given. Our part is to take the first step toward this gift by how we think, act, and live on a daily basis!

Loving God, may I reach for your kingdom and your glory today and help me to be open to living a life that is worthy of you. Amen

APRIL 10

Great Grace

> Now the whole group of those who believed were of one heart and soul, and no one claimed private ownership of any possessions, but everything they owned was held in common. With great power the apostles gave their testimony to the resurrection of the Lord Jesus, and great grace was upon them all.
>
> Acts 4:32–33

This passage is taken from the earliest days of the community of believers who wanted to follow Jesus. This period was shortly after the day of Pentecost when the Holy Spirit was given to the community. This early community spent time in prayer, were bold in their testimony, and they lived in harmony. The entire group was of one heart and soul; though they were many, they acted as one. It's difficult for us looking through our modern-day lens to believe that something like that could actually happen. In our world, today, yes even in a faith community, it is extremely hard to get a group of people to be of one heart, mind, and soul about anything. Thus, this early community had something special, something divinely given.

Sadly, it didn't last and over time the community started having issues and disputes. However, it doesn't take away from what they did have. They were together at one point, gave their testimony about Jesus Christ, and there was great grace upon them all. *Great grace!* The way in which they lived, prayed, and gave testimony allowed them to continue to bring the kingdom of God to that place and time. This great grace came to them not because they looked for it, or planned for it, or thought they were so good that they should get it. Rather it came because of how they lived and walked on their spiritual pilgrimage.

We may not often experience a time like they had then, but God's grace and love are still available to us because God is love and can't help but extend this love and grace to us. On your own pilgrimage, or during your faith community's journey, may you be open to receiving God's love and grace as you live, pray, and witness to Jesus' life!

Lord of infinite grace, guide me along my path so that I can receive your grace and love, and may my life reflect this to those that I meet today! Amen.

APRIL 11

A New Heaven

> For I am about to create new heavens and a new earth; the former things shall not be remembered or come to mind.
>
> ISAIAH 65:17

Please be encouraged to read this entire passage, from verse 17 to 21. It is a marvelous picture of what was to come. However, for anyone who wants to gain something new, like a new heaven or new earth, something has to be given up. To receive this new heaven the former things will not be remembered or come to mind. For some of us today that can be a very challenging situation to comprehend or even begin to accept.

Sometimes we think the past was the best of all times and we want to hang onto that way of living no matter what. Having fond memories of the past can be a good thing if done with an appropriate balance, for it is important to know where we came from and all of the people that have helped us to get where we are today. When my late wife, Judy, and I were raising our children, we moved away from our extended family, including both sets of parents. Thus, our daughter and son were not around them that much when they were growing up. However, we wanted them to stay connected with their grandparents and their roots.

Therefore, we made a strong effort to stay in touch with the grandparents with phone calls, pictures, and visits whenever possible. A neat thing we did was to make a picture collage of our parents, grandparents, and great grandparents (if we could find their pictures) and hang them on our wall in a visible spot so our children and visitors could see them. I also worked on our family tree, and outlined the history as far back as I could. In that way, our children could, as much as possible, know something about their family history, where they came from, and the important people in their lives. Our children were able to see what these people looked like and what features they'd inherited. Because we had a mixed marriage, this was even more important for us. We couldn't remain in the past but we could honor it, while at the same time moving on.

On your spiritual pilgrimage, as you strive for God's kingdom where you are today, the Lord may be leading you to something new in your life. May you be ready to receive and embrace it, while honoring the past, as you adapt to what the new creation brings. As you read in this passage, even though the past was going to be left behind, the future brought with it a wonderful new life!

Lord of a new heaven and a new earth, help me to listen to the quiet voice of the Holy Spirit when it directs me to a new creation in my life. May I be willing to let go of the former things that are not needed any longer! Amen.

APRIL 12

Live to the Lord

> We do not live to ourselves, and we do not die to ourselves. If we live, we live to the Lord, and if we die, we die to the Lord; so then, whether we live or whether we die, we are the Lord's
>
> ROMANS 14:7–8

In the verses immediately preceding those cited above, the Apostle Paul is warning about the importance of not passing judgment on the eating habits of others or upon the days in which they've chosen to honor the Lord. Paul wants those to whom he is writing to refrain from judging the actions of others. Passing judgment on others was a waste of time according to Paul because we all will be judged and will be accountable to the Lord.

The key point here is that in everything we do, we do it for the Lord. He didn't want his audience spending time and energy focusing on details that were unimportant and that would pass away. As humans on this earthly journey we too easily become fixated on aspects of life that are right in front of us rather than on God's kingdom because that takes more effort to see and connect with. But Paul wants us to try anyway, to live and die each day for the Lord, versus being distracted by the world.

Being on this spiritual pilgrimage and attempting to daily strive for God's kingdom takes courage, faith, persistence, and trust. On your journey, you may encounter those who may judge you because they disapprove of or dislike some of your habits that you feel are important. Trying to please others can be a never-ending endeavor. However, when we attempt to live to the Lord, we move toward becoming a lifelong disciple of Jesus Christ, and in the process, we are doing our part to continue to bring the kingdom of God into this time and place. May you find encouragement each day to remain on your path, maintaining your focus on the Lord's will in your life!

Creator God, please help me to have the faith to trust that when I live for you, you will be with me and your love will surround me regardless of what is happening around me! Amen.

APRIL 13

God's Spirit Causes Growth

> For I [the Lord] will pour water on the thirsty land, and streams on the dry ground; I will pour my spirit upon your descendants, and my blessings on your offspring. They shall spring up like a green tamarisk, like willows by flowing streams.
>
> Isaiah 44:3–4

This was written to indicate that the Lord's Spirit would be poured out on the descendants of the Israelite nation and they would grow and blossom. It is a wonderful image for us today who can so easily be weighed down by so much of the negative news that comes our way on a daily basis. This message from Isaiah is both refreshing and uplifting and gives us hope.

I have often noted that being married or being in a committed relationship is one of the more difficult things to do on a day-to-day basis. Getting people from dissimilar backgrounds to work together over an extended period takes effort, compromise, patience, prayers, grace, and the ability to laugh at oneself. These are among some of the qualities that go into a living, growing relationship.

Probably just as challenging is being a parent, teacher, guardian, or a mentor for young people as they're maturing and being formed. No matter how many books you read, or how much help you can get from others, or how smart you think you may be, this is a role where there are no perfect answers or ways of helping a person grow up. There are just too many different things that come up which have to be worked through on the spot. You can't stop the world and ask for a committee meeting, or think about it for a week. Sometimes no matter what you do, the situation remains a difficult one. Finally, the time comes when the young person goes off on their own and you can only hope and pray that they have what they need to make it. However, at that point they are in God's hands and your influence decreases as time goes on.

Whenever you've worried about your family, especially your children, reread this verse and pray that they will be open to letting the Lord's Holy Spirit guide and comfort them. For according to this passage, God's Spirit can be poured out on your descendants, and the Lord's blessing will be on them, and they will spring up like trees by flowing streams. As you attempt to strive for God's kingdom where you are today, pray that all those you love and help, the young and old, will be willing to let this Spirit lead them as it is leading you!

Lord of new life, may your Spirit water and nourish me and all those I love, including my offspring, and may this growth be a witness in my life to those that I meet today! Amen.

APRIL 14

Exceeding the Righteousness of the Scribes and Pharisees

> For I tell you, unless your righteousness exceeds that of the scribes and Pharisees, you will never enter the kingdom of heaven.
>
> MATTHEW 5:20

In this passage, Jesus is saying that those who break one of the commandments and teach others to do the same will be called the least in the kingdom, and those who keep the commandments and teach them will be called great in the kingdom. Keeping the commandments and teaching others to do likewise seems to be a requirement for helping to bring God's kingdom into our present time. We know that Jesus brought the kingdom when he came; however, we all have a part to do to continue to bring it into the world today.

From what Jesus said, we have to exceed the righteousness of the scribes and Pharisees, in order for us to be part of this kingdom. It appears that these righteous leaders kept the letter of the law but not it's spirit. Thus, if we want to do our part we have to keep the spirit of the commandments and then teach others to follow them.

During Jesus' public ministry he went about teaching, healing, praying, worshiping, and making his way to the cross, to do what he came to earth to do. If we want to become a lifelong disciple of Jesus Christ we are to follow his example as led by the Holy Spirit, for each of us has been called to fulfill a specific role in bringing God's kingdom into this time and place. May your spiritual practices give you the discernment, courage, and wisdom from the Holy Spirit to do what you were called to do in order to keep the spirit of these commandments!

Lord of all creation, may your Holy Spirit enlighten and enrich my journey so that I may keep the spirit of your commandments and teach others to do the same! Amen.

APRIL 15

Draw Near to God

> Submit yourselves therefore to God. Resist the devil, and he will flee from you. Draw near to God, and he will draw near to you.
>
> JAMES 4:7–8A

The Bible tells us over and over again that God is love, and if God is love, it stands to reason that God can't help but love us and wants to be near to us. However, God has given humankind free will and thus will not force God's love upon us. It appears to be up to us to be receptive to this love and then to put ourselves in a position spiritually to receive this love.

One way this can happen is by our striving for God's kingdom where we are today, turning toward God on a daily basis. When we submit ourselves to God by our actions, which could include taking part in the spiritual practices of prayer, Bible study, and reflection, we can in fact be drawn near to God and become more open to receive that love. God loves us and wants to be near to us on a daily basis. May your spiritual pilgrimage condition your heart and soul to become a welcoming vessel of God's presence!

Holy Spirit, please guide me to be open to being drawn near to God today, so that I can receive God's love, and may I share that love with those whom I meet today! Amen.

APRIL 16

Praising God

> Pray then in this way: Our Father in heaven, hallowed be your name.
> MATTHEW 6:9

Jesus was talking to his closest disciples when he taught them about prayer in this passage that has come to be called the Sermon on the Mount. He also relates the proper attitude and place for praying. This prayer is known as the Lord's Prayer and is considered a perfect prayer because it covers areas for which we should pray. Think of including the Lord's Prayer in your spiritual practices, and even if you can't do anything else, pray it on a daily basis.

Jesus is encouraging us to keep God's name holy. One way in which we can do that is by praising God. There are countless books that have been written over the centuries about the need to praise God; the book of Psalms is full of verses doing just that. Praising God doesn't have to be just for the major things in life, but the small things as well.

My late wife, Judy, had two operations to remove a brain tumor. The first surgery basically went fine; however, after the second she couldn't walk, talk, or move her right side. It took a long time before she relearned these basic skills. During that time, I obtained a new appreciation for how wonderful the human body is that God created. I began to give thanks for being able to wake up in the morning and put my feet on the ground and walk.

Being able to feed myself, being able to walk up and down the stairs, and to get in and out of a car, etc., were things that I began to praise God for.

At some time during Judy's last few years she couldn't do these and other tasks, or she needed help in doing them. All of this made me realize how amazing the human brain is and how it functions the way it does and causes our body parts to operate as they do, almost without us thinking about it. I have been very fortunate to be as heathy as I am; however, going through the experience with Judy gave me reason to praise God for the large and small gifts of life that come my way on a daily basis.

Today, praise God for some gift of life that comes your way, and this can be done at any time or place, or for any reason!

God of creation, help me to praise your name in all times of my life! Amen.

APRIL 17

God's Kingdom and Will

> Your kingdom come. Your will be done, on earth as it is heaven.
>
> MATTHEW 6:10

Today we continue looking at the prayer that Jesus taught, that we know as the Lord's prayer. Jesus wants us to pray that God's kingdom comes into our present time and space, and that God's will be done on earth and within us, as it is in heaven.

When we pray for something to happen, in most cases we as humans look for that to take place; however, we need to do our part to bring about what we are praying for. If we are praying for healing of some type, then we should do all we can to bring about healing, such as seeking medical help for physical, mental, or emotional healing, and then following the advice given. If we are praying for discernment, then we should try to be open to what the Holy Spirit is telling us, and to wait with patient hope, trusting that the direction will come.

In the same manner when we pray for God's kingdom to come into our present time and God's will to be done now, as well as in the time to come, we must act accordingly. Many spiritual scholars have written that we all have a certain role or vocation to fulfill on our spiritual pilgrimage. We all have been gifted with certain talents and skills that are meant to be used throughout our lives. What I am called to do is different from my wife, Shirley, and different from you. By taking part in the spiritual practices of prayer, Bible study, and reflection we can better determine what our role may be, and what we are being called to do at the present moment. Also, we need to be aware that our role will probably change over time. Thus, we should always be seeking the Holy Spirit's guidance.

Whenever you pray this prayer, think of what you are being called to do to make this passage a reality where you are today!

Holy Spirit, as I pray this prayer, help me to fulfill my calling on this journey. May I be a light to others and help to bring about God's kingdom and will to the people I meet and situations I encounter this day! Amen.

APRIL 18

Daily Bread

Give us this day our daily bread.

MATTHEW 6:11

This short verse from the Lord's Prayer is probably one of the more challenging passages for me and many others. First of all it can be confusing, because what is daily bread? Does it include housing, heat, clothing, etc., or does it just mean the food we eat? Also, what is the daily supposed to be? Does that mean we have to go to the store every day to buy our food, as it may have been in Jesus' time, or does it mean we can shop for more than one day at time, which is the more practical thing to do?

Probably we need to look at this verse in context with the passages around it, especially Matthew 6:33–34 where Jesus talks about not worrying about tomorrow, for tomorrow will take care of itself for we have enough to worry about today. One could say that daily bread includes all of the things in life that we need to live each day. This may involve housing, heat, clothing, and food, depending on where we live in the world and what our status is at the present moment.

As noted before, the Sermon on the Mount was for Jesus' closest followers, those who wanted to become lifelong disciples of his; it was for those disciples then and now who want to follow Jesus' example about how to live. Those who follow Jesus have their focus on God's kingdom in their lives and strive to do God's will on a daily basis. This can be a difficult message to understand especially given the mind-set of our modern society that stresses the importance of long-term planning and taking care of oneself, above all else.

When we pray asking for our daily bread, we are trusting God for today's needs, acknowledging that is all we need to be concerned about. Thus, we are also saying that we are trusting God about the future. This type of thinking requires a real walk of faith, and one that is certainly challenging.

I personally don't think that it is harmful to think about and plan for the future. However, in reality today is the only day that we can live. We can't live tomorrow until it comes. We may think about tomorrow, but our trust and hope are in the Lord, and as a disciple we live today trusting God for all that we need!

Lord of all life, who provides my daily bread, give me the strength and courage to trust that you will take care of what comes tomorrow! Amen.

APRIL 19

Debts

> And forgive us our debts, as we also have forgiven our debtors.
>
> MATTHEW 6:12

In this passage from the prayer that Jesus taught us, we are told to ask God to forgive our debts, as we forgive those who are debtors of ours. In verses 14–15 of this passage the word trespass is used, and in some modern-day translations of the Lord's Prayer the word sin is also used. However, no matter whether debt, trespass, or sin is used we need forgiveness for the wrong things that we have done.

As fallible human beings with many faults and warts, we will make mistakes, fail, and act in ways that we will later regret, and basically do things that need to be forgiven by God and by those around us. No matter how hard we try to do otherwise, there are times in our lives when we fall short of behaving like we hope that we would. We can't get around the fact that on this side of God's kingdom, our earthy journey involves forgiveness.

Jesus knew that for us to move forward from our missteps, forgiveness was and is part of the process. God wants to forgive us, and the Lord's mercy is always there for us. Jesus also knew that once we are forgiven and we truly forgive others we can live more freely without carrying that guilt and baggage with us. In this manner, we are daily able to become more of the people that we were created to be.

On your spiritual pilgrimage as you strive for God's kingdom, remember that God wants to daily forgive you of all shortcomings, and as you forgive others, you are able to live a life freed of many of the burdens that may weigh you down!

Loving Lord, please forgive me and help me to forgive others so that I can be a witness of your infinite grace, love, and mercy! Amen.

APRIL 20

Trials and Evil

> And do not bring us to the time of trial, but rescue us from the evil one.
>
> MATTHEW 6:13

In Matthew's last passage given to us about this prayer from Jesus, we are told to pray so that we are not brought to a time of trail (or temptation) and that we are delivered from the evil one (or from evil).

There is evil inside all of us and all around us and there are more temptations and trials facing us every day than we can count. Sometimes it is easier to give in to these temptations than to resist them. We need the spiritual help of the Holy Spirit to aid with our physical and spiritual journey and we are encouraged to pray for help. Sometimes it may be a long time until we are ready to accept the help and guidance from the Holy Spirit to do this, but it will be given. It took me many years regarding one aspect of my life before I realized I needed the Spirit's help and was open to it.

One of my areas that has been a trial or temptation my entire life has been that of overeating, especially regarding the eating of sweets and foods high in carbohydrates. This issue is both a temptation for me and one where I can be overcome with the evil forces in me and around me to overdose on certain foods. I have been on more diets than I can count, and over the years I have lost and gained back more weight than I care to add up. This is because I have had times when I could control what I ate and times when I had little self-control.

For example, when I was a marketing representative in California my job was to travel around and visit the agents that sold our insurance, thus I was on my own during the day. I can remember stopping by a store or bakery to buy goodies and I'd eat them all in my car and a little while later would stop somewhere else to load up again. After years of positive thinking, prayer, and reading many books about my issues, it dawned on me that my physical makeup wouldn't allow me to eat just one of those foods. If I ate just one that was one too many and I would be on the road to many more.

I realize that countless people have similar issues with other kinds of food, drugs, and alcohol, whereby once you start you can't stop. I also understand that what I have may not be as life destroying and life changing as what others have had to deal with. However, this issue has caused me to have many moments of temptation, when what I know is best for me in the long run is overridden by my desire. Therefore, in my mind the best thing I can do is to not eat anything that will cause me to continue eating, and, hopefully, I will be able to do that more often than not. However, I cannot do this alone, for my impulse is to eat and enjoy the moment, and I need the Spirit's support to overcome my physical desires.

On your spiritual pilgrimage, continue to pray the Lord's Prayer and ask the Holy Spirit to be with you and to lead you not into a time of trial, but deliver you from the evil that is in you and all around you!

Gracious Lord, help me, guide me, comfort me, and keep me from all harm and danger on this earthly journey! Amen.

APRIL 21

Praising God—Where We Are Today

> Then I heard what seemed to be the voice of a great multitude, like the sound of many waters and like the sound of mighty thunderpeals, crying out, "Hallelujah! For the Lord our God the almighty reigns. Let us rejoice and exult and give him glory."
>
> REVELATION 19:6–7

The book of Revelation is written in an ancient style of writing known as apocalypse, which refers to a revealing or unveiling of something previously hidden. In Scripture, an apocalypse tells of an experience with the supernatural world in which the author is guided by a mystical being.

A popularized view of the book of Revelation in our present day wants to make the book a "history told in advance" with a series of hidden clues embedded in the narrative to warn its readers about events that will supposedly happen during their lifetimes. The real question at the heart of the book, however, is: Who or what is at the center of Christian life?

In this passage, we have a great multitude praising God. They created a sound like many waters, basically, they were really loud in their praise of God. Which means they didn't hold anything back, they were using their loudest voices in this praise.

Someday we'll be part of the great multitude around the heavenly throne praising God, but because we already know the end of the story, the story of God's triumphant victory over sin and death, why don't we live a life of praise here and now in our present time, individually or as a community? Why not praise the Lord where we are today as we are striving for God's kingdom in this time and place? If you can read this, give praise for your eyesight. If you got out of bed this morning by yourself, give thanks for being able to do that, and if you needed help getting out of bed, be thankful for the help you received. Get in the habit of giving praise for all aspects of life, both the large and small areas of life!

Praise God, Hallelujah! For the Lord our God the almighty reigns. Let us rejoice and exult and give God glory! Amen.

APRIL 22

The Word of God Stands Forever

> A voice says, "Cry out!" And I said, "What shall I cry?" All people are grass, their constancy is like the flower of the field. The grass withers, the flower fades, when the breath of the Lord blows upon it; surely the people are grass. The grass withers, the flower fades; but the word of our God will stand forever.
>
> ISAIAH 40:6–8

This passage reminds us that the word of our God will stand forever, but humans are like grass and flowers that are here today and gone tomorrow. As we take part in our spiritual practices of prayer, Bible study, and reflection, we daily seek to learn more and more about what the Holy Scriptures have to say to us. On this spiritual pilgrimage the Holy Spirit continually leads, guides and enlightens us to the things that God's word is revealing to us. This process is not done in a vacuum but daily as we strive for God's kingdom here and now.

How we view God's word changes over time as well as what we receive from studying the word. What we saw in a certain passage ten years ago will be different today, and probably something entirely new ten years from today. Over time we change, the environment around us changes, the world changes, and thus how we see Scripture and the message that it has for us will definitely change as well.

As you continue your spiritual journey it's important to remain open and receptive to the fact that even though humans change and will eventually die, the word of God stands forever and will continue to inform and enlighten us!

Lord of all creation, help me to be open to hearing the message that your word has for me, and may that word take hold in my life and comfort and guide me today! Amen.

APRIL 23

Set Your Mind on Divine Things

> But turning and looking at his disciples, he rebuked Peter and said, "Get behind me, Satan! For you are setting your mind not on divine things but on human things."
>
> MARK 8:33

In this passage Jesus is teaching his disciples about his journey and the suffering that was coming. Verse 32 notes that Jesus said all of this openly. He wasn't going to sugarcoat or put a positive spin on what he was about to face, he was honest and up front. Peter couldn't handle the message and wanted Jesus to alter the direction of his ministry in the hope of changing the outcome.

Jesus, however, wanted to get his message across and didn't want those closest to him to miss his point and so he turned and looked at them directly. It appears that this specific message was just for his disciples and not the crowds that were around him.

Second, he called Peter Satan, the same Peter who earlier had said that Jesus was the Messiah. Jesus wanted Peter to stop acting as a stumbling block, an agent of Satan.

Third, Jesus was attempting to get Peter and the others to focus on the bigger picture, the things of God, rather on human things. He may have thought that Peter was more worried about what the people around them thought about their mission instead of doing what God expected of them.

Jesus' message to Peter and the disciples is also meant for us where we are today, in that our minds should be set on divine things—the aspects of God's kingdom to which we are called to strive, rather than on human things that come to us in many different forms and shapes. May your spiritual practices help you to stay focused on these directions from Jesus!

Lord of all life, help me to listen to the guidance of the Holy Spirit and first set my mind daily on the things of your kingdom and not on the human aspects of life! Amen.

APRIL 24

Jesus Appoints the Twelve to Be with Him

> He went up the mountain, and called to him those whom he wanted, and they came to him. And he appointed twelve, whom he also named apostles, to be with him, and to be sent out to proclaim the message, and to have authority to cast out demons.
>
> MARK 3:13–15

In the public ministry of Jesus Christ, the calling of the twelve was an important act, signified by the fact that he went up the mountain where other major events had previously occurred, and appointed the twelve who would become his closet followers. He understood that even though he was the Son of God he couldn't do his ministry alone. The twelve would be with him to hear his words, witness to all that he did, support him and journey with him. They were chosen to be the extension of his ministry by proclaiming the message of God's love that came to earth in the form of Jesus.

As we talk about striving for God's kingdom today, we all ought to look at what we are being called to do to bring God's kingdom into the place where each of us is living and working. No matter what age we are, what point we're at in our spiritual pilgrimage, what our economic status is, how much or little education we might have, or what Christian community we belong to, we are all called, as where the Twelve.

I firmly believe that all of us are called by God to some ministry or mission that only we can fulfill. This call may change over time, but it's always there. The ways that we can be called are as numerous as the stars. On your journey, may you listen to the Holy Spirit calling you to take part in bringing about God's kingdom where you are today!

Gracious Lord, help me to listen and respond to your call in my life. Help me to be open to wherever it may be leading me! Amen.

APRIL 25

God's Kingdom Is Near

> From that time Jesus began to proclaim, "Repent, for the kingdom of heaven has come near."
>
> MATTHEW 4:17

Jesus began his public ministry with some really powerful words. He wanted those who would become his followers to repent of the things that were holding them back from becoming the people that God created them to be. Because God's kingdom is near, Jesus knew that his followers must seek God and what mattered most in their lives.

Jesus brought the kingdom when he came and it is with us now, but not in the fullness that will happen at the end of the time. Jesus expects all of us who want to become a lifelong disciple of his to continue what he started, to do our part to support the kingdom in this time and place as guided by the Holy Spirit, and to turn away from those things that may be holding us back.

Sometimes we try to make things in this spiritual pilgrimage more complicated than they need to be. In this verse, Jesus' words were short and sweet: repent for the kingdom is near. He didn't say to build a lot of structures, or start a worldwide movement, or come up with a lot of wise sayings, nor write countless books, his one word command was repent.

May this be a starting point as you strive for God's kingdom and will in your life, in order to become the person God wants you to be. Repent and turn away from those things that are keeping you from turning toward this kingdom!

Lord of the present and future kingdom, help me to leave behind those things that are a barrier to seeking you and that prevent me from striving for your kingdom in this time and place. May my striving allow me to be a reflection of what Jesus taught us! Amen.

APRIL 26

Human Glory versus God's Glory

> Nevertheless many, even of the authorities, believed in him. But because of the Pharisees they did not confess it, for fear that they would be put out of the synagogue; for they loved human glory more than the glory that comes from God.
>
> JOHN 12:42–43

In this passage, we again have Jesus causing problems for the religious leaders with his words and actions. However, part of the crowd came to believe in his message and his life, and supposedly a few of the religious authorities secretly believed in him as well. However, they were afraid that if they decided to follow him, they would be thrown out of the synagogue. This verse makes it clear that they were more concerned about what other humans thought about them than following Jesus.

If they followed Jesus, their words and actions would be changed and that would indicate they believed in Jesus. They would then begin to strive for God's kingdom and will in their lives and would be ostracized by the Jewish leaders.

As we move along on our spiritual pilgrimage and take part in the spiritual practices of prayer, Bible study, and reflection, we are called to do the same thing as the early disciples. We are to be less concerned about human acclaim and more focused on God's glory, kingdom, and will in our everyday lives. We must decide where our focus is going to be, on the world and its glory or on following Jesus. We may not be as popular by worldly standards when we try to follow Jesus' words and deeds, but we'll be following his call and living as his faithful disciples.

On this journey, may you be deliberate in where your spiritual inner being is focused and what you daily strive toward, God's kingdom and will in your life!

Lord of all creation, may I strive for your glory versus that of this earthly world, and may that striving allow me to become a witness to those I meet today. May doing your will be foremost in my life! Amen.

APRIL 27

The Kingdom of God Taken Away and Given to Others

> Jesus said to them, "Have you never read in the scriptures: 'The stone that the builders rejected has become the cornerstone; this was the Lord's doing, and it is amazing in our eyes?' Therefore I tell you, the kingdom of God will be taken away from you and given to a people that produces the fruits of the kingdom."
>
> MATTHEW 21:42–43

In this chapter the chief priests and elders of the people were again after Jesus asking questions in an attempt to trap him. They were always trying to challenge him especially as his fame grew and increasingly more people began to follow and believe in him. He was a threat to their power structure and so they needed to discredit him. The chief priests and elders felt that the kingdom of God belonged to them because of their knowledge of the laws and the religious practices they maintained.

However, Jesus thought otherwise and his words caused them to be fearful and concerned. He let them know that God's kingdom would be taken away from them and given to those who produced the fruit of the kingdom. Thus, because they were only interested in increasing their own power and influence rather than striving for God's kingdom and its righteousness, they weren't going to be part of the kingdom.

On our spiritual pilgrimage, striving for God's kingdom where we are today is something that is done with our hearts and minds as they focus on God's will in our lives, versus our own desires. We aren't doing this to increase our power or influence, but rather to be part of something that is much bigger and wider than anything that we can do on our own. This striving doesn't involve our knowledge about religious practices or how much power we think we may have, as the religious leaders in Jesus' time believed about themselves. Jesus is teaching that bearing fruit is an outgrowth that comes from how we live each day.

We are part of a movement that includes many that have come before us, many who are walking with us now, and many who will come after us. May you strive for God's kingdom in everything you do, asking the Holy Spirit for guidance about your daily steps and becoming a lifelong disciple of Jesus Christ, as reflected in how you live, think, and pray!

Lord of all creation, help me to strive for your kingdom where I am today. May my daily actions be a reflection of your grace, love, and mercy! Amen.

APRIL 28

The Kingdom Is Like Yeast

> He told them another parable: "The kingdom of heaven is like yeast that a woman took and mixed in with three measures of flour until all of it was leavened."
>
> MATTHEW 13:33

Yeast is an amazing ingredient in that a small amount causes a large measure of dough to rise. I am not much of a cook, but for a period of time our family made Christmas wreaths and candy canes out of flour and yeast and decorated them for the holidays. They were fun gifts to give friends. The packages of yeast weren't much to begin with, but with a little warm water, flour, and time it was the beginning of something wonderful. Jesus used examples of everyday life as parables for the people of his time to help them understand what the kingdom of God was all about.

Jesus talked about the kingdom of God more than any other subject and he wanted those around him to know of its importance. The kingdom of God comes to us and those around us when we strive first for this kingdom in our daily lives. It's present when we pray and worship and through our actions toward others as we seek to do the Lord's will in our lives. Even the smallest act of kindness, compassion, or forgiveness on our part brings God's kingdom into the lives of others as well as our own.

Jesus gave us many stories and parables about this kingdom and how to be ready for it. As we pray and study the Scriptures we begin to see signs of God's kingdom here in the present time. If you are always looking for it and expecting it, you will indeed see it each day and also when it comes in the fullness of time!

Lord of life, may your Holy Spirit guide my spiritual practices to help me look for moments where your kingdom is happening all around me today, tomorrow, and in the time to come! Amen.

APRIL 29

God's Word in Our Mouth and Heart

> No, the word is very near to you; it is in your mouth and in your heart for you to observe.
>
> DEUTERONOMY 30:14

As you look at this verse I would also encourage you to read verses 11–13 of chapter 30 from this passage. The verses tell us that God's word isn't too difficult to understand or far off, nor in heaven or beyond the sea, but rather very near to you, in your mouth and heart.

Sometimes we put up barriers for ourselves when we try to do something that takes us out of our comfort zone or when we are challenged in some manner. These barriers may arise for any number of reasons, some real and some that are only based on the fear of the unknown.

Striving for the kingdom of God, wherever we find ourselves, is about making God's will and kingdom the focus of our everyday life. This means that God's kingdom is foremost in our lives, and each day we need to take time to connect with God's word deep within our hearts.

We have God's promise that the word lives within us, and taking part in our practices each day opens us to God's presence in the very core of our being. Knowing that God's word is always with us gives us strength and courage to keep walking on our spiritual journey toward God's kingdom, trusting that the Holy Spirit will always reveal the next step.

Loving Lord, help me to be open to your word. Be always in my mouth and in my heart and may that give me the courage today to follow where you are leading me! Amen.

APRIL 30

Walking Humbly with God

> He has told you, O mortal, what is good; and what does the Lord require of you but to do justice, and to love kindness, and to walk humbly with your God?
>
> MICAH 6:8

This passage has often been used to indicate how humankind should treat each other and about how God wants us to live and move in our lives. In the verses just prior to this one, Micah is stating that God doesn't want our burnt offerings or any of the material things of this earthly life; rather the Lord wants us to do justice, love kindness, and to walk humbly.

When we attempt to walk humbly with our God we are also attempting to strive for God's kingdom in our lives in this present time. When we do this, we are trying to put God's will first in our lives before anything else. As I have stated often, this is a very challenging concept for me that I'd had to learn over and over again. As a fallible human being I daily must turn my focus to walking with God.

When I was going to college part time and working in the steel mill full time, I was dismissed from school twice for having a grade point average that was too low for the number of hours I was taking. At that time college work was challenging for me and when I tried to take too many courses while working I didn't do well. My focus was on my own time table rather than walking humbly with God and having my focus on God's kingdom and a realistic time frame that was actually better for my well being.

After almost being dismissed a third and final time I was very embarrassed and humbled and had to take a different approach if I wanted to continue. I had to step back and look at what I had done that hadn't worked and try to do something new. Thus, over the next three quarters I only took one course each quarter in order to concentrate my efforts on that one course, in order to work my way off of probation. I was able to do that and after that period I took a more reasonable number of classes and was able to obtain my bachelors' degree.

Being humbled in this case helped to get my focus off of what I thought I wanted, versus walking with God toward God's kingdom in my daily life. There may be times in your life when you have to humble yourself before the Lord as you strive to become a lifelong disciple of Jesus Christ; may your spiritual practices give you the courage and wisdom to do just that!

Holy Lord, please help me to do justice, love kindness, and to walk humbly with you! Amen.

May

Prayer—How, What, and Why

MAY 1

Quiet Places to Pray

> But now more than ever the word about Jesus spread abroad; many crowds would gather to hear him and to be cured of their diseases. But he would withdraw to deserted places and pray.
>
> LUKE 5:15–16

Jesus often went away to pray. He knew that he needed to do that to stay connected with the Lord and to be renewed in his spirit and physical body. Having structured daily prayer and reflection habits are extremely important on this spiritual pilgrimage. For centuries desert mothers and fathers have set aside specific times and places to pray and reflect.

Some of us may try and fool ourselves into believing that having a specific prayer time and place isn't important. We may wonder how in our fast-paced and very noisy society we can take time out of a busy day for prayer, but like anything else in our lives we will find time to do the things that are really important for us. I wish you well in setting aside a time and place to spiritually stay connected with God!

Today, Lord, show me how to set aside a quiet time and space to be renewed in my spiritual and physical body! Amen.

MAY 2

Praying Always

> Then Jesus told them a parable about their need to pray always and not to lose heart.
>
> LUKE 18:1

God wants us to keep on praying as we walk on this spiritual pilgrimage because it draws us closer to the Lord. Sometimes God does answer our prayer in one form or another. However, I can't begin to count the number of times that I have fervently prayed for some outcome and it didn't turn out the way I wanted. You can probably say the same thing.

That doesn't mean, however, that God doesn't love us or isn't concerned about our daily needs. God is love and can't help but love us, but the Lord isn't required to answer every request we make in the manner that we make it. However, as Jesus' parable from Luke 18 expresses, we should continue to pray and not to lose heart. During your journey, may your prayer efforts continue even when any response appears to be far off!

Loving Lord, help me to pray always and to not lose heart even when you appear to be quiet! Amen.

MAY 3

Praising God with a Joyful Noise

> Make a joyful noise to God, all the earth; sing the glory of his name; give to him glorious praise.
>
> PSALM 66:1–2

I like most any kind of music and enjoy those songs that have a good beat with some depth of meaningful soul. My favorite type of music is gospel, which became a vital part of my life during my early years in my hometown Baptist church. No matter what type of music you like to sing or listen to, hopefully, it brings joy to you and to those around you.

When we are praising God in song it can make us joyful and bring joy to those around us. When we praise the Lord, we are also joining all of the creation in giving glory to God's name. Today, may you find time to make a joyful noise to the Lord!

God of all creation, may my voice, heart, and soul make a joyful noise to you and bring joy to me and others as well! Amen.

MAY 4

The Lord's Prayer

> He [Jesus] was praying in a certain place, and after he had finished, one of his disciples said to him, "Lord, teach us to pray, as John taught his disciples."
>
> Luke 11:1

In Luke 11 Jesus gives his disciples the words of what is now known as the Lord's Prayer. "Father, hallowed be your name. Your kingdom come. Give us each day our daily bread. And forgive us our sins, for we ourselves forgive everyone indebted to us. And do not bring us to the time of trial."

It is the perfect prayer that covers all things for which we should pray each day. It is used during many worship services across the Christian world and many learn it as a small child. I use it in my own prayer routine and would encourage any of you who want to start or enhance your spiritual practices to use it also.

Loving Lord, give me the discipline to pray daily, to seek your will in my life, and to trust the words of this prayer given to us by Jesus Christ! Amen.

MAY 5

Meditating Day and Night

> Happy are those who do not follow the advice of the wicked . . . but their delight is in the law of the Lord, and on his law they meditate day and night.
>
> Psalm 1:1–2

I am a big sports fan and have also read my fair share of sports stories and biographies. One of the common themes that frequently appear is that the very best in any field devotes a great amount of time in developing their abilities. A person can't rely solely on their natural gifts, a great deal of hard work is also required.

Likewise, when a person proclaims that Jesus Christ is Lord of their life, in order to develop a closer, more loving relationship with Jesus, one needs to devote time to develop this relationship. This verse mentions meditating day and night, which could be interpreted as this practice becoming part of the very fiber of one's life. May you find the time, every day, to meditate!

Lord of my life, may my daily spiritual practices allow me to develop a closer relationship with you and in the process become the person that you want me to be! Amen.

MAY 6

The Lord Hears

> O Lord my God, I cried to you for help, and you have healed me. Weeping may linger for the night, but joy comes with the morning. To you, O Lord, I cried, and to the Lord I made supplication; . . . "Hear, O Lord, and be gracious to me! O Lord, be my helper!" You have turned my mourning into dancing; you have taken off my sackcloth and clothed me with joy, so that my soul may praise you and not be silent. O Lord my God, I will give thanks to you forever.
>
> PSALM 30:2, 5B, 8, 10–12

This psalm assures us that God hears us when we cry out to the Lord. The title of this psalm from the NRSV Bible is "Thanksgiving for Recovery from Grave Illness." As we go through life, most of us will have times when we or someone we love is ill, or have friends who are facing some medical crisis. Often the first thing we say is that we will be thinking about and praying for the person who is ill.

Deep down a number of us know prayers are needed and often helpful in times like that. However, we should bring everything to God in prayer each day, praising and thanking the Lord for hearing the cries of our hearts every day of our lives!

Gracious Lord, please provide me the guidance and discipline to daily pray to you, in good times and periods of pain and suffering, for you always hear me! Amen.

MAY 7

Prayer of Deliverance

> Deliver me, O Lord, from evildoers; protect me from those who are violent.
>
> PSALM 140:1

This psalm is explained by a footnote in the HarperCollins Study Bible in this manner: "An individual prayer for help against those who have slandered and falsely accused the one who prays."[1] If you take the time to read this entire psalm, you find that the writer is very upset with some enemy and wants God to do something about the situation.

All of us at some time have felt like this. No matter how much we pray, study the Bible, have reflection time, and try to love our neighbor, at some point in life we will be angry and ask God to do something. May your anger be changed to praise as it was for the psalmist!

Loving Lord, please give me the love and patience to react to those evil forces around me by trusting that you will deliver me! Amen.

MAY 8

Calling for Help

> My steps have held fast to your paths; my feet have not slipped. I call upon you, for you will answer me, O God; incline your ear to me, hear my words.
>
> PSALM 17:5–6

The title of Psalm 17 from the NRSV Bible is "Prayer for Deliverance from Persecutors." This passage is a plea for help from someone who has tried to walk uprightly but who is set upon by persecutors. Of course, in our lives we could replace persecutors with things like: cancer, the evil in the world, a death of something or someone, a lack of employment, war, basically any storm of life.

Even when we try to do what we think is right in our lives, when we try to love our neighbor as ourselves, and even when we daily practice our spiritual disciplines, we will have times when we feel persecuted. Like the

---

1. Wayne A. Meeks et al., eds., *HarperCollins Study Bible: New Revised Standard Version* (New York: HarperCollins, 1993), 929.

writer of Psalm 17, we can call upon God trusting that the Lord will hear and answer our prayers. May your spiritual practices give you the courage to keep on calling and believing!

I pray that I am given the courage to call upon the Lord and truly believe that my prayer will be heard! Amen.

MAY 9

Spiritual Food

> And so, brothers and sisters, I [Apostle Paul] could not speak to you as spiritual people, but rather as people of the flesh, as infants in Christ. I fed you with milk, not solid food, for you were not ready for solid food.
>
> 1 CORINTHIANS 3:1–2

One of the aspects of the spiritual pilgrimage is that all of us are at a different stage in our journey. What may seem basic for some may be very challenging for others. The Apostle Paul is writing to acknowledge that fact. It doesn't matter where you are on the spiritual journey, because you're on the path.

We begin with milk and progress to solid food as we're able to digest it. Often it only takes a few minutes every day, with something as basic as saying the Lord's Prayer, as a way to get started with spiritual practices. Start with something, no matter how small, and try to make it a habit and see where the Holy Spirit takes you!

May I be unafraid of the shortcomings in my spiritual practices, and gracious Lord help me to start somewhere and try to make it a daily habit! Amen.

MAY 10

Praying in Secret

> But whenever you pray, go into your room and shut the door and pray.
>
> MATTHEW 6:6A

This passage is part of what has become known as the Sermon on the Mount. Jesus is teaching those close to him about how he wants them to live and pray. This section is about practicing one's piety before others. Many of the religious leaders in Jesus' time liked to pray in the synagogues and streets so that they would be seen and praised by others.

However, Jesus wanted his closest followers to pray in secret behind closed doors, so that only God could hear them. It's not wrong to pray in public and many of us do that in many different ways. In this teaching the focus is upon the attitude of one's heart; we are not to pray publicly in an attempt to impress others with our piety, our holiness. Praying alone, out of the sight and hearing of others, allows our relationship with God to grow and deepen!

Heavenly Lord, may my prayer time bring me into a closer relationship with you! Amen.

MAY 11

A Time of Distress

> Therefore let all who are faithful offer prayer to you; at a time of distress, the rush of mighty waters shall not reach them.
>
> PSALM 32:6

Having a prayer life of some type is one of the main aspects of this spiritual pilgrimage. Whether the length is only two minutes a day or up to several hours, turning our heart and mind to God and God's will in our lives is what is important. Having a relationship with anyone requires time, energy, and effort; the same is true of our relationship with the Lord.

In Psalm 32:6 we read that when the faithful pray to God in a time of distress, the waters will not reach them. Mighty waters here could also refer to the challenges of life that may overtake any of us. Many scholars believe that having a strong prayer life will not keep us from having problems, and we suffer just like anyone else. But, we believe that the Lord's love will surround us and walk with us through the valley times of our lives!

May my prayer times enable me to have a growing awareness of your love, O God, and especially during times of distress may this allow me to feel your presence! Amen.

MAY 12

Praying

> Out of the depths I cry to you, O Lord. Lord hear my voice! Let your ears be attentive to the voice of my supplications! . . . I wait for the Lord, my soul waits, and in his word I hope.
>
> Psalm 130:1–2, 5

The writer is crying out asking the Lord to hear the prayer and be attentive to it. The writer waits with hope that the prayer will be heard. There are countless books written on prayer and all that prayer entails. Many writers have noted that God does indeed hear all of our prayers; however, one can ask *if* God hears our prayers why aren't they always answered.

God is love and can't help but love us, and walks with us throughout our life. However, that doesn't mean that all of our prayers will be answered in the manner and method that we have prayed for. The most important part about prayer is that it strengthens our relationship with our Lord and helps us to become the person God wants us to be—everything else is secondary.

I remember after my late wife's second operation to remove a brain tumor she couldn't talk, walk, or move her right side. I prayed and prayed that I could get the former Judy back. That prayer wasn't answered the way I wanted. However, after she went under hospice care, I prayed that she would die without any pain and I think she did.

From what I have read about prayer and from my own experiences, the Lord does want us to cry out at any time and as often as we can, because when we pray we are drawn ever deeper into God's love, grace, and mercy!

Today, may my prayers go up to the Lord, and may my soul and heart wait in hope for whatever comes from them! Amen.

MAY 13

The Prayer of the Righteous

> Therefore confess your sins to one another, and pray for one another, so that you may be healed. The prayer of the righteous is powerful and effective. Elijah was a human being like us, and he prayed fervently that it might not rain, and for three years and six months it did not rain on the earth. Then he prayed again, and the heaven gave rain and the earth yielded its harvest.
>
> James 5:16–19

Prayer is the cornerstone of this spiritual pilgrimage, together with Bible study and refection. If one reads about the lives of past and present spiritual mothers and fathers, it is easy to see that they practiced daily prayer, of many types and methods. They have left us and continue to leave a wonderful example of the importance and use of prayer. Think about reading about their practices.

This passage indicates that the prayer of the righteous person is powerful and effective. In this context if someone is righteous they could be striving for God's kingdom and God's will in their lives. They probably have some understanding of their relationship with God and they are aware that prayer only enhances it. With that connectedness their prayer is likely centered on God's will and where they think God may be leading them, versus their own agenda.

They know that everything they pray for may not be given in the manner or method that they prayed. However, they know that God loves them and it is important to continue their prayer life, even when no answer is forth coming.

That may be where the powerful and effective part enters in. To continue praying even when we are not sure of the outcome can be powerful and effective, for our trust is in the grace, love, and mercy of the Lord, and not in our own efforts or what comes from our prayers!

May I start or enhance my prayer life today, so that my relationship with God begins or is strengthened, and may it continue throughout all the times of my life, and in time become powerful and effective! Amen.

MAY 14

God's Plans for Us

> For surely I know the plans I have for you, says the Lord, plans for your welfare and not for harm, to give you a future with hope. Then when you call upon me and come and pray to me, I will hear you. When you search for me, you will find me; if you seek me with all your heart.
>
> JEREMIAH 29:11–13

This passage is from a letter from the prophet Jeremiah to the Israelite exiles in Babylon. The letter outlines how false prophets had been claiming to be God's prophets. However, God said that these false prophets should not be believed because they were not conveying God's word.

This passage indicates that God does have a plan for the Israelites, one that is for their welfare and with a hopeful future, even if it may take a long time to bring it about. They are encouraged to call upon and pray to God, then search with their entire heart and they will find God.

Sometimes we feel like we are in a desert period that has gone on for a really long time. At times like these, God can seem far off or even nonexistent. While I was caring for my late wife (Judy) at home after she went under hospice care, the hospice staff strongly encouraged me to maintain the routine that I had prior to her illness. Doing that would help me keep a balance of some sort in my life. Of course this was a real challenge that took a lot of effort to do; however, I did try.

In the same manner, please be encouraged during all of the times of your life, no matter if in the desert or on the mountaintop, to continue your spiritual practices. God has a plan for you just like the Israelites had. They may be revealed over a long period, hopefully not seventy years as with the Israelite people!

May I call upon, come to, and pray to the Lord with my whole heart today, so that God's plans can be revealed to me! Amen.

MAY 15

Rejoice, Pray, and Give Thanks

> Rejoice always, pray without ceasing, give thanks in all circumstances, for this is the will of God in Christ Jesus for you.
>
> 1 THESSALONIANS 5:16–18

The Apostle Paul wrote this letter to the church community that he and his followers had started in Thessalonica. When he wrote that they should rejoice always, pray without ceasing, and give thanks in all circumstances, he hoped that those actions would nurture good relationships within the community. I would imagine that those early Christians had found it challenging to do those things on a daily basis.

They like us would have been involved with the everyday matters of work, family, cultural pressures, health issues, financial stresses, etc., and thus would have thought that they didn't have a lot of time to rejoice, to pray, and to always give thanks. However, Paul knew that it would be important for this new community to come together, and as they grew in their faith, being involved in these activities would be a vital step to that happening.

The meaning for us today is that by rejoicing always, praying without ceasing, and giving thanks in all circumstances, we are becoming the person God wants us to be, and strengthening the community of which we are a part.

Please be encouraged, as part of your spiritual pilgrimage, to look for ways to rejoice, pray, and give thanks at different times of the day. I try to find small ways to rejoice in the Lord: when I see a colorful part of nature, a pretty sky, a smiling baby, or think about my overall health, whatever is a wonder to me is something to rejoice in and give thanks for. Often, I pray while driving, jogging, walking, or when preparing a meal. I pray for family members and friends, for things that I might be involved with, for some hurting person, or for some painful situation around me or in the world. Try to find everyday situations in which to pray and you might be surprised about how quickly this practice becomes a habit!

Loving Lord, in my daily walk help me to look for ways to rejoice, pray, and give thanks and may these actions bring me closer to you and to those around me! Amen.

MAY 16

Seed Sown on Good Soil

> But as for what was sown on good soil, this is the one who hears and understands it, who indeed bears fruit and yields, in one case a hundredfold, in another sixty, and in another thirty.
>
> MATTHEW 13:23

In this passage from Matthew, Jesus is giving another parable to the crowds, this time about a sower of seed / the word. Again, his disciples have a difficult time understanding what this parable means and Jesus has to explain it to them, which he does in Matthew 13:18–23.

According to the parable the seed that doesn't bear fruit is compared to the person who hears the word about the kingdom of God but doesn't comprehend and follow it. It isn't understood because the evil one comes and takes away what is sown (the word), or because the root isn't deep enough, or because the cares of the world choke it. In all these cases the seed/word yields nothing.

However, what is sown on good soil bears fruit. In the same manner when the word about the kingdom is heard and grasped it becomes embedded in a person's heart and soul. We have the potential to be this good soil especially when we are actually engaged in our spiritual practices of prayer,

Bible study, and reflection. When this is done, we are on the road to becoming a lifelong disciple of Jesus Christ and we can also bear fruit and share this message about God's kingdom right now, right where we are.

Blessings on your spiritual pilgrimage as you allow this word to take a root in your inner being, which prevents it from being taken away, and where the cares of the world are put in their proper place in your life!

Lord of all creation, guide me to be good soil so that your word takes a strong root in me, and enables me to share the message of your kingdom with those I meet today! Amen.

MAY 17

God's Words Bring Joy and Delight

> Your words were found and I ate them, and your words became to me a joy and the delight of my heart; for I am called by your name, O Lord, God of hosts.
>
> JEREMIAH 15:16

In this verse, the prophet Jeremiah tells us how he has been called by the name of the Lord. Also, the Lord's words have been placed in his month and these words brought his heart joy and delight. The first chapter of Jeremiah tells how Jeremiah was consecrated before he was born, how he would speak for God, and how the Lord's words were put into his mouth.

All of us are called, as well, to take some role in bringing God's kingdom into this time and place. What I am called to do is different from you, and each of us has been gifted with the skills and abilities to carry out whatever we have been called to do. As we take part in our spiritual practices our prayer time opens up our hearts and minds so that God's words are able to guide and comfort us. This might also bring joy and delight to our hearts as it did for Jeremiah.

We may not be called to be prophets, however, each function that we are given is something that contributes to the will of God being done today. This calling may change over time and may very possibly take us to places that cause us to grow spiritually. Hopefully, your prayer time allows you to trust and to have faith in these promises of God that just as the Lord was with Jeremiah, God will be with us as well!

God of hosts, help me today to listen for your call, to pray about it, and to seek guidance from your word. May my heart's joy and delight that comes from this be shared with those I meet today! Amen.

MAY 18

The Lord's Voice in the Sheer Silence

> He [the Lord] said, "Go out and stand on the mountain before the Lord, for the Lord is about to pass by." Now there was a great wind, so strong that it was splitting mountains and breaking rocks in pieces before the Lord, but the Lord was not in the wind; and after the wind an earthquake, but the Lord was not in the earthquake; and after the earthquake a fire, but the Lord was not in the fire; and after the fire a sound of sheer silence. When Elijah heard it, he wrapped his face in his mantle and went out and stood at the entrance of the cave. Then there came a voice to him that said, "What are you doing here, Elijah?"
>
> 1 KINGS 19:11–13

In this passage the Lord told Elijah to stand on the mountain for God would be passing by. The main point from this reading is that the Lord wasn't in the great wind, or the earthquake, or in the fire. Wind, earthquakes, and fire in the Old Testament were often ways in which God's presence was revealed. However, in this case God chose not to appear to Elijah in any of these forms, but here it is in the *sheer silence*.

The writer of 1 Kings doesn't come right out and say that God is in the quiet, however it is strongly implied that this is what happened, because Elijah wrapped his cloak around himself and stood on the ledge and then the Lord spoke to Elijah. God appeared to Elijah while he was alone on a mountain and God came to Elijah *in the silence*.

Sometimes, in order to hear God's voice as Elijah did, we have to be alone or go to a quiet place to hear what God wants to tell us. On our spiritual pilgrimage, we are encouraged to take part in the spiritual practices of prayer, Bible study, and reflection, which often requires that one find quiet time to engage in these practices.

My encouragement to you is that you take time and reflect on this passage and think about your own practices. Think of ways that you can look for and listen to God's voice and word coming into your life; it takes energy, effort, persistence, and commitment for it to be meaningful. God through the Holy Spirit can speak to us when we are alone, or on a mountain or it may come in ways that we may not expect, such as in the *sheer silence* or even in the midst of a raging storm.

As you take part in this spiritual journey be open to where God may be leading you. The Lord may be asking you to take part in some great event, or it may be something as simple as praying for someone in need!

Holy Spirit, help me to be ready to listen for God's voice in all areas of my life, and may that voice direct and guide me today! Amen.

MAY 19

Praying Boldly

> Let us therefore approach the throne of grace with boldness, so that we may receive mercy and find grace to help in time of need.
>
> HEBREWS 4:16

When we talk about praying boldly that could strike some of us in the wrong way because it may indicate an attitude that isn't humble and one that causes us to think more highly of ourselves than we ought. However, the verses around this passage inform us that because of what Jesus has done, we are able to pray in this manner.

Thus, our boldness in prayer doesn't come from our station in life, or from anything we have done, nor from our piety. Our ability to pray with confidence comes from what God has done for us through Jesus Christ. As you take part in the spiritual practices may you pray with the trust that they will be heard and will be answered in God's time frame, manner, and method. Our part in becoming a lifelong disciple of Jesus Christ is to continue praying boldly and trusting the results to God!

Lord of all creation, help me to be bold in my prayers and know that you created me to grow to trust in you more each day. May this trust and faith in you be shared with those I meet today! Amen.

MAY 20

Meditating on God's Creation

> Every day I will bless you, and praise your name forever and ever....
> On the glorious splendor of your majesty, and on your wondrous works, I will meditate.
>
> PSALM 145:2, 5

The passage that these verses were taken from expresses praise and thanksgiving for the greatness of the Lord and for all that has been made. The psalmist talks about meditating on all of these wonderful works. As you take part in the spiritual practices always remember to give thanks for all of God's creation, which hopefully will become a natural outcome of your prayer life. As we experience various aspects of the universe that impact us we can bring those images to our minds during our meditation time. In this manner, we can praise God for all that has been created for us to see and enjoy.

I have been fortunate enough to have either lived around or been able to visit some really awesome places and sights over my lifetime. Mountains, oceans, lakes, rivers, deserts, forests, and wild flowers equally awe me. Being present to each moment as I experience it, give me a reason to praise God and be thankful for all of creation.

During your spiritual pilgrimage, may you find time to reflect upon and then give thanks for the small and large marvelous aspects of this world that touch your very being and help you to realize how beautiful God's creation is!

Lord of all life, may your Holy Spirit open my eyes to see the wondrous works of your creation, and may that awareness be shared with those I meet today! Amen.

MAY 21

God Does Not Reject My Prayer

> But truly God has listened; he has given heed to the words of my prayer. Blessed be God, because he has not rejected my prayer or removed his steadfast love from me.
>
> PSALM 66:19–20

The book of Psalms is full of places that note how the Lord hears our prayers. In this passage the writer talks about how God does not reject our prayers. For any number of reasons some of us may feel uncomfortable praying. We may not want to pray for we feel God would reject our prayer because we think that it should be done in a certain way, or the words don't flow very easily, or we may not feel worthy of praying to the Lord, or something from our past is blocking our inner spirit from reaching out. You can probably think of other things that may hold you or others back from praying.

However, God is love, and as this passage notes, God's steadfast love hasn't been removed from us, and thus will not reject our prayer. That doesn't mean that everything we pray for is granted, but they are heard. If we can just focus on the fact that the Lord loves us no matter what we do, or how we think others see us, or how stumbling our words may be, that knowledge might help us. When we have doubts about prayer, if we can just start in some way or fashion, no matter how small, God's love and the Holy Spirit will help us in the process.

If you are challenged in your prayer life, be encouraged to simply start, and let God's Spirit show you the next step. Also, consider making prayer a habit in your life and in that way, it gets easier every day to begin and continue!

Loving Lord, help me to trust in the promise that you don't reject my prayers, and may that fact help me to freely pray to you with an open heart, mind, and soul! Amen.

MAY 22

Raised Arms in Prayer

> I call upon you, O Lord; come quickly to me; give ear to my voice when I call to you. Let my prayer be counted as incense before you, and the lifting up of my hands as an evening sacrifice.
>
> PSALM 141:1–2

The thing about prayer is that there is no *one* way that fits everyone and people are unique in their prayer routine. From what I have read and personally experienced, the most important thing is to simply begin in some matter, and try to make it a daily routine.

Another thing I've read was to try raising one's hands during part of the prayer time, as it helps to keep one better focused while praying. I have tried to do that for a few minutes during my prayer time. Try lifting up your hands at some point during your prayer time; it could be counted as a sacrifice of praise to God!

Gracious Lord, help me to focus on you and your will in my life during my prayer time and throughout the day! Amen.

MAY 23

Growth in Prayer

> When I was a child, I spoke like a child, I thought like a child, I reasoned like a child; when I became an adult, I put an end to childish ways.
>
> 1 CORINTHIANS 13:11

This passage is taken from the chapter in 1 Corinthians that is known as the "love chapter" (ch. 13) and emphasizes the importance of love and of its everlasting quality. There are many wonderful messages in this chapter and one of them is embedded in verse 11. When we are young in age or less mature we generally act, and think in one way; after we age or grow in maturity we act and think in another manner. The same can be said about our prayer life and the steps that we take along our spiritual pilgrimage.

Many spiritual writers have said that having a life of prayer will change us and cause us to see things in a different way as we continue with our spiritual practices. I know that is certainly the case for me. My prayer life has often changed over the years as I have added and dropped certain aspects of my prayer routine. One of the biggest changes is that I now pray for my family, things that I'm concerned about, and for others during the day; this is in addition to the specific prayer times that I observe. I often pray when I am going for a walk, jogging, riding in a car, or waiting for an appointment. Somewhere along the way I was guided to carry a small piece of paper in my pocket with the names of my family members and close friends and a few issues that are a concern to me. While waiting in line or for an appointment, I pull out the paper and pray for those that are on it.

How we did things while young in our faith will not be the same as how we do things when we move along on our walk. As this passage states, when we were a child we thought like a child, but when we became an adult the childish ways were put aside. Be encouraged to find creative ways to have prayer be an ever-changing aspect of your spiritual pilgrimage. Know that as you mature in your journey how you pray and live will change, evolve, and grow!

Lord of all creation, help me to be open to your Spirit changing and moving me to new places on this pilgrimage! Amen.

MAY 24

Morning Prayer

> In the morning, while it was still very dark, he got up and went out to a deserted place, and there he prayed.
>
> MARK 1:35

In the passages before and after this verse Jesus is healing the sick and ministering to many that came to him or that he met along his travels. It's understandable that such activity caused him to seek some quiet time to be alone and pray. In this case in the morning before the sun was up, he went to a deserted place to pray. He did this before things got too hectic for him and his followers, and he left those closest to him so that he could be alone to pray.

Certainly, this is a wonderful example for us. However, people often say that they don't have time to set aside a specific period to pray in quiet without multitasking and trying to pray while doing three other things. In our modern society doing more than one thing at once is a sign of good time management and often we can pat ourselves on the back for this. We tell ourselves that we can pray as we go through our normal activities and we can and it's a wonderful habit to acquire.

However, as lifelong disciples of Jesus Christ we might think of following his example and have a specific time of prayer. We generally are able to make time for those things that are really important to us. From this passage, it appears that Jesus knew that everyone would be looking for him, yet he went away for this quiet time of prayer anyway.

On your spiritual pilgrimage, may you find a specific time to be alone to pray. Just begin with a few minutes if that is all you can do; the main thing is to just start in some manner. Jesus set the example for us to follow and the desert mothers and fathers, as will, felt this was important to do. May you, too, be open to this vitally important practice!

Holy Spirit, give me the guidance and courage to set aside some time during the day to be alone, to be quietly in your presence so that I may grow in knowledge and love for Jesus and his will in my life! Amen.

MAY 25

Waiting in Silence

> For God alone my soul waits in silence; from him comes my salvation.... For God alone my soul waits in silence, for my hope is from him.
>
> PSALM 62:1, 5

The psalmist wanted to get the point across about waiting alone in silence for God. The first half of both verses 1 and 5 are exactly the same. This person was intent on just waiting for God and for no one and nothing else, because their faith was in the Lord alone. They knew that their salvation and hope came from God.

This advice is also good for us today because we have a lot of noise, messages, and activities coming at us in our nonstop media world. Trying to wait in silence for anything takes a lot of effort. The desert mothers and fathers knew the importance of getting away from the world in order to hear the Holy Spirit's voice. Jesus often went away from everyone including his closest followers to be able to do this.

As you take part in the spiritual practices of prayer, Bible study, and reflection know that part of the process is sometimes waiting in silence for whatever needs to come to you. Maybe in the process you will be able to say as this writer noted that God alone is your hope and salvation!

Lord, during my prayer and reflection time, help me to strive to wait in silence for your message, and in that quiet may I continue to become the person you want me to be! Amen.

MAY 26

Listening

> And now, my children, listen to me: happy are those who keep my ways. Hear instruction and be wise, and do not neglect it. Happy is the one who listens to me, watching daily at my gates, waiting beside my doors.
>
> PROVERBS 8:32–34

Wisdom is something that can't be bought, stolen, or achieved because one is powerful or in a place of importance. Wisdom in most cases is obtained by living and experiencing all that comes about in one's life and learning from those events. Wisdom usually comes with age, but it can also come from listening to people who are wiser than we are and faithfully trying to put into practice what has been taught. This chapter from Proverbs talks about wisdom and its part in creation and in the life of humankind.

This specific passage tells us to listen to wisdom's voice and watch and wait for it at the gates and doors. Often in our fast-paced society we don't want to pray, watch, and wait for anything, because we've become accustomed to getting most anything we want in an instant. However, learning about wisdom and receiving guidance and discernment for our spiritual pilgrimage can only come when it's meant to come, and not before.

Thus, that can be one of the more frustrating aspects of our prayer life, being patient enough to wait for guidance, discernment, and wisdom to come our way as we take part in our spiritual practices. Praying, listening, watching, and waiting take courage and persistence when everyone around us seems to be getting what they want a lot faster than we do. May you be willing to pray and then listen with an uncluttered ear to what the Holy

Spirit may be trying to convey to you, and may that listening provide the wisdom needed for today!

Lord of all creation, help me to continue with my prayer practices and be a very patient listener to what I need to hear for the next step on my pilgrimage. May that wisdom help me to become the person you want me to be! Amen.

MAY 27

Loud Prayers

> I cry aloud to God, aloud to God, that he may hear me. In the day of my trouble I seek the Lord; in the night my hand is stretched out without wearying; my soul refuses to be comforted. I think of God, and I moan; I meditate, and my spirit faints.
>
> Psalm 77:1–3

Most of us don't want to cry aloud, but there are times in life when it may come and we don't have any control over it: times such as when a newborn baby loudly cries because she/he needs something from their parent or caretaker, or the cries of someone in pain, grief or sorrow. Sometimes we just have to let it out!

The writer of this psalm definitely wants to get the point across that they are crying aloud to God so that the Lord will hear them. I have done that several times in my life, and the most painful period was after my late wife's (Judy) second operation to remove a brain tumor. The first surgery had little or no effort on her body. However, after the second surgery she couldn't talk, walk, or move her right side. After a few days she seemed to make a little progress, but then her medication was changed and she slipped back into a comatose state again. I about lost it!

The next few days were extremely difficult and painful for my family and me as we saw Judy every day lying in this state in the hospital. That is one time I most surely cried to the Lord, loud and long, asking that Judy would recover from the operation and be well again. I prayed, wept, and was at one of the lowest points of my life. She did slowly recover, but was extremely limited as to what she could do; she couldn't drive or work outside of the home ever again. Over time the tumor returned and she went under hospice care.

You may have times on your spiritual pilgrimage where you feel like crying aloud to the Lord. Go ahead, God is love, can't help but love us, and hears our prayer. We may not get the result we want from the prayer, but be assured that they are being heard, and that we are loved! As this passage states: cry aloud, in the day of trouble seek the Lord, stretch out your hands, moan and meditate. Trust in God as you continue your spiritual practices, as you are able, in the midst of whatever is happening in your life.

Dear Lord, please hear me when I cry aloud to you in my pain, sorrow, or grief. Help me to feel your love, no matter what I might be going through at the moment! Amen.

MAY 28

Double-Minded, Unstable Prayers

> But ask in faith, never doubting, for the one who doubts is like a wave of the sea, driven and tossed by the wind; for the doubter, being double-minded and unstable in every way, must not expect to receive anything from the Lord.
>
> JAMES 1:6–8

As young parent I was very nervous about how to deal with a newborn, our first daughter seemed to be so tiny and helpless. Over time I got used to holding, feeding, and changing her. As I have grown older and become more used to being around babies I now love holding infants and being around young children. Part of my wonderment came about after my late wife's battle with brain tumors as I learned more about how marvelous our human bodies are and how they function. Newborns are awesome reminders of God's wonderful gift of creation to us!

I once read that a baby can sense the nervousness or fear of the person holding them and may begin to cry. But if they are held by someone who is secure in holding them, there is less fear and the baby feels safe. In the same way, God knows when we are timid or doubting in our prayers.

This passage tells us that God wants us to have faith when we pray, never doubting that we are being heard and held in God's love. Therefore, we can trust that God will always hear our prayers and is full of love and only wants the best for us. Our prayers may not be answered in the ways we want or expect but we can always trust that the Lord hears us and wants us to have faith, not doubting or being fearful of our loving God, who only wants the best for us!

Gracious Lord, help me to not be double-minded, unstable, or doubtful in my prayers to you, knowing that you always hear me, and that the Holy Spirit will help me and provide what I need for my spiritual pilgrimage! Amen.

MAY 29

Being Devoted to Prayer and Alert with Our Thanksgiving

> Devote yourselves to prayer, keeping alert in it with thanksgiving. At the same time pray for us as well that God will open to us a door for the word, that we may declare the mystery of Christ.
>
> COLOSSIANS 4:2–3

Devoting oneself to prayer often seems like a lot of work! It's easy to convince ourselves that having regular times of prayer may deprive us of time to devote to other things that may be more fun. However, once you set aside a specific prayer time, praying during the day can quickly become a routine to which you look forward with anticipation.

Keeping alert with thanksgiving may take a little effort as well. Depending upon how we look at life, finding things for which to give thanks could, at times, be a challenge. It is really easy to get weighed down with all of the pain, human suffering, and struggles that are part of our own daily lives as well as what we see through the media-focused world. We can learn about what happens around the world as it is occurring and this gives us much with which to concern ourselves. Thus, finding the time or energy to be thankful can be extremely challenging. It is important, however, to take time to be thankful for the many very wonderful gifts in your life and the lives of those around you that God gives each and every day.

I try to jog several times during the week and over the years have established certain routines that I do while jogging. I always pray for my family and my extended family, as well as use the time to memorize my Bible verse for the week. On the Saturdays that I jog, in addition to my prayers for others, I also try to give thanks for the things that happened to me during the previous week. I always give thanks for my sound mind and healthy body and for the mere fact that I am able to run.

Another area that I give thanks for is the gift of eternal life present here and now and in the time to come because of what Jesus did for all believers through his life, death, and resurrection. Giving thanks for guidance, safe travels, family, daily bread, shelter, etc., are some of the other areas for which I praise God.

Find ways that you are comfortable with, which fit your personality and lifestyle, and devote yourself to prayer and thanksgiving. Pray that the Holy Spirit will guide all of your spiritual practices!

God, guide my spiritual steps that I may devote myself to my prayer life, and in the process, help me to always be willing to give thanks for your infinite grace, love, and mercy! Amen.

MAY 30

Bold Asking

> And this is the boldness we have in him, that if we ask anything according to his will, he hears us.
>
> 1 JOHN 5:14

There have been countless books written on prayer, and I have read my share of them both for my own personal use and for my ministry. One of the common themes in many of those books is that of believing that our prayers are heard, even when all we hear is silence. Praying with boldness means that we know that no matter what else is going on around us, and even when our lives seem to be in a very low period, the Lord still hears us.

Praying in a bold manner with a humble heart doesn't necessarily mean that we know what will come from our prayer. Rather, we trust that God loves us and only wants the best for us and will hear our prayers; and whatever comes, God is with us.

Often, more than I care to mention, I have boldly prayed with an intense persistence about some major issue in my life and silence is what I heard for a long period of time. Eventually the path was shown to me, but it came in its own time and way, and not when I thought it should come. However, I can be bold in my prayer life because my trust is in God's love for me and all of creation.

Take courage, be bold in your prayer efforts knowing that you can trust God's love and compassion for you and others in your life, even when the answer you receive isn't necessarily what you are praying for. Being open to prayer that moves you toward striving for God's kingdom and will in your life may allow you to accept what God wants for you, rather than just looking for those aspects of life that you want and even demand!

Lord, help me to be bold in my prayers with a humble heart and may I be willing to listen to what comes from those prayers, even if it takes me to places that I never thought I would ever want to go! Amen.

MAY 31

The Righteous Cry for Help

> When the righteous cry for help, the Lord hears, and rescues them from all their troubles. The Lord is near to the brokenhearted, and saves the crushed in spirit.
>
> PSALM 34:17–18

If we established a routine of prayer but thought that we weren't heard, would we continue? Most of us would probably state, *no way!* No way would I continue to pray to someone or something if I didn't believe that anyone was listening. At some point, we would just stop and not worry about offering appeals up to the thin air, where they aren't heard anyway.

Isn't that the way with most things in this life? If we continue to do something and nothing comes of it, at some point we eventually stop or try a new way of doing it that might, hopefully, be more successful. Most of us would rather not keep hitting our heads up against a stone wall, so to speak, if it doesn't get us anywhere.

We have many examples in life in general and in our own specific lives where we can state without a doubt that the Lord does hear our prayers. Additionally, there are countless places in the Scriptures where it states in many different ways that our petitions are heard. This entire passage from Psalm 34 is a good illustration of this point about God listening to us and coming to us in our need.

As you take part in the spiritual practices of prayer, Bible study, and reflection may your prayers be sent up with a strong confidence and assurance. We know that whatever comes will, in the end, be best for us, because God loves us. Of course, the answer that comes may not be in the manner or timing that we would have hoped for; however, all of our prayers regardless of whether they are large or small, detailed or general, are heard!

Loving Lord, help me to be bold in my prayers and supplications to you, knowing that you welcome all of them no matter in what stage of life I happen to be, and your love surrounds me and you hear all of my pleas! Amen.

June

Prayer—How, What, and Why

JUNE 1

Prayer—How, What, and Why

By his words and actions Jesus left us a vast wealth of knowledge and guidance concerning what our prayer life might become.

In Matthew chapter 6 and Luke chapter 11, as well as other places, Jesus talks about how to pray and that it is done in secret or in a quiet place. He indicates that it should be done so that it doesn't draw attention to the person praying, but rather is focused on God. There are many recorded times where Jesus went off to pray by himself away from the crowds and from the stress of daily living. He apparently knew that he needed this time to stay connected to his heavenly Father, and that he needed to keep his focus on what he was being led to do.

In these chapters, Jesus gives us the Lord's Prayer. This prayer is a model of what our prayers should include. The words in this prayer are very powerful and helpful to us on our spiritual journey. There are countless books written about the Lord's Prayer; consider reading and reflecting on them.

In Matthew 26:41, we are given a very good reason as to why we should pray. Jesus said to three of his disciples in the garden at Gethsemane, "Stay awake and pray that you may not come into the time of trial; the spirit indeed is willing, but the flesh is weak." In this scene, Jesus wanted his disciples to stay awake with him as he went off to pray, however three different times he returned to them, only to find them sleeping. Often as fallible human beings we can't stay awake or stay alert when we need to. Our prayer life and spiritual practices can help us get through these times. We pray because our spirit may indeed be willing, but our flesh is weak.

According to Jesus we should most often pray alone, follow the model of the Lord's Prayer, and pray because we are in need of God's strength and guidance each day of our lives!

Lord Jesus, give me the wisdom in my prayer life to follow your model, and may my prayer life provide me the faith to be a loving and prayerful example to those I meet today! Amen.

JUNE 2

Finding Time to Pray

> But I call upon God, and the Lord will save me. Evening and morning and at noon I utter my complaint and moan, and he will hear my voice.
>
> Psalm 55:16–17

One of the most frequent comments about starting or enhancing one's spiritual practice is, "With so many things vying for my attention, how can I possibly add more things to my life?" You know all of the rationalizations and they probably sound something like this: there are too many work things that have to be done; I am caring for a sick child or parent; I am a single parent with no extra time; there is too much noise around me to have quiet time; etc. All of these reasons are certainly valid ones; however, it has been said that we always find time to do the things that are really important to us.

I would encourage you to start praying daily no matter how small the amount of available time might be. Consider starting by simply praying the Lord's Prayer as a beginning step. We can pray at any time during the day: in the shower, at meal time, while doing dishes or laundry, in our car, hiking, etc. Form the habit of thanking God for everyday miracles and then begin to listen and talk to God daily. At some point find a specific space and time to quietly enhance or begin the spiritual practices of prayer, Bible study, and reflection.

The desert mothers and fathers knew the importance for their spiritual growth of having their day revolve around worship and prayer, and they were very intentional about centering their daily lives around such activities. Many faith communities continue this practice today. I made a silent retreat at the Abbey of Gethsemani where their normal day consisted of eight specific worship times beginning at 3:15 a.m. and ending with the last one at 7:30 p.m. These scheduled times were in addition to other times during the day set aside for personal prayer and study. This routine is maintained every day of the year. I didn't attend all of these worship services while I was there, but I could have.

My point is that there are groups yet today who believe in worshiping at various times of the day, as a way to become a person of prayer and to carry out their vocation. Psalm 55 encourages us to cry out to God—evening, morning, and noon. Hopefully you are able to set aside a specific time during the day to turn your heart and soul to the Lord in prayer. Pick a time that works for you and begin to make it a habit!

May I set aside time for prayer today, O God, and may that draw me closer to you! Amen.

JUNE 3

Prayer and Life's Decisions

> Now during those days he went out to the mountain to pray, and he spent the night in prayer to God. And when day came, he called his disciples and chose twelve of them, whom he also called apostles.
>
> LUKE 6:12–13

In this passage, Jesus left us another blueprint about prayer. He was on the verge of making a really important decision for his ministry and he knew that he had to get away from the noise and stress of things that were going on around him in order to hear God's voice.

We have many stories in the Bible where God's wisdom, revelation, and guidance were given on mountains, and for Jesus, mountains were a place of solitude, peace, and reflection. He spent the entire night on the mountain in prayer. Jesus is the Son of God, in whom the Lord was well pleased, and yet Jesus felt the need to pray all night before calling his disciples.

It's important to daily seek God's guidance, but especially when making life decisions, no matter whether they're large or small ones. Jesus' example reinforces the need for going off to a quiet place to have sincere, heartfelt prayer. We may not have a mountain to go to; however, if we look hard enough we can certainly find something that fits into our lifestyle, a place that is quiet and allows us the ability to both talk to and listen to God.

We may never have to choose twelve disciples as Jesus did, but daily we make choices about various aspects of our life. These daily decisions determine the direction of our spiritual pilgrimage. May you find the outer and inner peace to enhance your walk with the Lord!

God of Life, today help me on my spiritual journey to find the place and time to pray and then listen for your word and direction! Amen.

JUNE 4

Persevere in Prayer

> Rejoice in hope, be patient in suffering, persevere in prayer.
>
> ROMANS 12:12

Romans 12:9–21 describes the characteristics of a true disciple of Jesus Christ. Among other things it refers to living a life of genuine love, serving the Lord with zeal, extending hospitality to strangers, blessing your enemies, living in harmony and peace with others, and forsaking vengeance, etc.

Take time today to read and reflect on these qualities. Attempting to fulfill all of these aspects can be quite overwhelming. However, many spiritual writers down through the ages have noted that when prayer is the cornerstone of one's life, these traits are frequently reflected.

Prayer can mean various things to different people and there isn't a "one-size-fits-all" model. Prayer can be thought of as a two-way conversation; it opens up our hearts and souls to give and receive. It can lead, guide, and comfort us. The most important part is that it strengthens our relationship with our Lord and helps us to become the persons God wants us to be—everything else is secondary.

Starting a prayer life takes effort and perseverance in our life. The main thing is to begin and try to make it a habit. Begin with the Lord's Prayer, maybe when you first get up or with your morning tea or coffee. Start your day by thanking God for everyday miracles. Listen and talk to God daily as you take part in your spiritual practices.

On your spiritual pilgrimage, may you find what is needed to persevere in prayer and in so doing be able to embody the characteristics in this passage!

Heavenly Lord, may my prayer life draw me closer to becoming the person you want to be and in the process, help my life bring others closer to you! Amen.

JUNE 5

Jesus Prays for His Disciples

In John 17 Jesus is praying for his disciples. He prayed for them because he was about to leave them and he was committing them to the care of his Heavenly Father. Just as Jesus prayed for his disciples, he continues to pray for all of us today. Jesus is a model for us to follow. Praying for those you love or who are in need is something that all of us on this spiritual pilgrimage should take very seriously and try to do daily.

During my prayer time, I have a list of family members, friends, church members, and situations around the world for which I prayed. Holding others up in prayer can cause us to reach out beyond ourselves to walk with others during their challenging times. Just as God through the Holy Spirit walks with you daily, you can walk with others as well. People realize that they are thought about and loved when they know they are being prayed for.

There are countless ways in which this can be done. As an example, during the year I place the Christmas cards that we have received in a basket and every couple of days I pull a card. The family whose card is pulled is prayed for during meal times and when Shirley and I pray together before we start the day. During my jogging time, I also have a list of people for whom I pray

Just as Jesus prayed for his disciples and he continues to pray for us, we, too, should try to please find ways to pray for others. May this practice help you in your spiritual journey to become a lifelong disciple of Jesus Christ!

Loving Lord, help me to pray for those that I love and for those in need and may this practice open my heart and soul to be able to receive more of your infinite grace, love, and mercy that I can then share with others! Amen.

JUNE 6

God's Peace from Prayer

> Do not worry about anything, but in everything by prayer and supplication with thanksgiving let your requests be made known to God. And the peace of God, which surpasses all understanding, will guard your hearts and your minds in Christ Jesus.
>
> PHILIPPIANS 4:6–7

When we pray with thanksgiving and let God know what is going on in our lives, we can have this peace that passes all understanding. During a time in my life when I was really struggling, God's peace came to me through prayers which gave me direction and insight.

My late wife, Judy, had two operations to remove brain tumors. The first one went fairly smoothly and she had little if any side efforts from it. However, the second surgery was another matter for it was a much more difficult one. Afterwards she couldn't talk, walk, or move her right side. Needless to say, it was a very trying time for all of my family, but especially for Judy and me. She spent twelve weeks in two hospitals and a nursing home recovering from the operation, undergoing radiation, and relearning many skills.

During her time at the nursing home she seemed to be getting a little better, however, every evening I hated to leave her there. It was very difficult for me because I felt so sorry that I couldn't do any more for her. I always prayed for her during the day and for guidance about this situation and was very thankful for any progress that she made. I was led by the Spirit to get a devotional book and started reading it to her before leaving at night. I read the scripture listed for the day, then the reflection part of the book, and the prayer at the end of the devotional.

That small act gave me some peace of both mind and spirit so that I felt somewhat better leaving her at night. The peace I received didn't change the situation that we were in, but it did allow me the ability to cope a little better with what was going on. After she came home, we continued to follow the same practice before going to bed. After Judy passed away, I continued that routine alone. During your prayer time let God know what is going on with you and may you experience the peace of God that passes all understanding!

God of all peace, guard my heart and mind as my prayers with thanksgiving go up to you! Amen.

JUNE 7

Praying for Space and Room in My Distress

> Answer me when I call, O God of my right! You gave me room when I was in distress. Be gracious to me, and hear my prayer.... But know that the Lord has set apart the faithful for himself; the Lord hears when I call to him.
>
> PSALM 4:1, 3

In the book of Psalms, we have many cases where the writer is pleading to God to hear their prayers and save them. In some cases, it is a prayer of deliverance from one's enemies, as in Psalm 4. The writer wants to be heard by God and rescued from whatever is causing harm.

This psalm notes that God had given them *room* in their distress. Apparently, the psalmist was feeling confined or trapped in this distress. That is an interesting concept for us today as we think about all of the different ways that our society can make us feel confined or trapped. There may be times in our lives when we may feel hemmed in by something inside us or around us that even causes us to have trouble breathing.

We may feel some comfort and relief in knowing that God is with us in the midst of the situation. During your prayer time always talk to God about your concerns, troubles, whatever is distressing you, because your prayers will most certainly be heard. Our prayers may not be answered in the manner and time frame that we would like; however, just having a little room to better cope with the challenges may be all that is needed to help us make it through another day!

Lord, hear my prayer and provide what is needed for me to get through this day. Help me to be open to the possibility that the answer is just a little room! Amen.

JUNE 8

My Waiting on the Lord Helps Others

> I waited patiently for the Lord; he inclined to me and heard my cry. He drew me up from the desolate pit, out of the miry bog, and set my feet upon a rock, making my steps secure. He put a new song in my mouth, a song of praise to our God. Many will see and fear, and put their trust in the Lord.
>
> Psalm 40:1–3

This psalm tells about a person who prayed for deliverance to the Lord, then waited patiently, was saved, had a new song given to them, and because of this, many then recognized what had happened and put their trust in God.

When we are involved with prayer and our faith journey, it may benefit others. People around us may be looking at how we handle tough situations in life. If they can see that we are asking God to walk with us in our challenges and attempting to embrace God's presence, they may be encouraged by that. Waiting for the Lord to help us or deliver us takes courage and faith to trust that God's love and mercy will be with us even we can't see or feel it at the present moment.

Waiting, of course, is one of the more difficult facets of this spiritual pilgrimage, especially for those of us who live in this modern society of instant everything. Because of technically, we can do things in a matter of minutes, tasks that used to take hours to accomplish. Thus, we can easily get in the habit of believing that everything operates that way. However, many aspects of human life, God's creation, and the spiritual realm do not occur right away. Some things happen when they happen and not in the fashion that we expect.

On your pilgrimage, be assured that when you pray you are putting the answer and also the timing of the response into God's hands. Also, realize that others may be encouraged to trust when they see how you are living out your faith!

Loving Lord, today help me to pray to you and then wait for your answer. May my actions help those around me to believe in you and then begin to pray to you also! Amen.

JUNE 9

Time Alone

> Now when Jesus heard this, he withdrew from there in a boat to a deserted place by himself.
>
> MATTHEW 14:13A

Matthew 14:1–12 records the death of John the Baptist. After Jesus heard this he was saddened and had to get away. Even though he was the Son of God this event greatly grieved him, and he had to be alone so that he could mourn the death of someone he loved very much.

We may have times in our lives when we have to be alone to think about, grieve, or contemplate something that has happened to us. Like Jesus we want to remove ourselves from the noise and demands of the world around us. However, notice what occurred in the verses that follow this one: Jesus was moved by the crowds and went to them and ministered to them. Thus, at some point after our periods of grief, rest, and reflection—and we are the only ones who know when that time is—we ought to think about becoming active again in our community.

I experienced something like this after my late wife, Judy, died following a long struggle with cancer. We had been married for more than twenty-eight years when she passed away in January, the middle of winter when the days are short, cold, and dark. My grief was made more difficult because of the decreased amount of daylight hours. I remember sitting in my living room alone after work, with the darkness outside, and feeling a pain and loneliness that I'd never known before. I was alone a great deal in the evenings—by choice, because I needed to grieve and process what had happened. I missed her terribly, and I had no idea how my life would unfold. It took all my energy to make it through each day. Spring did come and I began to feel somewhat better. Looking back, I know that time away from doing a lot of unnecessary activity was really important for my healing and for being able to move forward with my life.

On your spiritual pilgrimage, you may have the occasion when you need to get away to pray, grieve, or reflect on events in your life. If that is needed, do so, remembering that Jesus did the same thing. However, realize that just as Jesus did, we may need at some point to get back into our surroundings in order to do the ministry that we have been called to do and to continue with our healing!

Compassionate Lord, when needed, help me to take the opportunity to be alone and reflect on the things that impact my life, and may that time allow me to share your love with those that I meet today! Amen.

JUNE 10

Daniel Prayed Anyway

> Although Daniel knew that the document had been signed, he continued to go to his house, which had windows in its upper room open toward Jerusalem, and to get down on his knees three times a day to pray to his God and praise him, just as he had done previously.
>
> DANIEL 6:10

If you don't know this story of Daniel and King Darius, consider reading Daniel 6 to get all of the details. Even though a document was signed forbidding anyone from doing so, Daniel still prayed to his God as he always had. His habit of praying three times a day on his knees was one that he continued to do regardless of the king's orders to the contrary. Daniel trusted in his Lord more than in the rulers of that time.

Those of us who live in the United States are basically free to pray and worship as we choose. Of course, there are many places around the world where this is not the case. Countless numbers of people have died down through the centuries and innumerable others are still being persecuted today in many countries because of their religious beliefs. Many who came to this country did so because of religious oppression.

Being able to freely pray and worship is a wonderful opportunity especially for those of us in the United States. Hopefully you are exercising this gift and are involved in some form of spiritual practices. Continue to be open to new ways of improving on your current routines. May Daniel's faithfulness and commitment encourage you in your spiritual journey!

Holy Spirit, help me in starting or enhancing my spiritual pilgrimage. May these practices draw me into a deeper relationship with you, so that I may be an instrument of your love to others! Amen.

JUNE 11

Prayer for the Really Tough Things of Life

> He [Jesus] said to them, "This kind can come out only through prayer."
>
> MARK 9:29

This story tells of the unsuccessful attempt of Jesus' disciples to cure a boy of an unclean spirit. Jesus commanded that this spirit come out of the boy and it did. The disciples asked him why they couldn't do it and Jesus replied that prayer was the only way to remove such a spirit.

This is a humbling story because even though the disciples had been with Jesus for some time and had heard his teachings and witnessed his miracles, they were unable to perform some of his feats. It wasn't until after the Holy Spirit came upon the disciples that healing was recorded in the book of Acts. In this case Jesus seems to imply that some things can *only* be done through the power of prayer.

Sincere, persistent prayer can help us do things that otherwise would be very challenging for us. Prayer causes us to change, to see things through the eyes of God's kingdom, and may lead us to take risks that we wouldn't otherwise take. Prayer can help us handle some of the really tough things in life, such as pain, sorrow, and trying times. A prayerful life can help us navigate the rough and uncertain waters of life.

Like the disciples, we probably won't be able to physically heal someone; however, we can listen, encourage, or pray for those who are struggling and in the process, bring them a sense of peace. Prayer enables us to handle situations and stresses that we previously weren't able to deal with because we are able to see life differently through the lens of God's eyes. Who knows, we may even be led to places, people, and opportunities that are new and exciting!

Lord of creation, help me to believe that through you and my prayer life I can be changed and empowered to do new and wonderful things for your kingdom, and in the process, help others to be changed as well! Amen.

JUNE 12

Praying in the Spirit

> Take the helmet of salvation, and the sword of the Spirit, which is the word of God. Pray in the Spirit at all times in every prayer and supplication. To that end keep alert and always persevere in supplication for all the saints.
>
> EPHESIANS 6:17–18

These verses are part of a larger passage whereby the writer of Ephesians talks about taking on the entire armor of God. Some of the qualities found in this armor are truth, righteousness, faith, and being able to proclaim the gospel of peace. Two other characteristics of this armor are the word of God and praying in the Spirit.

Studying the word of God and praying in the Spirit are very important rituals of this spiritual pilgrimage. Verse 18 gives us some specific direction about our prayer life. According to this verse we should pray in the Spirit at all times and should try to keep alert and persevere in our prayer efforts.

One way to do that is to begin your prayer time asking the Holy Spirit to direct and guide your prayers. We can't begin to understand how the Spirit functions in our spiritual lives, just as we can't see where the wind comes from, however, we know that it is still all around us. We ask the Spirit for guidance, and then trusting, we wait until the direction comes.

It is essential for us to wait, stay alert, and persevere, for we don't know where our prayer time will lead us nor how long it may take before discernment comes. So, we have to remain ready and faithful in our prayer practices. This is extremely challenging in today's society where we have instant everything, but walking along the spiritual path is the very opposite of our culture's current mind-set.

On your spiritual pilgrimage, may you put on the entire armor of God, including the study of the word of God and praying in the Spirit in a consistent, patient manner!

Holy Spirit, direct and guide my study and prayer time that it be a time in which I can become the person that you created me to be, and in that process become a witness of God's grace to those I meet today! Amen.

JUNE 13

The Lord Accepts My Prayer

Depart from me, all you workers of evil, for the Lord has heard the sound of my weeping. The Lord has heard my supplication; the Lord accepts my prayer.

PSALM 6:8–9

As you read these daily devotions I would encourage you to read the verses preceding and following the passages selected. In that way, you can obtain a better understanding of what the Bible writers were attempting to say overall. In Psalm 6 the writer describes a situation in which a person is in great physical pain and whose life is full of moaning.

The Lord has been asked to heal and deliver this person. All of us may have been in situations in which we cried ourselves to sleep, our eyes were red from our grief, our pain or the pain of someone we loved was overwhelming, and we didn't know if we could get through another day.

During times like this it is important to know that God hears our prayers, "For the Lord has heard the sound of my weeping. The Lord has heard my supplication; the Lord accepts my prayer." We may not be cured of all of our diseases, or be delivered from all of our troubles; however, knowing that the Lord has accepted our prayers can comfort and sustain us through these times.

Take courage and continue, if at all possible, your spiritual practices, even in the midst of extremely demanding periods of your life. For the Lord, will hear your prayer and be with you!

God of all hope, help me to cry out to you in prayer at all times, especially when life is the most difficult, and allow me to realize that all my prayers are accepted by you! Amen.

JUNE 14

Being Humble in Prayer

He [Jesus] also told this parable to some who trusted in themselves that they were righteous and regarded others with contempt: "Two men went up to the temple to pray, one a Pharisee and the other a tax collector. The Pharisee, standing by himself, was praying thus, 'God, I thank you that I am not like other people: thieves, rogues, adulterers, or even like this tax collector. I fast twice a week; I give a tenth of all my income.' But the tax collector, standing far off, would not even look up to heaven, but was beating his breast and saying, 'God, be merciful to me, a sinner!' I tell you, this man went down to his home justified rather than the other; for all who exalt themselves will be humbled, but all who humble themselves will be exalted."

Luke 18:9–14

In this parable, Jesus is giving us more direction about our prayer life. This passage is fairly straightforward in that our attitude toward God and ourselves determines how and what we pray. According to this parable even though we may fast, tithe, and do other wonderful things, it shouldn't be done with a boastful or arrogant attitude in order to exalt us.

The tax collector in this story kept his words simple and humble, "God, be merciful to me, a sinner," while the Pharisee went on and on about how wonderful he was. We are all sinners in need of God's mercy and forgiveness, and may that be reflected in our prayers!

Lord of infinite grace, help me to know that your mercy is able to overcome any shortcomings on my part, and may that knowledge influence the manner in which I come to you in prayer! Amen.

JUNE 15

Hearing What the Lord Speaks

Let me hear what God the Lord will speak, for he will speak peace to his people, to his faithful, to those who turn to him in their hearts.

Psalm 85:8

God can speak to us in many ways. How the Lord speaks to you is probably different from how God communicates with others. Also, over time how God speaks to us will probably change as we mature in our prayer lives. The messages may come during our prayer time, while worshiping with others, through our friends or family members, through events happening in the world around us, or on a walk, you name it, for the Holy Spirit can speak to us in countless ways. The key part for us is to be faithful and to turn our hearts toward God.

An example of how God's guidance came to me through other people was at the time that when we put my late wife, Judy, under hospice care. She had already had two surgeries to remove brain tumors and radiation when the same dreaded tumor-like symptoms returned. This time our options were limited and chemotherapy would only slow the tumor's growth and could cause unwelcome side effects. We talked to her doctors about what to do and prayed about it.

My son, Kevin, said that you hate to see a loved one suffer, and thus we made the choice to make her as comfortable as possible but not try anything else to prolong her life. If we hadn't been open to God's Spirit coming to us through others, we may have continued treatments that would not have cured her but simply kept her alive for a few more weeks or months. But we did what we believed was best for her. I firmly believe that God spoke through other people to guide our family and me during that time to make that very difficult decision.

As you take part in this spiritual pilgrimage, may you be faithful and turn your hearts to the Lord and look for the many ways that God may be speaking to you about all areas of your life!

Holy Spirit, please help me to hear the voice of God coming through you to me, and may I be open to where this voice is leading me! Amen.

JUNE 16

God's House of Prayer

> ... for my house shall be called a house of prayer for all peoples.
>
> ISAIAH 56:7c

This passage teaches us the importance of being open to others who are welcome into the Lord's house even though they may be different from us. We sometimes look at others through the lens of our own experience and beliefs. Thus, we may judge others based on our own expectations, and in the process, may attempt to place boundaries upon those with whom we have opportunities to interact.

But it is important to know that God's house of prayer is for all peoples who seek to do the Lord's will. We are imperfect humans and will make mistakes and have shortcomings. However, when we sincerely take part in the spiritual practices of prayer, Bible study, and reflection we may slowly begin to see life and those around us through the lens of God's will and purposes, versus how we think things ought to be. We begin to understand that even through others may be different from us, they are welcome in the Lord's house of prayer just as we are!

Lord of all peoples, help me to view others as you see them and guide me to welcome them with open arms into your house of prayer and into my life! Amen.

JUNE 17

God in the Quiet

We live in a period and culture that create a lot of noise, flashing images, commotion, stress, and situations that didn't previously exist for our grandparents and great grandparents. Today it takes more energy and effort just to keep up with what is happening all around us. These distractions often get in the way of having quiet time to think about, reflect on, and process life.

God is still talking to us and walking with us today; however, because of all of the diversions of the world around us, we often fail to hear God's voice. Jesus and the desert mothers and fathers practiced the art of seeking solitude in order to be able to listen and learn from God. Hopefully they can be an example for us.

Please be encouraged to try and find the time and space to be able to hear in the silence around you and within you God's voice speaking to your heart and spirit. Try finding a room in your house where you can be alone or an open church or quiet park, or going on a retreat, or giving up some of your TV/internet time to sit quietly or go for a walk alone. There are countless ways to find quiet spaces and time, but it takes energy, effort, and persistence to make that happen.

As you take part in the spiritual practices of prayer, Bible Study, and reflection, ask the Holy Spirit to help you create an environment so that you're better able to listen to the voice of the Lord!

Lord of the silence, guide me to look for ways to be quiet during my prayer times, so that I can hear your voice and feel your love all around me! Amen.

JUNE 18

Remaining Alert through Our Prayers

> Be alert at all times, praying that you may have the strength to escape all these things that will take place, and to stand before the Son of Man.
>
> Luke 21:36

In this passage, Jesus talks to his followers about the future destruction of Jerusalem and the coming of the Son of Man. He goes on to note the importance of not letting their hearts be weighed down by the worries of this life. He encouraged his followers to be alert, praying for the strength needed to deal with what was coming. Being alert and praying is the cornerstone of this spiritual pilgrimage for those of us are who are striving to become a lifelong disciple of Jesus Christ.

Praying for the strength to not let our heart be weighed down by the worries of this life is very challenging, at best. There are so many situations in life that can bring us down mentally and emotionally; things like war, violence, property, disease, the unfair treatment of vulnerable peoples, weather-related events, and an increase of cynicism in our society as it relates to dealing with other humans. This of course is made more dramatic because of the increased level of communications whereby we can instantly learn about what is happening on the other side of the world. Sometimes we may feel as if we have information overload when it comes to learning about world events. Thus, what Jesus was expressing about being alert and praying is definitely good advice for us in this fast-paced culture.

Of course, just because we try to stay alert and pray for strength to deal with these issues doesn't mean that we are exempt from all of life's happenings. As long as we are on this side of God's kingdom we will be subject to the events mentioned above and then some. However, by trying to guard our hearts from the worries of the world through our spiritual practices, we can have hope that no matter what happens to us today or in the future the Lord's presence and love will be with us and surround us. May you stay alert and pray for strength and may your heart be encouraged!

Lord of love, help me to trust you and pray for strength so that my heart is not weighed down with the worries of this life, and may my spiritual pilgrimage be a witness to those I meet today! Amen.

JUNE 19

Prayer Answered in God's Time

> But as for me, my prayer is to you, O Lord. At an acceptable time, O God, in the abundance of your steadfast love, answer me.
>
> PSALM 69:13

The writer of this psalm is expressing a faith that is hard for most of us to comprehend—that at an acceptable time the answer to our prayer will be forthcoming. In our world of instant everything in which we can learn about what is happening anywhere in the world right after it occurs, where we can get information about most any topic in a matter of seconds, and where most of us grow impatient when we forced to wait for something, this verse might cause us some anxiety. Unlike the fast-paced world in which we live, our spiritual pilgrimage unfolds at a more gentle, unhurried pace.

Declaring that we would be willing to have God's answer at some unknown "acceptable time" goes against our very nature. However, that is in fact what the writer of this passage and countless other spiritual writers have been saying for centuries. God's timing is not the same as our timing. A large part of this spiritual journey is learning to trust the fact that the Lord does indeed love us and knows what is best for us and those around us.

This is a very challenging aspect of this pilgrimage and one that has caused me concern more times than I care to count. On your spiritual walk, trust that God will answer in the best time because God's love is abundant and steadfast!

Lord of overflowing love, help me to trust that you hear all my prayers, and that no matter how or when my prayers are answered your love it always surrounding me! Amen.

JUNE 20

Gathered in Prayer

> For where two or three are gathered in my name, I am there among them.
>
> MATTHEW 18:20

I have been very fortunate to have been a part of a number of Christian communities over my lifetime. They all have contributed to my spiritual growth and have been a supportive part of the ups and downs of my life and that of my family. My family and I have always participated in regular worship services wherever we lived. Over the years, I have been involved in an American Baptist Church, a few Roman Catholic parishes and several ELCA Lutheran congregations in six different states. Of course, no community is perfect and at times some of them have caused unintended pain to me or my family. However, like most things in life, if something is important to us we try to work through the difficult times.

I realize others may view being involved in a community in a very different light, especially if they're been a part of a very difficult or challenging situation and been hurt because of it. That happened to my mother when I was a young teenager. For a while she was given a very hard time for something that was going on in her life, and while she felt that she was doing the right thing, others in the community thought otherwise. Even though that was a very painful time for her, she stayed in that faith community, and over time things got somewhat better. She remained a faithful member of that congregation for many more years until she passed away.

Jesus wants us to pray individually and with others and assures us that whenever two or three are gathered in his name, he will be in their midst. In this extended passage, he is talking about how to deal with issues that arise in the church. If you are already involved with a spirit-filled community, continue to allow them to be a part of your journey in all of its joys and challenges. If you're not actively involved in a Christian community, may this verse encourage you to pray for guidance about finding one and then becoming an active part of the worship practices and mission of that particular body of Christ. For when people are gathered together in Jesus' name, there he is also!

Lord of life, help me to embrace my current community or pray for guidance about how to find one that can walk with me on my spiritual pilgrimage! Amen.

JUNE 21

Prayer and Persistence

> I tell you, even though he will not get up and give him anything because he is his friend, at least because of his persistence he will get up and give him whatever he needs. "So I say to you, Ask, and it will be given you; search, and you will find; knock, and the door will be opened for you."
>
> LUKE 11:8–9

In this passage from Luke, Jesus' disciples ask him to teach them to pray. Jesus goes on to give them Luke's version of what has come to be called the "Lord's Prayer." He then tells them about the need of being persistent in one's prayer with a story about a friend coming at midnight asking for bread. Jesus lets them know that the friendship isn't why the request is granted but rather because of the persistence of the person doing the asking. He further relates to them that asking is the key, and that God who is love knows how to give good gifts and especially the Holy Spirit to those who ask.

For most of us who live in this modern society being persistent in our prayer life can be challenging because we are programmed to expect instant answers and gratification. We are a culture that has become used to getting information when we want it, communicating with someone across the world in a few seconds, and finding out what is going on anywhere as soon as it happens. Thus, reading about waiting for answers to prayers, being patient, and being persistent in our prayer life goes against the mind-set of the world around us.

However, that is exactly what Jesus was telling his disciples many years ago, and also us today. He isn't telling us this in order to frustrate us in our prayer life or because he doesn't love us and wants us to suffer in the waiting. Rather, as many spiritual writers have written, waiting and being persistent in our prayer life is part of the process of becoming a lifelong disciple of Jesus Christ. Our faith grows not because we can get instant answers or because our prayers are answered in the way in which they were asked, but because our hope and trust are in the Lord. Our prayers are meant to draw us into a deeper relationship with our Lord, and according to verse 9 of this passage, we are meant to ask, search, and knock, for in doing that we learn that God does indeed know what we need and when we need it.

On your spiritual pilgrimage, may you be persistent in all your prayers, but at the same time be patient, knowing that they are heard by a loving Lord who only wants the best for you!

Lord, in my prayer life, help me to keep on asking, searching, and knocking. Guide me to trust that whatever comes will be what is needed for me today! Amen.

JUNE 22

Open the Door

> Listen! I am standing at the door, knocking; if you hear my voice and open the door, I will come in to you and eat with you, and you with me.
>
> Revelation 3:20

The first twenty-seven years of my life I belonged to and was a very active member of Jerusalem Baptist Church, which was on the far eastern side of Youngstown, Ohio. It was built near a steel mill and a number of the members worked in various mills around town. The vast majority of the families that were church members had moved to the area from the Southern states to get jobs in the steel industry or some related business. They were hard-working people who were looking for a better life for themselves and their families. The church was a very important part of their life and helped shape who they were.

At some point when the church was built or remodeled, I don't know which, a large window was installed at the front of the church behind the pulpit area. The picture on the window was of Jesus standing in front of a door, ready to knock on it. Anyone who worshiped there saw the window and would probably reflect on what it meant for them, and for the congregation.

This verse and the window are basically saying the same thing. Jesus is knocking at the door of our heart, soul, or spiritual core, and wants to be with us. Jesus wants to be a vital part of our lives, each minute, each hour, through both the good and the difficult times of life, but we have to be willing to let him in. We can daily open the door through our prayer practices and by striving for God's kingdom in our lives versus our own agenda.

Imagine for a moment that Jesus is knocking at your door, then envision you opening the door to let him in to be with you and to daily walk with you!

Holy Jesus continue to knock at the door of my life and may the Holy Spirit give me the courage and guidance to daily open it! Amen.

JUNE 23

Praying with a Companion

> One day Peter and John were going up to the temple at the hour of prayer, at three o'clock in the afternoon.
>
> ACTS 3:1

For some of us, doing things with another person is often easier than doing it alone. Organizations like exercise groups, book clubs, sewing circles, travel tours, and various other groups have been around for a long time. Such gatherings allow people the opportunity to join with others to do a certain task, activity, or to share a common experience. Such groups don't appeal to everyone, but others enjoy sharing things with like-minded people.

In this passage, Peter and John are going up to the temple to pray at three o'clock in the afternoon, which was a regular time of prayer. They went up together and both knew the importance of maintaining their prayer practice or routine. Some of you may find it difficult to begin and continue a daily prayer habit. Think of joining with another person or a group to support you in your desire to pray daily. Also, look for an open church or quiet place where your prayer time can be done if you aren't at home.

Try different methods and places until you find something that is comfortable for you and your personality. The main thing is to start and to do your best to continue. If you have already started and have a routine, be open to where the Holy Spirit may be leading you next on your spiritual pilgrimage. We can pray at any time of the day or night, but many spiritual writers note the importance of having a specific quiet time where the only focus is on our relationship with our loving God!

Holy Spirit, help me to look for ways that I can begin a regular prayer life and once started may I remain open to where you may be asking me to go next! Amen.

JUNE 24

John the Baptist

> John answered, "No one can receive anything except what has been given from heaven. You yourselves are my witnesses that I said, I am not the Messiah, but I have been sent ahead of him. He who has the bride is the bridegroom. The friend of the bridegroom, who stands and hears him, rejoices greatly at the bridegroom's voice. For this reason my joy has been fulfilled. He must increase, but I must decrease."
>
> JOHN 3:27–30

Each year on June 24 many liturgical churches celebrate the Festival of John the Baptist. John the Baptist prepared the way for Jesus by telling all who would listen that the Son of God was coming. After Jesus and his disciples began teaching and baptizing in the countryside, some asked John about Jesus. John replied that he wasn't the Messiah.

John states in one of the key points in this passage that "he [Jesus] must increase, but I must decrease." It appears that there is no ego at all in John's ministry because he is perfectly aware of his role. John was sent ahead of Jesus to prepare the way and when Jesus came, John knew that his importance would diminish.

One of the more important aspects as we move along on our spiritual pilgrimage is the concept that the Lord of our life, Jesus Christ, grows in importance and our interests become secondary to his will for our lives. As John stated, Jesus must increase and we must decrease. This is a very difficult concept to comprehend because our culture is based upon looking out for #1. May John the Baptist be your model along this journey, and may you be open to the Holy Spirit guiding you to allow Jesus to increase in your inner being!

Lord of all creation, enable me to seek more of Jesus in my life so that he becomes the dominant aspect of my spiritual essence! Amen.

JUNE 25

Jesus Our Example Concerning Prayer

> And after he [Jesus] had dismissed the crowds, he went up the mountain by himself to pray. When evening came, he was there alone.
>
> MATTHEW 14:23

We have many recorded passages where Jesus went alone to pray. Mark 1:35, Mark 6:46, Luke 22:41, and Luke 9:18 are just a few of the passages where this is noted. A lot of his ministry was done publicly; however, it seems as though he had a deep desire to get away from the crowds, and even his disciples, so that he could pray, spend time in solitude, and stay connected with his heavenly Father. It certainly appears that he knew that he needed time away from everything that was going on around him in order to stay focused on his mission as the Son of God.

If we are serious about taking part in this spiritual pilgrimage, shouldn't we attempt to get in the habit of doing as Jesus did by being intentional in finding space and time to get away and focus on our relationship with our Lord? Even a few minutes each day of solitude and prayer would be a wonderful starting point.

Think of creative ways to make this happen; possibly getting up a bit earlier each day; praying at lunch time; decreasing the time spend watching TV in the evening; finding a room in your home and putting up a "do not disturb" sign on its door as you are praying; finding a park or quiet outside setting; seeking an open church, etc. Discover what works for you and try to make it a habit!

Holy Spirit, help me to follow the example of Jesus. Guide me to find ways to be alone and quiet during my prayer time so that I may grow in my relationship with my Lord! Amen.

JUNE 26

Praying Early in the Day

> Give ear to my words, O Lord; give heed to my sighting. Listen to the sound of my cry, my King and my God, for to you I pray; O Lord, in the morning you hear my voice; in the morning I plead my case to you, and watch.
>
> PSALM 5:1–3

Much has been written about the subject of prayer: when and how to do it, methods for effective prayer, and devotionals and other resources to help one become centered. Prayer can certainly be entered into at any time of the day and for any reason, such as the need for guidance, or to give God thanks and/or praise. Many spiritual writers, as well as the practices of many faith traditions, emphasize the importance of having a set routine so that a specific time is allotted for this very important aspect of the spiritual pilgrimage.

The psalmist is expressing the need to pray to the Lord in the morning and then wait and watch, trusting that God will hear the prayer. The morning often provides a time free of the many messages and concerns that come our way later in the day. At the beginning of the day our minds and hearts are often the most alert and least cluttered. Thus, some form of morning prayer, devotions, or spiritual practices would be a good way to start the day.

On your spiritual journey continue to look for ways to enhance your relationship with our loving Lord who always wants to hear from us. You can talk to God at any time; however, beginning the day in this manner is a wonderful start to the day!

Loving Lord, help me to communicate with you whenever I can, and may that conversation begin in the morning, so that it can continue throughout my day! Amen.

JUNE 27

Proper Prayer

> You ask and do not receive, because you ask wrongly, in order to spend what you get on your pleasures.
>
> JAMES 4:3

One of the pitfalls of being on a spiritual pilgrimage and involved in the practices of prayer, Bible study, and reflection is that we may begin to believe that we are special people God looks more favorably upon than others and may therefore grant anything that we ask for. The Lord indeed does hold us with a loving embrace; however, God loves all people and indeed all of creation. As fallible humans, we act at times in ways that grieve God's heart, but the Lord never stops loving us, because God is love and can't help but love us.

The purpose of our prayer life is to bring us into a closer relationship with God. That is very different from praying so that we can get our sometimes, selfish requests granted. God will *always* hear our prayers and answer them in some manner. However, they may not be answered according to our time frame, or in the exact way we want. Sometimes the answer may be a *big fat no*, because God knows what we really need in order to become the people we were created to be.

This passage also tells us that we may be asking for own pleasures, versus sincerely striving for God's kingdom in our lives and to follow the Lord's will. I can't tell you what you should be praying for, but continue praying while trusting that the Holy Spirit will guide you and direct your prayers, and will help you keep your focus on God's will versus your own pleasure!

Lord of all creation, help me to daily pray and to keep my prayer focus on your will instead of my own pleasure, and to realize that you always hear my prayers and know what is best for me! Amen.

JUNE 28

God Hears Us Before We Speak

Before they call I will answer, while they are yet speaking I will hear.

ISAIAH 65:24

In the beginning of this chapter God wants to be sought after by those who aren't asking, and to be found by those who aren't seeking. The Lord said "Here I am" to a nation that didn't call upon God's name. The Israelites weren't living as the Lord had commanded them, therefore, God was pronouncing judgment through the prophet Isaiah upon the nation of Israel. However, God's righteous judgment outlines what will be done and how a new heaven and a new earth will be created.

Verse 24 is a wonderful example of how much God's love was poured out upon the Israelites even when they failed to live up to the standard that was set for them. It is the same for us today; even though we often fall short of what God expects of us, we will still be heard. In fact, we will be heard even before we speak. Think about that for a moment, *heard before we speak!*

This should encourage all of us to begin or continue with our spiritual practices of prayer, Bible study, and reflection. Praying on a regular basis is one of the ways to strengthen our relationship with God. We can communicate with God at any time of the day or night, for God wants to hear from us.

Of course, just because we pray and call out to the Lord, that doesn't mean that our lives will become perfect or constantly full of mountaintop experiences. We will indeed have such joys, but because we are on this side of God's kingdom we will also have pain, sorrow, and the desert periods in our lives. However, God's love and the Holy Spirit will be walking with us every step of our pilgrimage.

This chapter emphasizes that the Lord wants to be sought after, to be found, and to be called by name! May you have the faith to trust that God cares about every aspect of your life and indeed of all creation. Remember that the Lord will hear you before you speak!

Gracious Lord, help me to continue in my prayer efforts knowing that you are aware of what I am about to say, even before I say it. May that awareness make me bold to share your infinite grace, love, and mercy with those I meet today! Amen.

JUNE 29

A Road Less Traveled

Normally you can find me jogging several times a week—that time includes a prayer routine that has changed over the years, as have my spiritual practices. My jogging has allowed me to see things that I wouldn't have seen if I hadn't been out and about in the early morning. I've seen all kinds of wildlife, met some really interesting people, and witnessed some awesome sunrises, the whiteness of freshly fallen snow, abundant vegetable gardens, and beautiful flowers. I try to jog in all of the seasons of the year, including the cold and snowy winter months.

Over the years, I have learned how to jog on many kinds of snow; however, ice and very hard-packed snow cause me to stay inside or to jog very carefully. One thing that I have found when the snow has been around for a while is that on certain roads that I use the edges are not as solidly packed as the middle part of the road; thus, isn't as slippery. Therefore, I generally have better traction on the part that is less traveled.

The "road-less-traveled" concept is a good one to keep in mind when you are beginning or enhancing your spiritual practices. Just because some learned spiritual writers or your friends suggest a certain routine as a way to get involved in these rituals doesn't necessarily mean that they are right for you. Seek the guidance of the Holy Spirit and develop habits that work best for you. It just may be a method or pattern that others may not have thought of before, in essence "a road less traveled." You may come up with something that offers more traction for you, just as jogging on the edges of the snowy roads provides a better grip for me. Be open and creative and not afraid to step out in faith if that is where you feel you are being led. The main thing is to start or continue by being open to change as you are being guided!

Lord of all creation, help me to strive for your kingdom on a daily basis, and may that striving allow me to try new ways to take part in prayer and the other spiritual practices! Amen.

JUNE 30

Worshiping God in Spirit and Truth

> But the hour is coming, and is now here, when the true worshipers will worship the Father in spirit and truth, for the Father seeks such as these to worship him. God is spirit, and those who worship him must worship in spirit and truth.
>
> JOHN 4:23–24

This passage is from the section in John that is commonly referred to as the story of "Jesus and the Samaritan woman at the well." Jesus and the woman engage in a conversation even though it was highly unusual in that culture for a man and woman to talk to each other. Jesus tells her about worshiping the Father not on a holy mountain, nor in Jerusalem, but in "spirit and truth."

Part of this spiritual pilgrimage is taking part in regular prayer and reflection and part of it involves our worship of God in spirit and truth. The Lord seeks those who are ready and willing to worship God with their entire being.

Worshiping in spirit is done with our heart and soul rather than solely with our intellect or with preconceived ideas of the "right" way to worship. The kinship that we have with God isn't a visible one, in which we see and touch with our human eyes and hands, but rather a relationship based upon the eyes of faith. Our prayer life puts us in a position to do this.

When we worship God in truth, we are acknowledging the fact the Lord already knows everything about us. All of our desires, needs, hurts, and shortcomings are known by God before we think or speak them. However, the Lord still wants us to seek and bring all of our thoughts in the form of prayer and worship. Thus, we come in truth knowing that whatever we communicate is already known.

During your prayer times, and through each day, may you bring everything to the Lord. Worship God with all your spirit and in the most truthful manner that you are able to do!

Spirit-filled Lord, help me to come before you to prayerfully worship you in spirit and truth knowing that you desire all of the creation to do the same! Amen.

July

The Holy Spirit

JULY 1

God's Spirit Poured Out on Everyone

> Then afterward I will pour out my spirit on all flesh; and your sons and daughters shall prophesy, your old men shall dream dreams, and your young men shall see visions. Even on the male and female slaves, in those days, I will pour out my spirit.
>
> JOEL 2:28–29

This Old Testament passage promises that God's Spirit will be poured out on all flesh, allowing humans to prophesy, dream, and see visions. The exciting part of this promise is that the Lord's Spirit would be for everyone, regardless of what one's social status or age.

When Jesus was baptized, this promise was initially fulfilled when he received God's Spirit and then on the day of Pentecost when all of Jesus' followers received it in Jerusalem. The promise that it would be for everyone was fulfilled on the day of Pentecost when Jews from every nation were present for the Jewish festival of the Feast of Weeks. Peter quoted this passage to those bystanders who were witnessing this event as a way of explaining to them what had just happened.

Additionally, as the gospel message was spread, believers throughout the world received the Holy Spirit freely and without regard to their station in life! May you be willing to embrace the gift of God's Holy Spirit on your spiritual pilgrimage!

God of the living Spirit, help me to be receptive to the activity of the Holy Spirit in my life! Amen.

JULY 2

Baptized with the Holy Spirit and Fire

> I [John the Baptist] baptize you with water for repentance, but one who is more powerful than I is coming after me; I am not worthy to carry his sandals. He will baptize you with the Holy Spirit and fire. His winnowing fork is in his hand, and he will clear his threshing floor and will gather his wheat into the granary; but the chaff he will burn with unquenchable fire.
>
> MATTHEW 3:11–12

John the Baptist had been preaching in the wilderness around Judea about the need for repentance because God's kingdom was near. As people confessed their sins, John baptized them in the Jordan River. However, John was quick to note that Jesus, who was coming after him, would baptize with the Holy Spirit and fire.

This is the first New Testament mention of the Holy Spirit and indicates that Jesus' baptism would be more powerful than John's. This baptism would include fire that would burn the chaff away. The image of the chaff being separated from the wheat would have been understood in that time period because of the process of winnowing—throwing wheat into the air so that the wind would blow away the chaff, the dry casings of the wheat seeds. Thus, the good wheat would remain and the chaff would be removed.

When we receive the Holy Spirit, it burns away the chaff of our lives. During our spiritual pilgrimage and through our spiritual practices, more and more of the chaff-like aspects of our spiritual essence are burned off, laid aside, or left behind, etc., as we become more and more of the person that God created us to be. Through our baptism, we receive the Holy Spirit, which can guide, comfort, and support us, and it can also help us become a lifelong disciple of Jesus Christ by removing those things that are a barrier to our relationship with our Lord!

Today, O God, help me to listen to the Holy Spirit's directions and be ready to leave behind the chaff-like aspects of my spiritual life! Amen.

JULY 3

Spirit of God

> And when Jesus had been baptized, just as he came up from the water, suddenly the heavens were opened to him and he saw the Spirit

of God descending like a dove and alighting on him. And a voice from heaven said, "This is my Son, the Beloved, and with whom I am well pleased."

MATTHEW 3:16–17

The Spirit of God came upon Jesus when he was baptized by John the Baptist in the Jordan River. God was well pleased with Jesus and called him God's beloved Son.

We too receive this Spirit when we are baptized. Titus 3:5–6 informs us that "he [God our Savior] saved us, not because of any works of righteousness that we have done, but according to his mercy, through the water of rebirth [baptism] and renewal by the Holy Spirit. This Spirit he poured out on us richly through Jesus Christ our Savior." We are given the Holy Spirit as a free gift, we don't earn it or receive it because of our good works, but solely because of God's infinite grace, love, and mercy. We receive this gift because we are God's beloved children.

The Spirit comforts and guides us on our spiritual pilgrimage. However, like a muscle of our body or any gift or talent we have, if we don't open ourselves to it, we never realize its full impact in our spiritual lives.

From my own experience and the writings of many spiritual writers, when we are receptive to the gift of the Spirit it becomes a wonderful and transforming presence in our lives!

Thank you, gracious Lord, for this free gift of the Holy Spirit and for leading me today and every day! Amen.

JULY 4

Being Led by the Spirit

Then Jesus was led up by the Spirit into the wilderness to be tempted by the devil.

MATTHEW 4:1

Being led by the Holy Spirit can take us to places that may cause us to become very uncomfortable or to places that we haven't been. The Spirit may change us more than we ever thought possible as it guides us into making daily choices that may move us closer to God's kingdom and will in our lives.

Jesus, in his humanity, probably would have preferred not to be led into the wilderness to be tempted, or to have an encounter with the devil. However, he trusted that the Holy Spirit and God's love would be with him no matter where he went, including into a dangerous desert area. Following his time in the desert he called his disciples and began his public ministry.

Notice the sequence of these events; he didn't try to start his ministry or call his disciples before going through this experience. He trusted the leading of the Spirit that the forty days in the desert were necessary to his eventual ministry.

In the same way in our spiritual pilgrimage, we may have experiences that prepare us for the next major step in our journey. May you willingly enter the adventure with the Holy Spirit leading the way!

Loving Lord, may I follow the leading of the Holy Spirit wherever it may take me, including going into a wilderness area of my life! Amen.

JULY 5

Spirit of Truth Promised

> If you love me, you will keep my commandments. And I will ask the Father, and he will give you another Advocate [Helper], to be with you forever. This is the Spirit of truth, whom the world cannot receive, because it neither sees him nor knows him. You know him, because he abides with you, and he will be in [among] you.
>
> JOHN 14:15–17

In this passage, Jesus is responding to his disciples' questions when he promises them the Holy Spirit. In John's gospel, the Spirit of truth refers to the Holy Spirit. Jesus asked his Father for another Advocate (Helper or Comforter) for those who loved him and kept his commandments. Jesus knew that the Holy Spirit wouldn't be received by the world anymore, than it had received him.

This promise is as real today as it was two thousand years ago, when Jesus made it to his disciples. The Holy Spirit is sent to be a helper and comforter to all who love the Lord. When our spiritual eyes are focused, and pointed toward God's kingdom and will in our lives, then we are able to see and know the presence of the Spirit of truth in our lives.

This Spirit of truth gave the disciples the courage and boldness to spread the gospel message of Jesus Christ to the entire world and the Holy Spirit can also do the same for us. May your spiritual habits enable you to experience this Spirit within and among you!

Holy Spirit, help me to see and know your presence in my life this day and may I share your help and comfort with those I meet today! Amen.

JULY 6

The Holy Spirit Teaches Us

> I [Jesus] have said these things to you while I am still with you. But the Advocate, the Holy Spirit, whom the Father will send in my name, will teach you everything, and remind you of all that I have said to you.
>
> JOHN 14:25–26

In this chapter, Jesus is preparing his disciples for the time when he no longer will be with them. He continues to answer their questions about what is to come, as well as assure them that he and his Father will make their home with those who love him and keep his commandments. The Advocate/Helper is promised again in the form of the Holy Spirit.

Jesus specifically tells them that the Holy Spirit will teach them everything they will need in order to carry out the mission they'll be given. Also, the Spirit will continually remind them of what Jesus had said and taught them while he was with them.

We weren't with Jesus as the disciples were, but we do have the Scriptures that detail his life. As with the disciples, the Holy Spirit reminds us of what the Scriptures say and then helps us apply Jesus' teachings to our current circumstances.

Besides being a helper and comforter, the Holy Spirit can also be a teacher, interpreter, and a guide for those who are taking part in this journey. May you be receptive to all that the Holy Spirit can offer you on your spiritual pilgrimage!

Gracious Lord, help me to listen for the Holy Spirit's voice and direction. Open my spirit so that the Holy Spirit can teach and guide me today! Amen.

JULY 7

Testifying

> When the Advocate [Helper] comes, whom I will send to you from the Father, the Spirit of truth who comes from the Father, he will testify on my behalf. You also are to testify because you have been with me from the beginning.
>
> JOHN 15:26–27

The Advocate/Helper continues to be promised in the form of the Spirit of truth (the Holy Spirit), and will come from Jesus' Father. In this passage, we hear that the Holy Spirit will testify on Jesus' behalf. Jesus lets the disciples know that they are to also testify on Jesus' behalf with the aid of the Holy Spirit, for there will be times when they'll be called upon to bear a witness to Jesus' life.

"When they hand you over, do not worry about how you are to speak or what you are to say; for what you are to say will be given to you at that time; for it is not you who speak, but the Spirit of your Father speaking through you" (Matt 10:19–20). Jesus wanted them to be assured that the Spirit would speak for them and they didn't have to worry about what to say.

In this same way, whenever we are led to testify, proclaim the gospel, or express our faith, we should trust that the Holy Spirit will guide our words and actions. It is important to remember that we are God's vessels and what flows out through us to others is the result of the indwelling Holy Spirit in our spiritual lives. On your spiritual pilgrimage, may you continue to be a willing vessel to the Spirit directing your words and actions!

O God, may I have the courage today to boldly testify about my relationship with the Lord Jesus as directed by the Holy Spirit! Amen.

JULY 8

Truthful Words

> Nevertheless I [Jesus] tell you the truth: it is to your advantage that I go away, for if I do not go away, the Advocate will not come to you; but if I go, I will send him to you. . . . I still have many things to say to you, but you cannot bear them now. When the Spirit of truth comes, he will guide you into all the truth; for he will not speak on his own, but will speak whatever he hears, and he will declare to you the things that are to come.
>
> JOHN 16:7, 12–13

Jesus' disciples, of course, didn't want him to go away. They were like most humans who want to maintain the status quo. Things were going somewhat okay, so why rock the boat? However, Jesus knew what lay ahead and he kept telling his followers about what was going to happen soon, but they didn't always understand what he was saying. He wanted them to know that he had to go away before the Advocate/Helper, i.e., the Holy Spirit, could come to them. This seems rather obvious to us who know about the Pentecost event, but to those around Jesus this must have been hard to grasp.

Jesus wanted to tell them more things about his life and their ministry, but he felt that the disciples couldn't handle any more information at that point. But when the Spirit came, they would be led to all truth and would understand what was to come.

In our society today there are so many false messages about what is truly important in our lives and what is required to have a soul-satisfying life. It is easy to get swamped with information that can skew the real truths of life.

The Holy Spirit or Spirit of truth helps us to recognize what is Truth. May the wisdom and truth of the Holy Spirit be your daily guide on your spiritual pilgrimage!

Spirit of truth, come into my inner being and direct and guide my beliefs and steps so that they take me toward God's kingdom and will in my life! Amen.

JULY 9

Peace, the Holy Spirit, and the Great Commission

> Jesus said to them again, "Peace be with you. As the Father has sent me, so I send you." When he had said this, he breathed on them and said to them, "Receive the Holy Spirit."
>
> JOHN 20:21–22

In this passage from the gospel of John, Jesus appears to his disciples who are behind locked doors because they are afraid of the Jews. Even though they'd heard Mary Magdalene's message of Jesus' resurrection, they still didn't fully comprehend what was happening. When Jesus appears to them they rejoice, and twice Jesus offers them peace to alleviate their fear.

He also breathed on them and told them to receive the Holy Spirit (this gospel writer's Pentecost story). The Holy Spirit and Jesus' peace would be needed for the tasks that were ahead of them, which was to fulfill the great commission to become Jesus' witnesses to the end of the earth.

We too are given the gift of the Holy Spirit at our baptism and Jesus' peace comes to us in many different ways. We, like the disciples, will have many times of doubt and fear and need this peace and the assurance it brings. This peace comes to us as we daily strive for God's kingdom, trusting in the promises of God to love us and be with us no matter what we are going through, and as we take part in our spiritual practices. Today may you experience the peace of Jesus Christ in your life, and may the Holy Spirit guide your spiritual steps!

Loving Lord, open my heart and soul to receive these gifts of peace, comfort, and guidance today and may I share these gifts with those around me! Amen.

JULY 10

Power from the Holy Spirit

> While staying with them, he [Jesus] ordered them not to leave Jerusalem, but to wait there for the promise of the Father. "This" he said, "is what you have heard from me; for John baptized with water, but you will be baptized with the Holy Spirit not many days from now. . . . But you will receive power when the Holy Spirit has come upon; and you will be my witnesses in Jerusalem, in all Judea and Samaria, and to the ends of the earth."
>
> Acts 1:4–5, 8

The events of the first chapter of Acts are a very dramatic time for Jesus' followers. They thought that they had lost Jesus and then he appears to reassure them and stays with them for forty days. Even with this, they were probably still a bit nervous about what had happened, and uncertain about the future. But Jesus wanted them to wait in Jerusalem for the promise of the Holy Spirit.

Jesus knew that he was leaving them and that the disciples would be facing many challenges without him, and that the faith and endurance they would need would be provided by the Holy Spirit. Their power would come from the Holy Spirit and would give them what was needed to be Jesus' witnesses to the entire world.

The Holy Spirit has come to us, as it did to the disciples, to give us comfort, guidance, and support on our spiritual pilgrimage. However, the primary reason it was given was so that those who want to be lifelong disciples of Jesus Christ would have the power to be Jesus' witnesses to the world. This Spirit's purpose is to spread the gospel message of the love of God through Jesus Christ so that it reaches everyone, everywhere!

Holy Spirit, may your power allow me to be a witness of the good news of Jesus Christ in all that I do and say today! Amen.

JULY 11

Praying Together

> All these [Jesus' Disciples] were constantly devoting themselves to prayer, together with certain women, including Mary the mother of Jesus, as well as his brothers.
>
> ACTS 1:14

The followers of Jesus did as he asked and they returned to Jerusalem from the mount of Olivet. According to Scripture they went to an upstairs room in the place where they were staying to wait for the promise of the Holy Spirit. What might easily get overlooked in this story is that before they received the Holy Spirit, they were together devoting themselves to prayer.

Please think about that for a moment, they "were constantly devoting themselves to prayer" together with the women who were there. They for once listened to Jesus and followed his directions. They didn't decide to start their ministry of being Jesus' witnesses to the entire world before they received the Holy Spirit.

"Constantly devoting themselves to prayer" came before anything else; this is a valuable example for those who want to start or enhance their spiritual pilgrimage!

May I know, O God, that before going into the world to be a witness to Jesus, sincere prayer is needed to receive the power and guidance of the Holy Spirit! Amen.

JULY 12

The Coming of the Holy Spirit

> When the day of Pentecost had come, they were all together in one place. And suddenly from heaven there came a sound like the rush of a violent wind, and it filled the entire house where they were sitting. Divided tongues, as of fire, appeared among them, and a tongue rested on each of them. All of them were filled with the Holy Spirit and began to speak in other languages as the Spirit gave them ability.
>
> ACTS 2:1–4

The first chapter of Acts tells us that Jesus' followers devoted themselves to prayer and in this passage from Acts all of Jesus' followers were still together in one place. They stayed and were praying together when the Holy Spirit was given to them. Luke, the author of Acts, probably struggled to describe the Pentecost event. To experience "divided tongues, as of fire" must have been both a frightful and awesome encounter with the Holy Spirit for those who were there.

Those over whom the "divided tongues of fire" hovered immediately began to speak in other languages as they were led. The Holy Spirit allowed them to do things that they were unable to do before receiving it. This ability to speak in other languages was a visible sign of an inward change in all those who received this Spirit. This was the power that Jesus had promised to them that enabled them to go out as directed to be his witnesses to the entire world.

As we take part in the spiritual practices connected with this journey, we, too, can receive this power as we witness to and become the person that God intends for us to be. May the Holy Spirit allow you to do new things that you've never done before, for God's kingdom now and in the future!

Holy Spirit, by your power give me what is needed to do things that I couldn't do before, in fulfilling my call as a disciple of Jesus Christ! Amen.

JULY 13

A Right Spirit

> Create in me a clean heart, O God, and put a new and right spirit within me. Do not cast me away from your presence, and do not take your holy spirit from me. Restore to me the joy of your salvation, and sustain in me a willing spirit.
>
> PSALM 51:10–12

In this short passage, "spirit" is used three times. There are many definitions of "spirit," and it can be looked at from many different angles. If one is on a spiritual pilgrimage, it could mean that invisible-inner power that can give guidance and comfort to us.

In a footnote of my HarperCollins Study Bible it shows that Holy Spirit in verse 11 means "God's sustaining, powerful presence."[1] No matter how it is defined, the writer of this psalm wants to have a right and willing spirit and wants the Lord and the Holy Spirit to be within. As we daily travel on our spiritual walk, may we also desire the same!

Create in me a heart that is clean, oh my God, and place a new and right spirit in me! Amen.

---

1. HarperCollins Study Bible, NRSV, ed. Meeks et al. (New York, 1993), 847.

JULY 14

Trusting the Spirit

> This will give you an opportunity to testify. So make up your minds not to prepare your defense in advance; for I will give you words and wisdom that none of your opponents will be able to withstand or contradict.
>
> LUKE 21:13–15

During my days in college and my time in the insurance industry I learned to plan ahead. I still have that skill to a certain extent. Sometimes it comes in handy, but every once in a while, it can drive some people, including my wife, up a tree! However, we all need to plan ahead at certain times in our lives.

Nevertheless, when one is on this spiritual pilgrimage there can be times when we just have to trust the Holy Spirit for the next step or for what we are to say in a certain situation. That can take patience and faith, especially when those around us want quick action taken or words to be spoken. On your spiritual journey, may you trust the Spirit for wisdom when a certain action or word is needed!

Lord, may your Holy Spirit daily give me the words that need to be spoken and the patience to speak them at the proper time! Amen.

JULY 15

The Spirit Intercedes

> Likewise the Spirit helps us in our weakness; for we do not know how to pray as we ought, but that very Spirit intercedes with sighs too deep for words. And God, who searches the heart, knows what is the mind of the Spirit, because the Spirit intercedes for the saints according to the will of God.
>
> ROMANS 8:26–27

The Holy Spirit has a number of positive characteristics that enhance, guide, and comfort us on our spiritual pilgrimage in becoming a lifelong disciple of Jesus Christ. One of the more important benefits that we receive from the Holy Spirit is help in our prayer life.

Our prayer life may be the most challenging part of the spiritual practices of prayer, Bible study, and reflection. Some of us may be timid about starting a prayer life, others may start and stop before making it a habit, while still others may do it only in a moment of crisis. Making one's prayer life a habit takes persistence, faith, and a willingness to sometimes fail again and again—but never quitting altogether.

Trying to explain the function of the Holy Spirit in one's prayer life is difficult to do and the explanation would be different for every person. However, take courage from the words of these verses, pray sincerely, make it a habit, and believe the promise of this passage. Trust that the Spirit will indeed intercede for you, believe that your heart will be searched, believe that the purpose of God will be done in your life, and believe that the Lord will hear your heartfelt prayers!

Gracious Spirit, hear my prayers, correct them, and intercede for me with my heavenly Lord. Help me to follow your direction during my journey today! Amen.

JULY 16

Knowing the Spirit of God

> Beloved, do not believe every spirit, but test the spirits to see whether they are from God; for many false prophets have gone out into the world. By this you know the Spirit of God: every spirit that confesses that Jesus Christ has come in the flesh is from God, and every spirit that does not confess Jesus is not from God. And this is the spirit of the antichrist, of which you have heard that it is coming; and now it is already in the world.
>
> 1 JOHN 4:1–3

It seems as if false prophets have been around forever and we shouldn't fool ourselves into thinking that they aren't among us even today. As recorded in the Old Testament, the true prophets were always dealing with the false ones who were constantly trying to undermine God's message. The life of a true prophet of God wasn't easy, as they were often required to deliver messages that the leaders and people didn't want to hear. However, the true prophets let it be known that their messages were from the Lord and outlined God's will for the people.

In the same way, there are evil spirits in the world that can tempt us, cause us to turn away from God and toward our own selfish motives, and may even cause us to worship something other than our Lord. The writer of 1 John wants us to know that no matter how much we would rather think otherwise, these false spirits are very much all around us.

In order to know the difference between a true and false spirit we need to test them. If a spirit is from God it will confess that Jesus Christ is Lord and came in the flesh to die for our sins. If a spirit can't or won't make such a confession it isn't from God. Often, we don't have the time to analyze everything to any great depth. However, there is one thing you can always ask yourself: does what the spirit is telling you bring glory and honor to God or to yourself, someone else, or something else? The answer to that question may provide the guidance you need.

Testing the spirits can be a challenging aspect of this spiritual pilgrimage; however, on your journey there may be times when this comes up. Pray for guidance about how to discern between the Spirit of God and all other spirits!

Spirit of God, give me the wisdom and direction to walk this spiritual path knowing that your spirit confesses Jesus as Lord! Amen.

JULY 17

Maintaining the Unity of the Spirit

> ... making every effort to maintain the unity of the Spirit in the bond of peace. There is one body and one Spirit, just as you were called to the one hope of your calling, one Lord, one faith, one baptism, one God and Father of all, who is above all and through all and in all.
>
> EPHESIANS 4:3–6

This passage from Ephesians is encouraging the community to live together in harmony and to make every effort to maintain the unity of the Spirit. The Holy Spirit was given to the early church community on the day of Pentecost, so that the disciples and followers of Jesus would be empowered to be Jesus' witnesses throughout the world. They were to go under the power of the Holy Spirit who would support, guide, and comfort them as they made disciples of all nations.

However, some of the church communities were experiencing divisions. This letter was an attempt to promote peace and unity by reminding its readers that through the Holy Spirit all who believed in Jesus were one in body and spirit. Therefore, there shouldn't be any division or discord, because there is only one body, one spirit, one Lord, and one faith.

As we strive daily on our spiritual pilgrimage there may be times when we encounter situations, barriers, forces, or people that may attempt to pull us away from the unity of the Spirit and cause us to lose the peace that is ours through the Spirit. These times are inevitable as long as we are living in this world as imperfect humans. However, our spiritual practices can assist us in getting through such times as well as helping us to seek the unity that the Holy Spirit makes possible. The Holy Spirit also brings us peace in our lives in the midst of dissension and disunity. May you be open to the Spirit dwelling within you as you endeavor to become the person that God wants you to be!

Holy Spirit, may your peace surround me today and may I be your instrument of unity and peace to all those I meet! Amen.

JULY 18

Speaking with Boldness

> And now, Lord, look at their threats, and grant to your servants to speak your word with all boldness. . . . When they had prayed, the place in which they were gathered together was shaken; and they were all filled with the Holy Spirit and spoke the word of God with boldness.
>
> Acts 4:29, 31

In the fourth chapter of Acts, Peter and John were arrested and warned not to preach or teach about Jesus. After they were released the community offered prayers that the apostles would speak with boldness about the word of God. As they prayed they were filled with the Holy Spirit and began to speak in a daring manner about the word of God. After they prayed, the Holy Spirit gave them support and courage to continue in their ministry without fear.

The lesson for those of us who are on this spiritual pilgrimage is that as we take part in the spiritual practices of prayer, Bible study, and reflection, the Holy Spirit will also give us the support and courage to do what we are called to do with boldness.

Walking as Jesus wants us to do, especially in this world that doesn't understand what we are all about, can quickly wear us out unless we're in constant communication with our Lord. When we acknowledge that all of our strength and direction come through the Holy Spirit—a gift from God, we, too, like the early Christian community will be able to live out our spiritual lives and speak with boldness. May you feel the presence of the Holy Spirit in your spiritual journey and may that presence give you the courage to become the person that God wants you to be, and in the process, may you become a bold witness!

Lord of new life, guide me in my spiritual practices and allow me to have the boldness to live out my life in such a way that your light of love shines through me to all with whom I come into contact with today! Amen.

JULY 19

Samaritans Receive the Holy Spirit

> Now when the apostles at Jerusalem heard that Samaria had accepted the word of God, they sent Peter and John to them. The two went down and prayed for them that they might receive the Holy Spirit (for as yet the Spirit had not come upon any of them; they had only been baptized in the name of the Lord Jesus). Then Peter and John laid their hands on them, and they received the Holy Spirit.
>
> ACTS 8:14–17

During Saul's persecution of the early church, Philip went to the city of Samaria and preached about Jesus to the people there who were hated by many of the Jerusalem Jews. Philip was reported to be a follower of Jesus who was full of the Spirit and of wisdom and was chosen with six others to help distribute food to the widows in the early Christian community.

Philip's preaching reached many, and those around Samaria came to believe in Jesus. This fulfilled the words of Jesus when he said in Acts 1:8, "But you will receive power when the Holy Spirit has come upon you; and you will be my witnesses in Jerusalem, in all Judea and Samaria, and to the ends of the world."

When Peter and John arrived in Samaria, those who had come to faith through Philip's preaching received the Holy Spirit. Thus, the generations-old barrier between the Jews and the Samaritans was dissolved when the Samaritans received the Holy Spirit.

The actions of Philip, Peter, and John show that the message about Jesus and the gift of the Holy Spirit is for everyone who believes. It isn't just for a select few or for those who feel that because of their heritage or background that they are more privileged than others!

Lord of all creation, may your Holy Spirit give me a willing heart and spirit to be able to share your gifts with all of humankind, and not just those who look and act like me! Amen.

JULY 20

Spirit of Adoption

> For all who are led by the Spirit of God are children of God. For you did not receive a spirit of slavery to fall back into fear, but you have received a spirit of adoption. When we cry, "Abba! Father!" it is that very Spirit bearing witness with our spirit that we are children of God.
>
> Romans 8:14–16

God's children are led by the Spirit of God. When we engage in the spiritual practices of prayer, Bible study, and reflection and invite the Holy Spirit to come into our lives, we come to realize that we are indeed children of God. That knowledge should influence how we live and interact with those around us. As the Lord's children, our focus is on God's kingdom and will in our lives versus the things of the world.

The point of being adopted by God holds special meaning for me and may also hold importance for those from divorced families. My parents were divorced, as were both sets of my grandparents, and this made for some challenging dynamics in our family. I am sure that a lot of people including myself were impacted by divorce. When I was younger I didn't fully understand about being a child of God and what that meant. However, as an adult on this spiritual pilgrimage, I am becoming increasingly more aware that as a child of God—the Lord loves me no matter what I do or what may happen in my life. Thus, even when humans cause me pain and fail me, God loves me and will never fail me.

It doesn't matter what your situation is in life—if you are from a divorced family, or if you yourself are recently divorced, or you have been hurt by a divorce, or you never knew your biological parents—you can be assured that you are a child of God and the Lord loves you with an everlasting love!

Spirit of Adoption, help me to realize that as a child of God I can also help others come to know that they, too, are children of God, as I share your love with all those I meet today! Amen.

JULY 21

The Gifts of the Spirit

> Now there are varieties of gifts, but the same Spirit; and there are varieties of services, but the same Lord; and there are varieties of activities, but it is the same God who activates all of them in everyone. To each is given the manifestation of the Spirit for the common good.
>
> 1 CORINTHIANS 12:4–7

First Corinthians 12:4–11 tells us that the Holy Spirit gives various gifts to all believers to use in serving God and others. We understand that there are different gifts and services, but it is the same Spirit and Lord that activate them for the good of the community. Any well-functioning community has people fulfilling different roles in order to operate in an organized manner. For the Christian community, the Spirit empowers and encourages us to use our gifts in the ministries of the faith community of which we are a part.

My early church years were spent at Jerusalem Baptist Church located on the east side of Youngstown, Ohio. It was a small congregation; however, the Spirit led me into a number of different functions while I was there. I was the youngest Sunday School superintendent, I taught the high school youth, and was involved with the junior ushers, among other things. It was a great learning experience for me and helped me develop skills that are still used today.

As you take part in your spiritual pilgrimage, may you be open to where the Holy Spirit may be guiding you regarding using your gifts in the service of your faith community. No matter what you may be involved with, God through the Holy Spirit will bring everyone's gifts together for the good of the faith community!

Spirit of Life, help me to know that when I use my gifts in service to my community, my efforts and those of others bring glory to our Lord! Amen.

JULY 22

Spirit of Power, Love, and Self-Discipline

> For this reason I remind you to rekindle the gift of God that is within you through the laying on of my hands; for God did not give us a

> spirit of cowardice, but rather a spirit of power and of love and of self-discipline.
>
> 2 Timothy 1:6–7

Over the years, I have tried to memorize a Bible verse a week, and this verse is one that continues to be a favorite of mine. When I was younger I struggled quite a bit with low self-esteem; and memorizing Bible verses in general, and this one in particular, helped me in that regard. Currently, when I have moments of doubt, verses such as this one continue to provide strength and hope for me.

This letter from Timothy is one of thanksgiving and also one of encouragement for its audience. In this short passage, there is a lot of wisdom and support for those who are on this spiritual pilgrimage. It lets us know that God did not give us a fearful spirit, but instead a spirit of power, love, and self-discipline.

Having a spirit of power allows us to have faith that when we are striving for God's kingdom the energy and strength sufficient for what we are called to do will be given to us. Additionally, the spirit of love will always be with us, whether we are on a spiritual mountaintop or in the lowest valley. God is love and can't help but love us. The spirit of self-discipline can be viewed from a number of different angles. However, it seems important to realize that without some form of self-discipline as it pertains to this spiritual walk, we aren't able to take part in the spiritual practices which help us to become the person that God wants us to be.

On your journey, may you become increasingly more aware that the Lord desires that you have this spirit of power, love, and self-discipline! Hopefully, verses like this one will help when you encounter life's doubts and fears.

Holy Spirit, daily allow me to be willing to receive your spirit in my life, and may I share that spirit with those I meet today! Amen.

JULY 23

Being Transformed by the Spirit

> Now the Lord is the Spirit, and where the Spirit of the Lord is, there is freedom. And all of us, with unveiled faces, seeing the glory of the Lord as though reflected in a mirror, are being transformed into the same image from one degree of glory to another; for this comes from the Lord, the Spirit.
>
> 2 Corinthians 3:17–18

Many spiritual writers talk about being transformed because of our relationship with God through Christ Jesus. When our lives are in his, we are transformed little by little into his image. The Holy Spirit transforms us when we strive for God's kingdom and will in our lives and when we attempt to see God's glory and grace daily in all creation.

Being transformed will cause us to be changed into becoming more of the person that God wants us to be. When we sincerely take part in the spiritual practices of prayer, Bible study, and reflection, the transformation may happen slowly over our lifetime, but it does come. This transformation and change might take us out of our comfort zone to places and situations we may never have thought about before. Just as the followers of Jesus were transformed on the day of Pentecost and sent out to follow Jesus' instructions to be his witnesses to the entire world, we, too, are to be witnesses to the transforming power of Jesus Christ in our daily lives.

During your spiritual pilgrimage, be receptive to being transformed by the Holy Spirit, and may this change empower you to embark on the ministry you have been called to do!

Holy Spirit, help me to be transformed by you and then share this change with those I meet today! Amen.

JULY 24

Guided by the Spirit

> By contrast, the fruit of the Spirit is love, joy, peace, patience, kindness, generosity, faithfulness, gentleness, and self-control. . . . If we live by the Spirit, let us also be guided by the Spirit.
>
> GALATIANS 5:22–23, 25

If we acknowledge the fact that the Holy Spirit lives within us and is a very important aspect of our spiritual pilgrimage, then according to this verse we ought also to be guided by this same Holy Spirit. This seems to be stating the obvious! However, if the Spirit is truly leading us, are the fruits of the Spirit present in our spiritual core?

Can we say that we attempt to love all those around us, do we have the joy and peace that come from knowing that God's infinite love is always with us, and do we have faithfulness in our spiritual pilgrimage? Taking part in this journey and being directed by the Holy Spirit will change us and enable us to grow spiritually and emotionally.

I know that I am more understanding of those who years ago I might have been inclined to look at from a very judgmental standpoint, and I know that I am more willing to let go of things that have happened to me and around me than I used to be able to do; these are but some of the ways that I have been changed. Some of these changes may have come about because of my life experiences; however, I believe that the Holy Spirit has greatly impacted and molded me. May you be guided by the Holy Spirit alive in you and, in the process, be changed also!

Holy Spirit, help me to be open to your presence in my life. Guide and enable me to share your presence and direction with those around me! Amen.

JULY 25

Saul (Paul) Filled with the Holy Spirit

> So Ananias went and entered the house. He laid his hands on Saul and said, "Brother Saul, the Lord Jesus, who appeared to you on your way here, has sent me so that you may regain your sight and be filled with the Holy Spirit." And immediately something like scales fell from his eyes, and his sight was restored. Then he got up and was baptized.
>
> ACTS 9:17–18

Acts 9:1–19 describes the conversion of Saul (later known as Paul). Saul, who was one of the early church's most fervent opponents, had a vision on his way to Damascus when he heard Jesus ask him why he was persecuting him. Following that dramatic encounter with the risen Lord, Saul was unable to see for three days.

A disciple named Ananias was directed to go to Saul and lay his hands on him so that Saul's sight would be restored. Ananias did as he was instructed, he laid his hands on Saul and something like scales fell from his eyes so he could see, and Saul was filled with the Holy Spirit. After that Saul turned from persecuting Jesus' followers to becoming a tireless apostle for the Lord Jesus Christ. He was once again able to see physically and his spiritual eyes could "see" that Jesus was indeed the Son of God!

Most of us won't experience such a spectacular conversion and healing. However, when we are involved in the spiritual practices of prayer, Bible study, and reflection, the Holy Spirit causes us to see the physical and spiritual aspects of this life in a different light because our focus is turned toward following God's will in our lives. We may in fact have times in our lives when something like spiritual scales fall from our eyes as it did with

Saul. May you be receptive to the Spirit's guidance and be willing to change direction if led to do so!

Holy Spirit, help me to see the vision that you have for me, and may this insight guide me to be your witness to those I meet today! Amen.

JULY 26

The Spirit Speaking through Us

> When they hand you over, do not worry about how you are to speak or what you are to say; for what you are to say will be given you at that time; for it is not you who speak, but the Spirit of your Father speaking through you.
>
> MATTHEW 10:19–20

This passage is recorded just before Jesus sends his twelve disciples out to the Gentiles to proclaim that the kingdom of God has come near. He gives them instructions for the journey and warns them that they may be handed over to the authorities; however, if that happens they shouldn't worry about what to say because the Holy Spirit will give them the words they'll need.

On our spiritual pilgrimage the Holy Spirit guides and comforts us when we are willing to receive the help. It can also speak through us when we are called to witness to our faith and when we are called to proclaim that the kingdom of God has come near.

A few years ago, I had the opportunity to lead two Lutheran (ELCA) synod workshops on the topic of *discipleship*, one in Michigan and one in Indiana, within a few weeks of each other. For both workshops, I had a handout with a presentation that I was planning to give. However, the sessions were right after lunch and people had listened to speakers all morning and I realized that it would be a challenge to keep their attention. After a brief overview, I asked them to quickly read over my handout and come up with topics that they wanted to hear versus what I'd planned to present.

In that way, they were more invested in the discussion and we let the Holy Spirit guide what would be covered. It was somewhat of a risk on my part to do it this way because I had no idea where the discussion would go. Both breakout sessions seemed to go well and those who attended responded positively to them. Whenever I'd done presentations in the past, I generally followed my outline in order to stay on track. I still had to keep the discussion focused on the topic and moving along, but I trusted the Spirit that what would be covered was what the people there needed to hear.

May you be open to the Holy Spirit's guidance on your daily walk and especially when you are speaking about your faith or proclaiming the gospel message. It takes courage to trust and to give up some control of the situation, but that is what Jesus asked his disciples to do. Hopefully, you'll be able to do the same when the time and situation arise to do so!

Holy Spirit, help me to trust and believe that you are guiding me and giving me strength, and may I be willing to let you speak through me when needed! Amen.

JULY 27

Glorify God in Your Body

> Or do you not know that your body is a temple [sanctuary] of the Holy Spirit within you, which you have from God, and that you are not your own? For you were bought with a price; therefore glorify God in your body.
>
> 1 CORINTHIANS 6:19–20

These two verses come at the end of a passage written by the Apostle Paul in which he writes about glorifying God in one's body and spirit. He wants his readers to know that their bodies are temples of the Holy Spirit and a gift from God—not something that they own, because they were bought with the price of Jesus' sacrifice. Therefore, God should always be glorified by the way they live their lives.

The implication is that because our body is the temple of the Holy Spirit we should treat it with respect, never intentionally doing anything that would cause it harm or abuse. This seems like something that should be fairly easy to do and yet, we all know how challenging it can be! We know that we should eat right, exercise, get enough rest, stay away from anything that can be harmful, be it certain foods, medications, or using too much of any additive stimulant that has adverse side effects, etc. However, because we are all imperfect human beings we constantly struggle in maintaining a healthy balance in this regard.

If we'll try to visualize the Holy Spirit dwelling in our bodies, which are the temples of God's Spirit, it may motivate us to honor, respect, and treat our bodies better. This is certainly an area that I have battled with my entire life. Even though I can be very disciplined in certain areas regarding my body, such as with exercising regularly, getting the rest my body requires, and having an annual physical, I struggle in other areas. A craving for certain foods has been my downfall countless times in my life. This struggle is something that I have prayed about and have tried to find different ways of dealing with throughout my life. Sometimes I am okay for a while, but it is still a real challenge for me.

No matter what your situation is in caring for your body, on your spiritual pilgrimage may you feel the Holy Spirit within you, and may that presence help you to glorify God in your body!

Holy Spirit, help me to treat my body with respect and keep it from all harmful habits so that it is truly your temple, your dwelling place, and one in which God is glorified! Amen.

JULY 28

The Spirit Blows Where It Chooses

> Jesus answered, "Very truly, I tell you, no one can enter the kingdom of God without being born of water and Spirit. What is born of the flesh is flesh, and what is born of the Spirit is spirit. Do not be astonished that I said to you, You must be born from above. The wind [spirit] blows where it chooses, and you hear the sound of it, but you do not know where it comes from or where it goes. So it is with everyone who is born of the Spirit."
>
> JOHN 3:5–8

In this passage, Jesus is talking with the Pharisee named Nicodemus about being born from above. Jesus tells him that in order for a person to enter the kingdom of God they first must be born of water and the Spirit and that the Spirit blows where it chooses.

On our spiritual pilgrimage the Spirit comforts and supports us. When we take part in our spiritual practices and engage in the process of becoming a lifelong disciple of Jesus Christ, we become more open to where and how the Spirit is blowing in our lives. The counsel may come in small matters or sometimes the instruction may be in the major affairs that we are involved with. We may not even be consciously aware of the Spirit's presence, but it is always with us.

A good example of this is on the day of Pentecost as recorded in the second chapter Acts. The Spirit came like the rush of a mighty wind and filled the entire house where Jesus' followers were gathered. Those who experienced the Spirit's power didn't know where it came from or what would happen next, but the community of believers was guided and empowered after that day to spread the gospel message and to bring the kingdom of God to that time and place and then beyond to the wider world.

Be open to where the Spirit may be leading you for it might lead you to people or places you never thought you would be asked to go!

Gracious Lord, help me to trust the promise that you will always be with me and through the Holy Spirit's presence I will be guided and directed in my daily walk. May this assurance allow me to be a witness to others of your presence in the world today! Amen.

JULY 29

Renewal of Our Spiritual Minds

> You were taught to put away your former way of life, your old self, corrupt and deluded by its lusts, and to be renewed in the spirit of your minds, and to clothe yourselves with the new self, created according to the likeness of God in true righteousness and holiness.
>
> EPHESIANS 4:22–24

Being on this spiritual pilgrimage does not exempt us from the daily highs and lows of life. As a disciple of Jesus Christ, we are still fallible human beings, surrounded by other frail humans, and we all live in a very imperfect world. We all get sick, have financial struggles, are impacted by the violence and disasters around the world, and at some point, have to face death just like every other earthly creature.

But we can renew our spiritual minds, which allows us to become the person that God created us to be. Verses 20–21 of this passage refer to the fact that through Jesus Christ we are able to put away our old self and its former way of life. We are renewed spiritually and clothed with a new self in the likeness of God.

This endeavor doesn't take us out of the world, but helps us to see our life and the world around us through the lens of God's kingdom that is present here and now, as well as the time to come. Such a focus gives us hope to trust in God's promise to be with us no matter what else is going on around us. This trust allows our faith to grow so that the Holy Spirit can renew our spiritual minds and help us to become more fully clothed with this new self.

May you be willing on this journey to leave behind your old self and way of living and to put on the new self being renewed in your spiritual minds so that you can become a lifelong disciple of Jesus Christ!

Loving Lord, help me to strive for the renewing of my spiritual mind so that I might have a new self, and may this new life change how I interact in the world today! Amen.

JULY 30

The Spirit Gives Life

> It is the spirit that gives life; the flesh is useless. The words that I have spoken to you are spirit and life.
>
> JOHN 6:63

Jesus is once again teaching the crowds that are following him. Some of the disciples were complaining that this teaching was very hard to understand and accept (v. 60). Other than the original twelve, some of the followers decided at this point that they couldn't follow Jesus any longer and left him (v. 66). The followers who left Jesus apparently weren't able to understand what his ministry was all about, and therefore were unable to continue being a part of his mission.

Trying to logically explain Jesus' ministry and mission isn't easy to do. Attempting to use our common sense and worldly knowledge may not do it. As Jesus said, it is the Holy Spirit who gives life. It is through the guidance of the Holy Spirit that we can best decide to follow Jesus and become a lifelong disciple of his.

The spiritual pilgrimage can be challenging even with the Holy Spirit's strength and guidance, but it daily leads to new life for us. On this journey, hopefully, you can remain receptive to wherever and however the Spirit may be guiding you. May it allow you to continue, rather than turn back as some of Jesus' followers in this passage decided to do!

Holy Spirit, open my heart, mind, and soul to receive your words of life, and may these words be shared with those I meet today! Amen.

JULY 31

Simeon and the Holy Spirit

> Now there was a man in Jerusalem whose name was Simeon; this man was righteous and devout, looking forward to the consolation of Israel, and the Holy Spirit rested on him. It had been revealed to him by the Holy Spirit that he would not see death before he had seen the Lord's Messiah. Guided by the Spirit, Simeon came into the temple.
>
> LUKE 2:25–27

This is a well-known passage wherein, at eight days old, Jesus is named and then presented at the temple, as was the custom according to the law of

Moses. This indeed was a significant time for Jesus and his family. It was a wonderful time for the community of faith, as well. However, sometimes its importance in the life of this man called Simeon can be overlooked. He had been promised that he would not see death until he had seen the Lord's Messiah.

What may also get lost in this passage was how crucial the activity of the Holy Spirit was to this event, especially in the life of Simeon. Notice that the Holy Spirit rested on Simeon, revealed information to him, and guided him. Simeon is a great example for those of us on our spiritual pilgrimage as lifelong disciples of Jesus Christ.

During our pilgrimage as we take part in our spiritual practices, may we seek ways to become more receptive to the Holy Spirit so that we become more and more aware of the Spirit alive and active in us—granting us wisdom and guiding our daily steps. We never know ahead of time where we may be directed to go, and maybe we, like Simeon, may even be given the opportunity to witness some wonderful event!

Holy Spirit, help me to accept your presence in my life, and comfort, encourage, and direct me today! Amen.

August

Discernment

AUGUST 1

Discerning the Will of God

> I appeal to you therefore, brothers and sisters, by the mercies of God, to present your bodies as a living sacrifice, holy and acceptable to God, which is your spiritual worship. Do not be conformed to this world, but be transformed by the renewing of your minds, so that you may discern what is the will of God—what is good and acceptable and perfect.
>
> Romans 12:1–2

Discerning the will of God can be both simple and challenging. It can be simple because we normally only get the next step shown to us versus many steps at a time. It can be challenging because often the discernment may come in ways that we might miss, or we may become impatient, or it might mean that we have to change some aspect of our lives that may be difficult to do.

Guidance regarding the will of God comes to those who are trying to listen to the Holy Spirit's direction as they take part their spiritual practices. This passage informs us that when we are not conformed to this world and when we are transformed by the renewing of our minds, we are able to discern the will of God.

We are still part of the world despite the fact that we are not conformed to it; rather, we realize that God's kingdom, in the here and now as well as the time to come, is what we are striving for. When we are transformed by the renewing of our minds we know every day that we are being changed and renewed so that we are continually becoming the person that God wants us to be.

On your spiritual walk, may you be in the world but not of it, and may you daily be a new person as you are transformed into becoming a lifelong disciple of Jesus Christ!

Lord of new life, on my pilgrimage help me to discern your will in my life, and in the process, may I help others recognize your will in their lives! Amen.

AUGUST 2

About Bible Verses

> But, as it is written, "What no eye has seen, nor ear heard, nor the human heart conceived, what God has prepared for those who love him."
>
> 1 CORINTHIANS 2:9

For many years, I have memorized Bible verses to help me on my spiritual pilgrimage. I generally do one a week and try to learn it during my jogging time. When I worked in the insurance industry, I would write a verse on the back of an old business card and place it on the dash of my car to help me stay focused on positive things when making agency visits. Later on when I had an office I began writing them on a white board behind my desk.

This verse is one of the earlier ones that I used to help me. We can't begin to conceive of what God has for those who love the Lord and who try to follow God's will. I would encourage you to use Scripture as an aid in your daily walk!

O Lord, your word is a life-giving part of my spiritual journey, may it take root in my heart and soul! Amen.

AUGUST 3

Direction

> I keep the Lord always before me.
>
> PSALM 16:8A

It is a fact of life that the direction we are facing is the way we end up going. Trying to face backwards while walking forward will only cause us to fall or stumble. As a lifelong disciple of Jesus Christ on this spiritual pilgrimage we are encouraged to strive for God's kingdom on a daily basis. This can be done in many ways and one way is through prayer, Bible study, and reflection.

When we place things in front of us that don't last or possibly even cause us harm, we may not end up where God wants us to be. However, when the Lord is always before us our life will still be a human one with all of its challenges, but we'll have a better chance of becoming the person that God wants us to be as we follow God's will and direction for our lives!

Lord, please provide the direction I need on this journey to keep you always before me. Help me daily to maintain my focus on your kingdom above anything else! Amen.

AUGUST 4

Wisdom and Understanding for Daily Life

By wisdom a house is built, and by understanding it is established.

PROVERBS 24:3

The book of Proverbs is part of the wisdom literature of the Bible. Wisdom and understanding were important and much-desired attributes in the varied eras and cultures of the Old Testament. In Proverbs wisdom is often referred to using the pronoun "she," referring to wisdom as a woman—a friend or sister. The book of Proverbs has many wise sayings that provide practical insights and instruction about right living and wise dealing.

No matter if you are building a house, a business, a career, a marriage, a family, or anything else, the words of Lady Wisdom can indeed provide wisdom and understanding for the process. When we look at life through the lens of Scripture, we are often given greater wisdom and understanding for our journey!

Lord, help me to be open to hearing your words of wisdom and understanding in Scripture and then applying them in my daily walk! Amen.

AUGUST 5

Laying Aside

Therefore, since we are surrounded by so great a cloud of witnesses, let us also lay aside every weight and the sin that clings so closely, and let us run with perseverance the race that is set before us, looking to Jesus the pioneer and perfecter of our faith.

Hebrews 12:1–2a

Hebrews chapter 11 gives many examples of the Jewish leaders and prophets who acted by faith; chapter 12 reminds us that these people are great witnesses for us on our faith walk. This passage notes the importance of leaving behind those things in our lives that are barriers to becoming the persons that God wants us to be. This laying aside or leaving behind isn't a one-time event, but an hourly/daily one.

On your pilgrimage, may your spiritual practices give the hope, discernment, and courage you need to run your race, keeping your focus on where God is leading you rather than your own plans and desires!

Dear Lord, give me the ability to lay aside the things which prevent me from becoming the person that you want me to be! Amen.

AUGUST 6

Cry for Help

Then you shall call, and the Lord will answer; you shall cry for help, and he will say, Here I am.... The Lord will guide you continually.

Isaiah 58:9, 11a

This passage definitely shows that when we call out to the Lord for help, God will hear us and guide us continually. However, from my experiences I have found that this guidance and help may not come in the time frame or manner that I want or would hope for.

However, that doesn't mean that God isn't with us nor have we been forgotten. Walking this spiritual pilgrimage doesn't guarantee that we will get everything that we ask for or want nor when we want it. But the journey will increase our faith to allow us to keep moving forward even when things are a little cloudy at the moment!

Answering Lord, give me the courage to look for your presence during all aspects of my life, even when you seem to be distant! Amen.

AUGUST 7

Daily Steps

> Commit your way to the Lord; trust in him, and he will act. . . . Our steps are made firm by the Lord, when he delights in our way.
>
> Psalm 37:5, 23

One of the challenging aspects of this faith walk is taking daily steps when we are not sure how things will turn out. When I was working in the business world, the majority of my time was spent in the marketing departments. Much of our time was focused on short and long-range planning. It was an expectation that plans would be put in place and then followed up with a lot of hard work to make those plans a reality.

That, however, is not always the case with our faith journey. In our spiritual pilgrimage, we can be directed to take steps that do not fit into our personal long-range goals. These steps can also take us to new places, once unknown to us. I left a career of more than twenty-seven years and went to Trinity Lutheran Seminary not fully knowing why I was going, only that I was meant to go. On your journey, may you commit your way to the Lord, take the daily steps as directed, and trust that God will make your steps firm!

Lord, give me the courage to commit my way to you and daily trust that my steps will in fact be firm! Amen.

AUGUST 8

Change and New Paths

> Many peoples shall come and say, "Come, let us go up to the mountain of the Lord, to the house of the God of Jacob; that he may teach us his ways and that we may walk in his paths."
>
> Isaiah 2:3

Another difficult part of this spiritual pilgrimage is that it can change us and take us to places and situations that may take us out of our comfort zone. The prophet Isaiah wants the people to go into the house of the Lord so that God can show them the path to take. When we seek the Lord's way in our lives the path we *may* be shown could be different than the one we might have taken if we hadn't sought this guidance.

Many spiritual writers have expressed the view that if we don't want to change or be taken to new places, then don't pray nor seek God's will in our lives. On your spiritual journey, may you be open to being changed and following new paths!

Loving Lord, help me to come into your house and make me ready to being changed and directed! Amen.

AUGUST 9

Immediately

> As he [Jesus] went from there, he saw two other brothers, James son of Zebedee and his brother John, in the boat with their father Zebedee, mending their nets and he called them. Immediately they left the boat and their father and followed him.
>
> Matthew 4:21–22

Sometimes when God calls, we may surprisingly find ourselves responding immediately or at least without the delay of months or even years. When I initially thought about going to Trinity Lutheran Seminary my plan was to go part time for the first year as I continued to work in the insurance industry. I had gone to undergraduate school part time while working full time in the steel mill and I thought that was the practical thing to do again. However, God had other plans!

I talked to my pastor about my plans and some things that he put into place together with other signs gave me the clear message that I was to go full time beginning with the fall semester. That decision ended up changing my life, because if I had gone part time rather than full time, Shirley and I wouldn't have been in classes together nor met and gotten to know each other, and we wouldn't have been married two years later. *Sometimes* being practical is not what God is calling us to do, instead we're called to take a leap of faith and follow Jesus even though we have no idea what the future holds!

God of surprises, may I be willing to receive your call in my life, knowing that it may cause me to act immediately; may my heart accept and heed your call, trusting always in your love! Amen.

AUGUST 10

God's Foolishness

> For God's foolishness is wiser than human wisdom, and God's weakness is stronger than human strength.
>
> 1 CORINTHIANS 1:25

Sometimes when we are on this spiritual pilgrimage we are asked to take steps that may seem odd to those around us. Prior to earning my undergraduate degree, I had been working full time at a steel mill and going to college part time. After eight years in college I finally graduated and began looking for jobs outside of the steel industry. I remember my late wife's father, Vito, really questioning if that was a good idea. He had worked on the docks in Ashtabula, Ohio, and he knew what seniority meant in a company. I had nearly nine years in the mill and he thought I should stay there because of how important those years of seniority were.

Vito wasn't the only one, however—many of my mill coworkers thought I would stay because the pay and benefits were very good. But God had other plans and after a long process I was offered a job in the insurance industry (for less money) and out of state. However, thankfully, my wife was willing to move. Like many such steel mills in the Midwest the one I worked in closed down a few years later, the years of seniority wouldn't have meant anything at that point. One never knows what God may have for us to do, it may seem foolish to the world, but can make perfect sense to us in due time!

May my spiritual practices give me the courage to trust God's foolishness, versus what others think maybe the wise thing to do! Amen.

AUGUST 11

God Calling Us

> Then Moses went up on the mountain, and the cloud covered the mountain. The glory of the Lord settled on Mount Sinai, and the cloud covered it for six days, on the seventh day he called to Moses out of the cloud.
>
> EXODUS 24:15–16

God spoke to Moses out of the cloud on Mount Sinai. One could say that this was recorded in the Old Testament and that the Lord doesn't really speak directly to humans today, at least not to me. I can't say that God has spoken to me directly either; however, many spiritual writers observe that God does speak to humans today in many different ways, if we are open to it.

Notice that in these verses Moses went up to the *mountain* and then *waited*. Could it be that we have to put our hearts and souls in a place that allows the Lord access to our inner being? Prayer, Bible study, and reflection can help us come to such a place on our spiritual pilgrimage. Waiting for God to speak to us can, at times be a real challenge in today's society because we are people of the moment, doing it now, getting it done sooner rather than later.

However, Moses went to the mountain and waited and we, too, should be willing to go where directed and then be willing to wait, rather than expecting to hear God's message instantly. May you put yourself in a position to listen and be given the patience needed!

O God, during this journey may my heart and soul be in a position to hear your message and be willing to wait for it! Amen.

AUGUST 12

Be Strong and Courageous

> This book of the law shall not depart out of your month; you shall meditate on it day and night, so that you may be careful to act in accordance with all that is written in it.... I hereby command you: Be strong and courageous; do not be frightened or dismayed, for the Lord your God is with you wherever you go.
>
> JOSHUA 1:8A, 9

After Moses died, God spoke directly to Moses' assistant, Joshua, and gave him instructions for the Israelites. One of the main aspects about this passage is the use of the phase "be strong and courageous." In this chapter, it is repeated in verses 7, 9, and 18. God clearly desired that Joshua and his people not be afraid about what the future held. If they focused their hearts and minds on God's law and meditated upon it, they wouldn't to be frightened or dismayed for they would know that the Lord was with them.

On our spiritual pilgrimage, it is important to take part in the spiritual practices of prayer, Bible study, and reflection. Through our prayer and Bible studies we learn how God wants us to live and when we reflect on these insights we are led and comforted by them. May you be able to be strong and courageous in your spiritual journey by trusting that the Lord will be with you wherever you go, also that God's Holy Spirit will give you the discernment needed for your next step, just as the Israelites were led!

Discerning Lord, may your Holy Spirit help me to be strong and courageous on my daily walk as I participate in my spiritual practices. Help me to share the strength and courage that I'm given with those I meet today! Amen.

AUGUST 13

Our Plans

> The plans of the mind belong to mortals, but the answer of the tongue is from the Lord. All one's ways may be pure in one's own eyes, but the Lord weighs the spirit. Commit your work to the Lord, and your plans will be established. . . . The human mind plans the way, but the Lord directs the steps.
>
> PROVERBS 16:1–3, 9

These verses are challenging for me because their planning message is a lesson I have to learn over and over again. During my years of working in the mill while going to college part time, and then in my years in the insurance industry, I became fairly adept at planning and then achieving those plans.

While I was in college I had to balance my classwork and exams while working forty hours a week in a steel mill, mostly on the afternoon or night shifts. After several years of the part-time school, a full-time work schedule I got married, which took even more adjustments and organizational skills. During my more than twenty-seven-year career in the insurance industry most of my time was spent working in various marketing departments in which I was required to make corporate plans and individual marketing goals for the agencies that sold our insurance. I got quite good at planning ahead, and doing what was necessary to achieve these goals. However, my ability to set goals in this manner came into conflict with how planning operates in my spiritual walk, and I often have to relearn the lesson in these verses of allowing the Lord to direct my steps, rather than my carefully thought-out plans.

On our pilgrimage, we are, of course, free to make plans and then think about the best course of action. However, as we take part in the spiritual practices of prayer, Bible study, and reflection we are in fact asking God through the Holy Spirit to direct our steps.

As this Proverb states, humans can do the planning, but the answer and direction are from the Lord. Additionally, if we commit our work to

God our steps will be established. On your journey, may you pray about and reflect upon where God may be leading you, and then trust that the Holy Spirit's discernment will come in the time and manner that are best for you, and for God's will in your life!

Holy Spirit, help me to trust in your guidance today, and may your direction assist me in striving for God's kingdom! Amen.

AUGUST 14

Waiting for Direction/Deliverance/Discernment

> The angel of God who was going before the Israelite army moved and went behind them; and the pillar of cloud moved from in front of them and took its place behind them. It came between the army of Egypt and the army of Israel. And so the cloud was there with the darkness, and it lit up the night; one did not come near the other all night.
>
> Exodus 14:19–20

This is a fascinating story of how the Lord had Moses lead the Israelites out of slavery to the promised land. The angel of God was in the midst of a cloud to both direct the people and to guard them from the Egyptian army. This is an excellent example of how God can both direct our steps and also walk with us through tough times. When the angel of the Lord was leading the way, guidance was given, and when in back, protection was provided.

One aspect of this entire story that may be overlooked is how long the Israelites prayed for and cried out for deliverance before it actually came. Often when we pray to God we lose patience when an answer or solution is not forthcoming in the time and manner that we think it should.

We usually expect an answer or solution to our requests as quickly as humanly possible, whether the issue concerns direction regarding which path to take on our life journey, or deliverance from some issue in our lives that is overwhelming us, or discernment about a school, a job, whom to marry, or about what type of ministry to become involved with. Generally, however, we may have to wait, as did the Israelites, and the waiting may be a long time.

But the good news is that God still loves us and cares about what we are going through. During this waiting period that may be very trying for us, our role is to continue our spiritual practices because this period can be an important part of our spiritual growth as a lifelong disciple of Jesus Christ!

Lord of direction, deliverance, and discernment, help me to be open to any waiting period in my life, knowing that your answers will come in the manner that is best for me and your will in my life! Amen.

AUGUST 15

An Understanding and Discerning Mind

> At Gibeon the Lord appeared to Solomon in a dream by night; and God said, "Ask what I should give you." ... [Solomon said,] "Give your servant therefore an understanding mind to govern your people, able to discern between good and evil; for who can govern this your great people?" ... I [God] now do according to your word. Indeed I give you a wise and discerning mind.
>
> 1 KINGS 3:5, 9, 12A

When I was younger, I read a lot of self-help books to help with my low self-esteem. These books were very helpful to me then, for they encouraged me to set goals for myself and helped me to see myself in a more positive light. I also read a lot of wisdom literature as well as writers who expressed thoughts about how to live a wise life, so that people who read and followed the direction given could receive guidance in their life's decisions. The belief was that if the wisdom dispensed was followed, one could, very likely, be spared from making too many mistakes in life.

As I got older, I continued to read and reflect about how one could best live this life. Of course, I was like everyone else and made my share of mistakes. But I continued to read and as I did so, I began to find more wisdom in Scripture—the very word of God.

In my life, God has never spoken directly to me as was the case with Solomon. However, I believe the Lord still communicates through Scripture, prayer, spiritual and grace-filled writers, and through our friends who know us well, for all are sources of direction and wisdom. We can have an understanding and discerning mind as Solomon received, it may just come from many different directions and sources.

In your spiritual pilgrimage, may you always remain receptive to receiving God's spiritual wisdom to live by. This wisdom will not make our lives perfect, devoid of the pain and sorrow that comes our way as humans on this earthly journey. However, even the difficulties of life can bring us closer to the Lord and to those we come into contact with on a daily basis!

God of all knowledge, help me to receive to your wisdom and understanding no matter how it comes to me! Amen.

AUGUST 16

A Wise Heart

> For a thousand years in your sight are like yesterday when it is past, or like a watch in the night.... So teach us to count our days that we may gain a wise heart.
>
> PSALM 90:4, 12

Discernment can come to us in many different forms and shapes because the Holy Spirit utilizes a variety of means to reach all types of people. The means and the message are unique to each individual or group depending upon the need. The particular message can come through prayers, our life experiences, friends and family, mentors, clergy, our reading of and reflecting on spiritual books, any number of ways. It can also come through the reading of and meditating upon the Scriptures.

The Psalms and Proverbs are two books of the Bible that can be a good source of wisdom, understanding, and guidance. During your spiritual pilgrimage, I would encourage you to take advantage of the wonderful insights that they have to offer. It takes a willingness, however, to invest time, energy, and effort in reading and reflecting on them, for often what may be received from them is not immediately evident, but rather lays deep within, which may require some digging.

These two verses in Psalm 90 offer up a number of different insights depending upon where we are in our spiritual journey and what is happening in our lives at a particular moment. Being aware that as mortals we all have only a limited number of days can help us gain a wise heart. When we realize that we are fallible human beings subject to all of the challenges of this earthly life and that our days are limited versus God's eternal time, we then view our existence in a humbler light, which helps us gain a wise heart. May your spiritual pilgrimage allow you to realize the gift of each day and enable you to fully live in the present moment!

God of a thousand years, help me to live for you today, and may that ability allow me to gain a wise and discerning heart that can be shared with those around me! Amen.

AUGUST 17

God's New Thing

> Do not remember the former things, or consider the things of old. I am about to do a new thing; now it springs forth, do you not perceive it? I will make a way in the wilderness and rivers in the desert.
>
> Isaiah 43:18–19

This passage begins back at in verse 14 that reads, "Thus says the Lord." The Lord is promising the nation of Israel that their exile in Babylon will be coming to an end. God was about to do a *new thing*—their nation was going to be restored. They were to believe in this promise and not dwell upon the trials and tribulations of their exile.

The Lord is always doing a new thing, is continually bringing about God's will for all creation. On our spiritual pilgrimage, we'll have times when God will present us with another way of thinking, walking, or living. On this journey, we may be given a fresh way to look at various aspects of our spiritual growth, we may be shown a different way to approach certain life situations, or we may be directed to go to places that might take us out of our comfort zone.

Our role is to be open to where the Holy Spirit may be guiding us, and to take the steps shown to us in faith, believing that God's grace, love, and mercy will be with us all along the way. Of course, this takes courage and isn't for the faint of heart. The Lord *is* doing a new thing—trust in the promises of God, for doing so will help you become the person that God wants you to be!

Lord of all life, help me to be ready to receive the new things that you have prepared for me along my spiritual journey, and may I be willing to share this with those I meet today! Amen.

AUGUST 18

A Good Work Completed

> I [Paul] am confident of this, that the one who began a good work among you will bring it to completion by the day of Jesus Christ.
>
> Philippians 1:6

Being on this spiritual pilgrimage takes courage and persistence for several reasons: often we don't know where this journey will take us; there are many people around us who don't understand why we are on this walk anyway; and there are any number of other things we could be doing with our time other than praying, studying the Bible, and reflecting.

A spiritual pilgrimage requires a willingness and commitment for the long haul for this isn't a one-time event, but rather a journey that is lived out each and every day. Thus, it's easy to become discouraged, which is why verses like Philippians 1:6 are so important to us as a means of encouragement and guidance.

The Apostle Paul wrote to the Christians in the city of Philippi to let them know that he was praying for them, and he wanted them to realize that he still had confidence in them, but even more importantly that he knew that God would bring their ministry to completion. They are to continue to share the gospel message—the result of their efforts is in the Lord's hands.

As you take part in your spiritual practices there will be times when you don't feel like going any further because at the moment you can't see any obvious results or the weight of the issues around you and inside of you seem to be blocking any spiritual activity. However, anything that you do in the name of Jesus Christ will come to completion in God's timing. Be encouraged by the words of Paul to continue today on your pilgrimage!

Lord, today may your Holy Spirit provide what is needed for me to continue my spiritual practices so that my life may be a witness to those I meet! Amen.

AUGUST 19

Called by Name

> But now thus says the Lord, he who created you. O Jacob, he who formed you, O Israel: Do not fear, for I have redeemed you; I have called you by name, you are mine. When you pass through the waters, I will be with you; and through the rivers, they shall not overwhelm you; when you walk through fire you shall not be burned; and the flame shall not consume you. For I am the Lord your God, the Holy One of Israel, your Savior.
>
> Isaiah 43:1–3a

The Lord, through the words given to the prophet Isaiah, promises that the nation of Israel will be redeemed. When they walk through the waters, the rivers, and the fire God will be with them and they will be delivered, for the

Lord is their God, their Savior. God's unique relationship with Israel, different from with any other group or nation, was evident by God's promises to them. Israel is also reminded that God has called them by name, being called by name makes any relationship closer and more personal.

One of the most important aspects of being a parent is naming your newborn baby. The name chosen will probably be with that person for the rest of their life and could in some cases help define their personality. I know when my late wife, Judy, and I had our two children we thought long and hard before coming up with their first names. What we are called is important and when someone mispronounces or consistently can't remember our name we may feel hurt.

Thus, when God calls us by name we are empowered, valued, cherished, and that is a big deal. The Lord calls each of us by name—beloved child—from our first earthly breath until our last. The Holy Spirit daily calls upon us to use our gifts so that all of us together are working to bring God's kingdom into the places where we live and work, so that all may know the Lord calls them by name, too. God is indeed calling us by name and will be with us no matter where we're asked to go!

Lord of life, help me to hear your voice calling me as I continue on my spiritual pilgrimage, and may I trust and hope in your promise of redemption! Amen.

AUGUST 20

God's Living and Active Word

> Indeed, the word of God is living and active, sharper than any two-edged sword, piercing until it divides soul from spirit, joints from marrow; it is able to judge the thoughts and intentions of the heart.
>
> HEBREWS 4:12

This is a very powerful and meaningful passage for anyone who takes part in the frequent reading of God's holy word. When we invest time and energy to really engage in Bible study it will affect us in many ways. It is like a two-edged sword that will give us insight and wisdom and may even cause us to let go of the things in our lives that prevent us from becoming the person that the Lord wants us to be. God's word can and will change us.

This verse also notes that the word of God is living and active; it isn't some centuries-old document that no longer pertains to our lives. The Bible is as current and relevant today as it was long ago and will continue to be in the future. We are given new insight every time we read it *if* we're willing and open to what it may be saying to us.

Consider setting aside a time each day to thoughtfully and prayerfully read and reflect up on God's word. Doing this can guide you as you discern the Lord's will for your life as well as providing spiritual nourishment for your spiritual journey!

Word of God, speak to me when I study your word, and reveal to me what I should learn today for my spiritual pilgrimage! Amen.

AUGUST 21

A Prayer for Discernment

> Teach me your way, O Lord, that I may walk in your truth; give me an undivided heart to revere your name.
>
> PSALM 86:11

Discernment comes to us in many forms and often appears in ways that may sometimes be hard for us to understand. We are all called by God to fulfill a particular role in bringing about God's kingdom into our present time. We all have certain gifts and talents that others don't have. Therefore, it is important for all of us to determine how those talents should be used and then be about that task. This verse is a wonderful prayer as you begin searching for how your gifts might be used.

My late wife, Judy, went into a Catholic religious order to become a sister right after high school. She joined the Humility of Mary (sisters—often called the Blue Nuns, because of their blue habits)—for she believed that was what God was calling her to do. The sisters of that particular order had taught her throughout her twelve years of school and she had become very close to them.

She was in the order for more than two years and the time was a very good one for her, for she grew spiritually and in many other ways. However, as time went on, she knew that this wasn't what she was called to do for the reminder of her life. She left the order, but she continued to discern her call as a disciple of Christ and tried to use her talents as she was guided. She was instrumental in helping me and my children grow in our faith and she also was deeply involved in the Christian Education program in her local parish. Her entire life became a witness of God's love to those around her and she continued to discern God's call throughout her life.

Discernment comes to all of us daily. May you be receptive to where it may be leading you, for the Lord is a God of surprises and each day is totally new and different!

Lord, help me to walk in your truth and give me an undivided heart, soul, and mind, to praise your name, and may I always trust you about the future! Amen.

AUGUST 22

The Lord Gives Wisdom

> For the Lord gives wisdom; from his mouth come knowledge and understanding; he stores up sound wisdom for the upright.
>
> PROVERBS 2:6–7A

Wisdom, knowledge, and understanding are words that we don't often hear discussed in our modern fast-paced society. Our discourses tend to center more on the latest electronic tool that is out, how our stocks are doing, how fast we're able to climb the corporate ladder, or our dreams of possibly being the next person to start up a company that will bring us fortune and fame. Our lives are often much more focused on us and what we can get out of life, rather than on the gifts that the Lord wants us to give us.

This certainly isn't the mind-set of everyone; many of us, including a lot of young people, are looking for meaningful careers that are both rewarding and at the same time give something back to the world around them. There are many who faithfully look to the Lord for guidance on how to live their lives as they put their trust and focus on God's will.

Wisdom, knowledge, and understanding are not something that you can see or feel directly; nor can we wear or drive them, put them in a bank account, or show them off to your friends. These qualities are something inside of us that grow and develop in various ways over a long period of time.

We can obtain these traits through life experiences, watching how others live, listening to and reading about the lives of those who are wiser and more knowledgeable than we are. Wisdom, knowledge, and understanding can also be gained by taking part in the spiritual practices of this pilgrimage. When we do this, we are open to receiving these traits from the Lord, who wants to provide these qualities to us. Our role is to be a willing vessel to receive them when offered!

Holy Spirit, help me to receive wisdom, knowledge, and understanding, and may those gifts enable me to discern where God is leading me next! Amen.

AUGUST 23

Asking

> My brothers and sisters, whenever you face trials of any kind, consider it nothing but joy, because you know that the testing of your faith produces endurance; and let endurance have its full effort, so that you may be mature and complete, lacking in nothing. If any of you is lacking in wisdom, ask God, who gives to all generously and ungrudgingly, and it will be given you.
>
> JAMES 1:2–5

Wisdom is something that can help us in so many different ways and can come to us in various fashions. Some of us may have more wisdom than others and some may have had it from a very young age. Often wisdom comes to us through life experiences that have taught us how to live based on the ups and downs of our life. Things that happen to us over time can give us insight regarding how to live with other humans and how to deal with the challenges that we face on a daily basis.

The very things that test our faith can produce endurance in us if we are open to the lessons that come wrapped in the struggles that we face. Endurance gives us the faith to keep on walking and trusting because we know that just as God was with us in yesterday's trials, the Lord will certainly be with us in all future tests as well. The wisdom that we gain comes out of our past experience.

Wisdom and discernment also come directly from God through the Holy Spirit during the times that we are faced with things that are new to us and we don't have any prior experience upon which we can lean. By asking the Lord for wisdom in all areas of our life we aren't guaranteed perfect lives, but we will have the assurance that God will generously give us the wisdom we need at that time.

As you take part in this pilgrimage, may your spiritual practices allow you to have a receptive heart and soul to be able to receive God's wisdom being given to you and may that give you the courage you need to continue on your faith journey!

Lord of all life, help me to be a person that is open to receiving your wisdom and discernment, and may that awareness be shared with those I meet today! Amen.

AUGUST 24

Following Instructions

> When he [Jesus] had finished speaking, he said to Simon, "Put out into the deep water and let down your nets for a catch." Simon answered, "Master, we have worked all night long but have caught nothing. Yet if you say so, I will let down the nets." When they had done this, they caught so many fish that their nets were beginning to break.
>
> Luke 5:4–6

In these verses, we have Jesus calling his first disciples. Jesus instructs Simon (Peter) to go out into the deep water and let his nets down again. Even though Simon had fished all night and had no fish to show for his efforts, he did what he was told. The catch was so big that his nets were strained and Simon had to get his partners to help out with the haul! Simon and the others were in awe at what had just happened. Jesus then tells these individuals that they would soon be fishing for people. After going ashore, all of them left their boats and followed Jesus.

As we take part in this spiritual pilgrimage we may also be asked to do something that, in human terms, seems as foolish as Simon and his friends putting their nets into the very same lake that had failed to yield anything after a full night of fishing. However, if the instructions and discernment come from the Lord through the Holy Spirit, hopefully, we will react as did the first disciples and do as we are guided.

Something like this happened to me the summer after I got out of high school. I didn't quite know what to do after graduation, as I wasn't drawn to either college or the military. I worked for a time at a few odd jobs. I didn't have a lot of self-confidence at that time and was somewhat shy. Going out and trying to find a full-time job, or determining what I was meant to get involved with was a very frightening task. A couple of men at my church helped me get interviews with two of the steel mills in town. I lived in Youngstown, Ohio, and the steel mills were still a going concern for the community. However, this was an industry that I knew little about; in fact I had never even been in a steel mill before. So, it took a lot of strength and faith on my part to enter this world.

I applied at one mill called Republic Steel and they told me that they would call me later on if they wanted to hire me. I also applied at Youngstown Sheet & Tube Company and they offered me a job on the spot and said I could start in a few days. A few days later Republic Steel called back and offered a job as well. I thought about it and decided to go with Youngstown Sheet & Tube.

That really worked out for me in the long run. I was laid off far less often working for them than I would have been at Republic Steel over the nearly nine years that I was employed in the mill. Over time I was also able to the work the afternoon and night shifts, which allowed me to go to college part time and eventually earn my college degree. I became somewhat comfortable in those surroundings; however, it wasn't very easy at first and took a long time before I got used to going to work there every day. The mill environment could be very daunting and sometimes dangerous.

Thus, interviewing for the steel position and then staying with that job took me way out of my comfort zone. But the instruction and discernment of the Holy Spirit helped me to walk a path that I wouldn't necessarily have chosen for myself and ultimately into a future I never dreamed of when I left high school.

As you take part in this pilgrimage may you, like the early disciples, listen for Jesus' voice coming through the Holy Spirit, calling you to do things for the kingdom of God that you never thought you could previously do!

Holy Spirit, help me to listen for your daily instructions. May this discernment allow me to become a lifelong disciple of Jesus Christ and in the process become a witness of God's infinite love for all of humankind! Amen.

AUGUST 25

Imitators

> Because our message of the gospel came to you not in word only, but also in power and in the Holy Spirit and with full conviction; just as you know what kind of persons we proved to be among you for your sake. And you became imitators of us and of the Lord, for in spite of persecution you received the word with joy inspired by the Holy Spirit.
>
> 1 Thessalonians 1:5–6

One of the popular activities that children and young people often engage in is that of imitating some famous person, be it an actor, world leader, or sports figure. Often people are idealized because of what they have accomplished or simply by how they are perceived by the general public. When I was young, I loved to act out scenes and pretended to be characters from different Western movies or TV shows that I liked. Each generation locks onto whatever or whomever is current at that time. I know that my children's interests were not the same as mine, and my grandchildren are different from both my children and myself. Everything changes with the times and what was in vogue ten years ago is generally old news today.

However, one thing that is just as essential and current today as it was long ago is the word of God that comes to us. It comes with the gospel message of God's infinite love for all of humankind in and through the life of Jesus Christ. In this passage the Apostle Paul is encouraging his readers to become imitators of himself, Silvanus and Timothy, and of the Lord Jesus Christ. The Christians in Thessalonica received the word of God with joy inspired by the Holy Spirit despite the persecution they suffered.

One way for us to be imitators of Jesus is to continue our spiritual practices even when we have things around us that become barriers to our pilgrimage. Unlike the things that are popular today and gone tomorrow, the love of God is everlasting and is just as necessary for us today as it was for our parents and grandparents. Hopefully you are able to filter out the noise of the world so that you can hear and see the word of God coming to you. May you then be ready to receive the inspiration, direction, and comfort of the Holy Spirit!

Lord of infinite grace, love, and mercy, may your Holy Spirit give me the discernment and guidance to become an imitator of Jesus Christ, and may my life reflect your love to all I meet today! Amen.

AUGUST 26

Divinely Guided

> When Herod died, an angel of the Lord suddenly appeared in a dream to Joseph in Egypt and said, "Get up, take the child and his mother, and go to the Land of Israel, for those who are seeking the child's life are dead."
>
> MATTHEW 2:19–20

This passage is the second recorded case where an angel of the Lord appeared to Joseph in a dream. The first time was when Joseph was told to take Mary as his wife. In both cases, they are major events in the lives of Jesus' family and especially in the case of the unborn child and later on in the life of the very young child.

To my knowledge an angel of the Lord hasn't come to me in a dream. However, like most people I have had my share of crazy dreams that I usually have a hard time remembering, and if I do remember them I have an even more difficult time understanding what they mean. Nonetheless, I believe that I have been given guidance throughout my life in many different ways. Some of the discernment has come through other people or things I've read, sermons I've heard, or as I've been praying/reflecting while walking or jogging.

However, increasingly it seems that I have been given direction or insights during my prayer and reflection time or right afterward. I don't hear any bells going off, nor do bolts of lightening appear around me—just thoughts that come to me during this time. Thus, for many years I've kept a pad and pen nearby to write down any thoughts so they aren't forgotten afterward. I also generally end my extended prayer times writing in my journal where I record any insights I've received.

We are all unique and therefore receive discernment, wisdom, and guidance in the way that is best for us. From what many of the spiritual writers have said is it important for us to be open to hearing and seeing what is out there for us. On your spiritual pilgrimage and in your quiet times of reflection, may you be like Joseph and be receptive to what an angel of the Lord or the Holy Spirit maybe trying to convey to you!

Holy Spirit, come and give me what I need for today to walk as a disciple of Jesus Christ! Amen.

AUGUST 27

Jesus Taught and Continues to Teach with Authority

> They went to Capernaum; and when the sabbath came, he entered the synagogue and taught. They were astounded at his teaching, for he taught them as one having authority, and not as the scribes.
>
> Mark 1:21–22

Much has been written about the many things Jesus did during his short three-year ministry. The miracles that he performed are the things that many focus on. What may get overlooked are the many times that he went up to the temple to pray and worship as he carried out the traditions of the Jewish faith. We also know that he taught, but we don't often hear about what he taught in the synagogue, only that it was with great authority and not as the scribes. Thus, his message, or how he delivered it, was obviously very different from the usual teaching that the people were accustomed to hearing.

Jesus continues to teach us today, especially to those who are open to his message. When we pray, study the Scriptures, and then reflect on what is being taught, we learn and are given discernment/insights for our journey.

One of the neat things about any journey that we are on is that our view or prospective of the information/knowledge presented to us changes as we move along the path before us.

Thus, what I read about and learned five years ago, could mean something totally different to me now as compared to then. What the Holy Spirit teaches us regarding Jesus also changes over time. Life is not static nor are wisdom, understanding, and discernment. Rather they are ever changing, evolving, and being created anew in our lives each day. May you receive what Jesus wants to teach you, today, tomorrow, and in the time to come!

Lord of all wisdom and discernment, help me to learn and grow in my knowledge of Jesus' life and teachings, and may that awareness allow to me become a lifelong disciple of his! Amen.

AUGUST 28

A Balanced Life on This Pilgrimage

> Two things I ask of you; do not deny them to me before I die: Remove far from me falsehood and lying; give me neither poverty nor riches; feed me with the food that I need, or I shall be full, and deny you, and say, "Who is the Lord?" or I shall be poor, and steal, and profane the name of my God.
>
> PROVERBS 30:7–9

The writer of this passage was asking the Lord for help to have a balanced life with enough to live on, without having to steal, nor having too much to deny that God is needed. I have been fortunate enough to have known people who only had enough resources to just barely make it, but were full of joy because of how they looked at life. I have also known people who were very wealthy and were only concerned with how to hold tightly onto their wealth, and in the process had missed the really important aspects in this life and the life to come.

On the other hand, one family I knew had great wealth but saw this as a gift from God and recognized that they were simply the stewards of. They felt that their resources should be used to help others and did so frequently. They used prayer as a way of determining how their funds should be used. They established a number of scholarships, provided aid for college students, and were always willing and open to helping others.

Praying for discernment on this spiritual pilgrimage to help us decide how best to use the gifts that have been given to us should always be our first step. Having a balanced life with neither too little nor too much is hard to sustain because of life's ebbs and flows. But, no matter what stage we happen to be at, when we look at everything as a gift from God we are in a better position to listen to the discernment coming our way and to live as we are meant to live as a disciple of Jesus Christ!

Lord of all creation, help me to treat all I have as a gift from you, and guide me to use these gifts in a balanced manner! Amen.

AUGUST 29

God's Understanding

> With God are wisdom and strength; he has counsel and understanding.
>
> JOB 12:13

Gaining wisdom and understanding is something that is not talked about much in our modern society. Most of the topics that are floating around the mass media circuits are how to become rich and famous, how to achieve greatness in one's own lifetime, how to look good despite one's age or station in life, or how to live a long life with enough saved up to be comfortable in retirement, you get the point. Seldom do we find those in the public eye encouraging us to seek wisdom and understanding so that our lives are enriched and more meaningful. Rather, the ongoing message focuses on "what's in it for me!"

The book of Job, together with the Psalms, Proverbs, and Ecclesiastes, are often referred to as the wisdom and poetry books of the Bible. As you take part in your spiritual practices of prayer, Bible study, and reflection, consider reading passages from these as a way to learn more about the wisdom, understanding, counsel, and strength that come from God. On this spiritual pilgrimage when we open ourselves up to learn and receive, discernment regarding the next step in our journey will be given to us through the Holy Spirit.

The Lord's wisdom and understanding can certainly come in many different ways, even through mass media methods; however, they are more easily found in and through our spiritual practices and Bible study. Our role is to remain receptive to where the Spirit may be leading us!

God of all knowledge, help me to receive your wisdom and understanding and may your Holy Spirit give me the discernment that is needed for today! Amen.

AUGUST 30

God Called Abram, Jacob, Jeremiah, and Us

Abram, Jacob, and Jeremiah are called by God in Genesis 12:1–3, Genesis 46:2–3, and Jeremiah 1:7–10, respectively. The Lord called these individuals to do something specific that only they were called to do. The call was a lifetime journey that included times of change, trial, and danger. Initially, they probably didn't understand why God had called them, but they accepted the call and tried to faithfully follow it.

Part of the discernment process of this spiritual pilgrimage is being open to where God may be calling you today. One way to hear this call is through the practices of prayer, Bible study, and reflection. Our first reaction may be to think that we are too young or too old, or that we don't have the right education, or the time isn't right, but when we trust in God rather than in our own abilities, we discover, as have countless others who have gone before us, that things work out because God, not us, is in charge!

I would encourage you to daily listen to and trust the voice of God calling, even when it may call you to some area of ministry or spiritual growth that may cause you to wonder, why me and how can I possibly do this? More than likely you are being called to do something that only a person with your experience, skill, and position in life can do. May the Holy Spirit give you the courage and wisdom to say, "Here am I Lord!"

Holy Spirit, help me to heed God's voice and then act on what has been heard, always seeking the discernment needed for the next step! Amen.

AUGUST 31

God's Light and Truth Will Lead Us

> O send out your light and your truth: let them lead me; let them bring me to your holy hill and to your dwelling.
>
> PSALM 43:3

Discernment is a word that most associate with being called to be a pastor, priest, a sister in a religious order, or ordained person in a church or faith community. However, discernment is a vitally important part of any call where one feels led to use their gifts to further God's kingdom here on earth, be it in a religious vocation or in a position like teaching, providing health care, working for social justice, or being the best plumber, electrician, postal worker, retailer clerk, parent, or guardian, etc., etc., that it is possible to be.

Discernment often involves experiencing God's voice, guidance, or nudging to take a path that may be somewhere you wouldn't have gone on your own, or in a direction that others may not understand. Sometimes following this direction may give us the courage to take risks, step out in faith, or even go to places that are new and challenging. It also might lead us to simply continue doing what we are already doing as we listen for the guidance of the Holy Spirit on a daily basis.

There are countless ways that discernment comes to us as outlined in the writings of many spiritual writers; however, Scripture is one of the best resources. The Psalms and Proverbs are valuable references for gaining wisdom and guidance. In this passage from Psalm 43, the psalmist is asking that God's light and truth would lead and direct them to the Lord's holy hill and dwelling.

Seeking God's light and truth—the light that illumines our path so that we know where to walk, and the truth to guide our thoughts and reflections—is a worthy request.

As we faithfully participate in our spiritual practices, discernment for our daily walk is there for us, if we are open to receiving it. On your pilgrimage look to God's light and truth to lead, comfort, and support you on a daily basis!

Lord of light and truth, help me to receive your discernment today. Lead me to where you want me to be! Amen.

September

Discernment

SEPTEMBER 1

Understanding God's Ways Requires Some Action on Our Part

> Teach me, O Lord, the way of your statutes, and I will observe it to the end. Give me understanding, that I may keep your law and observe it with my whole heart. Lead me in the path of your commandments, for I delight in it. Turn my heart to your decrees, and not to selfish gain.
>
> Psalm 119:33–36

This short passage has a number of action words in it, a few of them are "teach" (v. 33), "give" (v. 34), "lead" (v. 35), and "turn" (v. 36). The writer of this passage also asks to be taught the Lord's statues, to have help in understanding the law, to be led in the Lord's commandments, and to turn heart and soul to God's decrees. Again, more action statements, all asking for wisdom, discernment, and understanding in determining God's desire for living the spiritual life.

Please read and reflect on this short passage, and the verses preceding and following it, and meditate upon what it may be saying to you today on your spiritual pilgrimage. God's wisdom, discernment, and understanding are always present as a free gift for all of us to help us grow in our faith walk. But, we have to ask God to teach us, give us those gifts, and direct us so that we may receive them. At the same time, we also have to turn our hearts toward the Lord to be open to receiving them.

This is a daily occurrence on this spiritual journey—it isn't a one-time event, but rather a lifelong journey. It requires effort on our part as we participate in our spiritual practices. May you remain receptive always to where the Lord may be leading you, and today may you strive for God's kingdom and will in your lives!

Lord of life, help me to move toward you by my actions and in the process, move to becoming your faithful lifelong disciple! Amen.

SEPTEMBER 2

Following God's Will Versus the World's

> Please test your servants for ten days. Let us be given vegetables to eat and water to drink. You can then compare our appearance with the appearance of the young men who eat the royal rations, and deal with your servants according to what you observe.
>
> DANIEL 1:12–13

The story found in the first chapter of Daniel is one from which we can all learn. Daniel and three other Israelites were chosen to serve in the court of the Babylonian king. They were to be educated and given fine foods to eat. However, Daniel didn't want to defile himself with those fine but ritually unclean foods; therefore, he asked if for ten days they could eat only vegetables and water to determine if afterward they were not better off from eating them. As the story goes, they were indeed healthier than the others at the end of the ten days.

"To these four young men God gave knowledge and skill in every aspect of literature and wisdom; Daniel also had insight into all visions and dreams" (Dan 1:17). Out of this situation God gave these four men knowledge and wisdom and they became very important people in the king's court, despite the fact that they refused to eat the food of the king.

You will no doubt have times in your life that you will be given choices that have to be made concerning things in your personal or professional lives. There may be pressures exerted from various factions that will cause you stress regarding the decision that you need to make. Be assured that as you pray the Holy Spirit will provide comfort, peace, and discernment in your daily life. The Holy Spirit speaks to us in many different ways, through people, through life events, and as we participate in our spiritual practices.

No matter what you may be facing today, remember that Daniel and his friends refused food that they knew would defile them and instead followed God's will rather than what the world was offering!

Loving Lord, may your Holy Spirit guide me and give me discernment on a daily basis and may this help me to do your will in my life! Amen.

SEPTEMBER 3

An Angel to Comfort and Lead

> I [the Lord God] am going to send an angel in front of you, to guard you on the way and to bring you to the place that I have prepared.
>
> Exodus 23:20

In this passage from Exodus, God is reassuring the Jewish nation about how they will be guided to the promised land. An angel of the Lord would be in front of them to direct them and they were to listen to and heed the angel's voice. As we talk about discernment on this spiritual pilgrimage, we often talk about how God will find ways to lead us.

Discernment can come from any number of people, places, or situations; from our family, friends, our faith community, or from something we read or experience. It can also come from angels like the ones who were with the Jewish nation. Now I am not sure if I have ever seen something that looked like an angel of old, however I have encountered some human-looking angels. The first time was in 1970 when my late wife, Judy, and I got married in Youngstown Ohio.

Judy was a second-generation Italian from Ashtabula, Ohio, and she had a strong upbringing in the Catholic faith. I was from an African American Baptist family in Youngstown, Ohio, about one hour from Ashtabula. For a number of reasons her parents and extended family had a hard time accepting the idea that we were going to be married. Her parents eventually accepted me and our marriage and over time were extremely supportive and loving to me. However, on our wedding day it was an entirely different manner.

No one from Judy's side of her family attended the wedding. Her friends, some of our mutual friends, and some of my family came. We had a priest perform the marriage in the Catholic church. The minister from my Baptist church took part, as well as a close friend who was a ministerial student. We definitely had some challenges to deal with, but we believed that was God with us; we also thought that we had an angel at the wedding.

A middle-aged Caucasian male, dressed for a wedding, sat in the back of the church for the entire service. The church was located on the east side of town where you would not normally see this type of gentleman. We didn't exactly remember what he looked like and *no one* knew who he was. We're not sure if anyone actually saw him come in or leave, only that he was there.

As we later reflected on that day, we felt that this gentleman was an angel. Judy and I knew that angels were used by God and we reasoned that he was sent to be with us at the beginning of our marriage. We thought that it was the Lord's way of showing us that God was with us then and would be with us throughout our marriage.

Be alert to the many ways that God may be supporting and guiding you on this journey. Help and discernment might just come to you in the form of a human angel!

Lord of creation, help me to be receptive to wherever you may be leading me and to be ready to follow that direction! Amen.

SEPTEMBER 4

What We Are to Be Is Unknown

> Beloved, we are God's children now; what we will be has not yet been revealed. What we do know is this: when he is revealed, we will be like him, for we will see him as he is.
>
> 1 JOHN 3:2

One of the more trying aspects about being on this spiritual pilgrimage and seeking guidance and discernment is acknowledging that we are not in control of certain areas of our life. When we determine that we want to become a lifelong disciple of Jesus Christ, we are in reality saying that the future is in God's hands and not ours. We begin to live each day making decisions and taking steps trusting that the Holy Spirit is directing our path. Our role is to strive for God's kingdom and then be ready to accept where we are being led.

As we daily walk the spiritual path, neither we nor others around us know what the future holds for us or what we may become. As this verse notes, what we will be has not been revealed yet. Think for a moment about what you thought you wanted to be when you were very young and compare it to what you are doing now and the person that you have become. It may very well be that your earlier thoughts and dreams are nothing like what your life has become.

In my own life that is most certainly the case, there have been many times in my life when what I became was nothing like what I had imagined. Your role on this pilgrimage is to be receptive to where the Holy Spirit may be leading you and through your spiritual practices be willing to listen to where you are being directed!

Lord of new creation, help me to be ready to go where you want me to go and to become the person you want me to be, so that I might be a witness to others of the new life that comes from being a lifelong disciple of Jesus Christ! Amen.

SEPTEMBER 5

Compassion

> When the Lord [Jesus] saw her, he had compassion for her and said to her, "Do not weep." Then he came forward and touched the bier, and the bearers stood still. And he said, "Young man, I say to you rise!"
>
> LUKE 7:13–14

Jesus felt compassion for this widow who had but one son, and in that culture, it would mean that she would be in a very difficult financial and social situation following the death of her son. Jesus brought her son back to life, an act that also restored the woman's life as well. However, in the amazement and joy of that miracle, we must not overlook the fact of compassion for the woman that motivated Jesus' action.

We are not able to raise people from the dead, but all of us can have compassion for those who are struggling with life's pains and sorrows. One of the definitions of compassion is to suffer with. When we are able to stand with another in their pain, struggles, discouragement, and even despair, we bring them the hope and love that are ours in Christ Jesus who *always* had compassion for the suffering of others.

Compassionate Lord, give me the guidance, love, and compassion to suffer with those around me and to walk with them in their pain! Amen.

SEPTEMBER 6

Discernment Is about Always Learning

> Give instruction to the wise, and they will become wiser still; teach the righteous and they will gain in learning. The fear of the Lord is the beginning of wisdom, and the knowledge of the Holy One is insight.
>
> PROVERBS 9:9–10

Discernment on our spiritual pilgrimage may come in many ways, some methods may be difficult to see or understand with our human eye and/or mind. It can also come in a manner that is directly opposite of how the world may view guidance and direction. On this journey the Holy Spirit may use a person, book, retreat, sermon, our prayer time, or any number of other ways to give to give us spiritual discernment.

Another aspect in this discernment process is that it may be ongoing with just enough direction to get you to the next step. The spiritual walk doesn't operate in the same manner as the long-range planning of the secular world. Spiritual discernment is something that is constantly evolving as we change and grow. Thus, having a wonderful, life-changing revelation is not usually sufficient for a lifetime of faithful discipleship. Rather, it takes many small daily steps in which we are given more and more direction over an extended period.

This passage tells us that when the wise are given instruction they become wiser still. However, they are not to rest on past instruction and guidance but continue to be open to being taught and growing in the knowledge of the Holy One. This pilgrimage is a walk of faith in which we trust God's promises about the future and believe that we will be given what we need for the next step, and the next step after that. May you be ready to receive the discernment and instruction that come your way each day as you are given new insight and wisdom in your pilgrimage as a lifelong disciple of Jesus Christ!

Loving Lord, you are the beginning of wisdom and insight, help me to receive your instruction and discernment needed for my spiritual pilgrimage! Amen.

SEPTEMBER 7

Following Jesus' Voice

> My sheep hear my voice. I know them, and they follow me.
>
> JOHN 10:27

In this passage from John, some Jewish leaders were following Jesus in order to challenge and discredit him. They kept asking him if he was the Messiah and wanted to hear the truth from his own lips. He responded that he had already answered them but they didn't believe him. He said that they didn't believe because they weren't part of his sheep fold, but that those who were his sheep heard his voice, knew him, and followed him.

Through the centuries since Jesus walked on this earth, his words have been translated into hundreds of languages and distributed all over the world. However, just like the people in this passage, there are those who aren't able to believe in him for one reason or the other. No one was forced to believe in Jesus during his earthly life and no one is forced today; belief is a gift of the Holy Spirit. We become one of his sheep by our response to the Spirit.

Jesus' voice gives us comfort and discernment for our spiritual pilgrimage. Our spiritual practices of prayer, Bible study, and reflection can help us to hear Jesus' voice more clearly. May you be open to hearing Jesus' voice and daily following where it is leading you on your journey as a lifelong disciple of Jesus Christ!

Good Shepherd, help me to listen to your voice coming to me through the Holy Spirit, and may this voice guide my steps today and every day! Amen.

SEPTEMBER 8

What Am I to Do, Lord?

> I asked, "What am I to do, Lord?" The Lord said to me, "Get up and go to Damascus; there you will be told everything that has been assigned to you to do."
>
> ACTS 22:10

This is a frequently told story about Saul's conversion when he was on the road to Damascus to persecute the followers of Jesus. As he was traveling a great light shone on him, and he heard the voice of Jesus asking, "Saul, Saul, why are you persecuting me?" After Jesus spoke to him, Saul said, "What am I to do, Lord?" Jesus commanded Saul to go to Damascus and there he would be told what he was to do next. Since Saul had been blinded by the light, he was led by his companions.

Discernment on this spiritual pilgrimage is about being open to where the Lord through the Holy Spirit may be leading us. We may not have an experience like Saul had, with the blinding light and unseen voice, however, the guidance may come in a dramatic fashion or in the gentlest of circumstances. Asking God what we are to do next may be the easy part; listening, and then willingly following the word we've been given can be the more challenging part. Our role is to position our inner being to receive this direction, and one way this can be done is with our spiritual practices.

May you, like Saul, be receptive to where you are being asked to go, and may you be willing to step out in faith, even though you can't see where you are going, only that God has asked you to go!

Loving Lord, help me to daily ask for your guidance and then have the courage to obey, even though I may not know where it will take me! Amen.

SEPTEMBER 9

Going as Instructed

> The word of the Lord came to Jonah a second time, saying, "Get up, go to Nineveh, that great city, and proclaim to it the message that I tell you." So Jonah set out and went to Nineveh, according to the word of the Lord.
>
> JONAH 3:1–3A

The story of Jonah is a well-known one. When we think of what happened, our focus is often on the section that reports Jonah being in the belly of a large fish. The real emphasis in the story is that Jonah was trying to run away from what God had instructed him to do. In fact, he went in the opposite direction toward Tarshish instead of to Nineveh where the Lord had instructed him to go. He eventually ended up in Nineveh and did what he was guided to do.

This also may be the case with many of us in that the Holy Spirit may have guided us in one direction and we made the decision to go elsewhere. The aspect about God's love is that we are not forced to heed the guidance, but it is *totally* our choice whether or not to follow. I know of a few people who felt called to a certain ministry but put it off for decades. The irony is that the call never went away—it was always there in the background, nagging at the subconscious. Eventually, like Jonah, it was fulfilled.

As part of this spiritual pilgrimage we might be given direction that could take us to places that we don't initially want to go, but may we always know that the Lord is patient and never fails to be with us!

Lord of the past, present, and future, help me to trust that when you call you will go with me whether I can go immediately, as instructed, or delay! Amen.

SEPTEMBER 10

Human Wisdom and Divine Wisdom

> Who is wise and understanding among you? Show by your good life that your works are done with gentleness born of wisdom. But if you have bitter envy and selfish ambition in your hearts, do not be boastful and false to the truth. Such wisdom does not come down from above, but is earthly, unspiritual, and devilish. For where there is envy and selfish ambition, there will also be disorder and wickedness of every kind. But the wisdom from above is first pure, then peaceful, gentle, willing to yield, full of mercy and good fruits, without a trace of partiality or hypocrisy. And a harvest of righteousness is sown in peace for those who make peace.
>
> JAMES 3:13–18

Taking part in this spiritual pilgrimage encourages us to become a lifelong disciple of Jesus Christ by striving for God's kingdom as part of our daily walk. When we look at life through the lens of God's kingdom and the Lord's will in our lives, we are guided to live differently because our focus is on God's kingdom versus the many aspects of the secular world.

In the same manner when we use our human wisdom to govern our daily steps the outcome often may be different from the result would be if we allowed divine wisdom to guide us. Sometimes *our* ideas of what seem best for us may very well be in opposition to God's will for us and at opposite poles from the Lord's kingdom. How we think about life determines our words and actions. As this passage indicates, things done in gentleness will have an entirely different outcome than things done with a heart motivated by envy or selfishness. Divine wisdom enables us to act and live in ways that are pleasing to God.

Our spiritual practices help us to see things from the Lord's perspective and then to live out of that divine wisdom.

The following century-old prayer for discernment has been a help to countless people down through the years. May it aid you on your pilgrimage today!

"*I believe I am always divinely guided. I believe I will always take the right turn of the road. I believe God will always make a way where there is no way!*"

SEPTEMBER 11

Beginning of Wisdom

> The fear of the Lord is the beginning of wisdom; all those who practice it have a good understanding. His praise endures forever.
>
> PSALM 111:10

This message is stated in a number of different places in the Old Testament Scriptures. The beginning of wisdom is derived from a fear *of* and reverence *for* the Lord for all of the wonderful deeds that God has done. The phrase "fear of the Lord" is common in Israel's teachings and writings; it sums up a proper relationship with God that includes worship, love, obedience, and reverence. As we seek discernment and wisdom along our spiritual pilgrimage, regarding all aspects of our life, it is encouraging to know that wisdom begins with a reverent attitude toward the Lord.

Discernment comes from life experiences, through the words and actions of our family and friends, through reading the writings of those spiritually wise persons from the past as well as of today, and through our spiritual practices. However, wisdom is born out of our relationship with God and is what all other wisdom that we receive is built upon.

Wisdom and understanding are qualities of spiritual life that can't be purchased, imitated, or stolen, only used or shared with those around us. God gives us these gifts to help us navigate on our spiritual journey. May your spiritual practices put you in a position to be able to receive these gifts as you fear and praise the Lord!

God of all wisdom, help me to be open to the gifts of wisdom and understanding that you have for me, and may these gifts help me as I attempt to live as a faithful disciple of Jesus Christ! Amen.

SEPTEMBER 12

Making a Home Wherever We Are Sent

> Build houses and live in them; plant gardens and eat what they produce.
>
> JEREMIAH 29:5

These words were given by God, through the prophet Jeremiah, to the Israelites living in exile in Babylon regarding how they were to live. They weren't to act as exiles but were to fully embrace the area and people among whom they were living. God indeed had other plans for them in the future as noted later in this chapter. However, at that time they were to build homes and plant gardens.

I've never been an exile in a foreign land, but I have moved a number of times as an adult. After completing college, my late wife, Judy, and my family made several corporate moves. During the years in which I worked in the insurance industry, I was employed by five insurance companies in four states—in two of these states I lived in two different cities. Since leaving the insurance industry and graduating from seminary I have moved to two different states where my wife, Shirley, has been called as a pastor.

Each time we relocated we tried to create a sense of being "settled in" for my family and me and we became active in the community. We bought houses, planted gardens, and tried to make wherever we lived our home. We also explored the community itself and on weekends and vacations we would travel throughout the surrounding areas.

Discernment on this spiritual pilgrimage involves living in the moment and trusting the future to God. That was the message the Lord was giving to Israel, that even though they were in exile they were to build homes, live in them, plant gardens, and basically settle down.

You may not be called to move to a new location as you listen to God's direction and guidance; however, you may be asked to attempt something new either in your professional, personal, or church-related life. No matter what it is, take it seriously and embrace the new adventure and live in the moment, knowing that the Lord has a plan for your future!

Creative God, help me to listen for your guidance and give me the courage to embrace whatever I am being called to. Show me how to live in this moment and trust the future to you! Amen.

SEPTEMBER 13

Strength and Understanding for the Pilgrimage

> Have you not known? Have you not heard? The Lord is the everlasting God, the Creator of the ends of the earth. He does not faint or grow weary; his understanding is unsearchable. He gives power to the faint, and strengthens the powerless. Even youths will faint and be weary, and the young will fall exhausted; but those who wait for the Lord shall renew their strength, they shall mount up with wings like eagles, they shall run and not be weary, they shall walk and not faint.
>
> Isaiah 40:28–31

This is a Bible passage that has no doubt encouraged people through the years. It promises that when we wait upon the Lord our strength will be renewed. As we deal with some of life's tougher challenges, we can become weary from the strain of whatever burden we are carrying. Knowing that God will renew our strength gives us hope for each day. I have also used these verses when I am jogging and my energy level is low, repeating this passage has helped me take the next step and the one after that.

These verses also remind us that we can't begin to understand how wonderful the Creator of the world truly is. The Lord does not faint or grow weary, and God's understanding is unsearchable. In this very sophisticated world in which new and ever more rapid technological systems are being developed daily, the Lord remains essentially a mystery to us. There are so many aspects of God that have to be taken on faith.

That is where our spiritual practices may help us. Not that we'll become expects about God, but daily we learn to trust in the Lord, communicating our every need. The Holy Spirit will comfort and guide us on our journey even when we don't have all of the answers about what is coming next!

Lord of life, renew my strength and give me the hope I need to trust in your promises regarding the future even when there is so much I will never know or understand about you on this side of your kingdom! Amen.

SEPTEMBER 14

Dying to Bear Fruit

> Very truly, I tell you, unless a grain of wheat falls into the earth and dies, it remains just a single grain; but if it dies, it bears much fruit. Those who love their life lose it, and those who hate their life in this

world will keep it for eternal life. Whoever serves me must follow me, and where I am, there will my servant be also. Whoever serves me, the Father will honor.

JOHN 12:24–26

In this passage, Jesus is talking about his upcoming death to his disciples. He is speaking to them in a manner to which they could relate by using the illustration of the wheat plant. I grew up in the city and wasn't around many farms in my younger days. However, over the years I have come to appreciate the faith that it takes to be a farmer or a gardener who plants vegetable or flowers. The seed is put into the dark earth and needs to be watered, weeded, and fed. Even with the best care there is no guarantee that the plant will grow.

In this passage, Jesus wants those who are following him to know that in order to become his disciple and to bear the fruit of God's kingdom they have to die to themselves. What does it mean to die to oneself? It involves dying to our desires, our self-centeredness, and seeking the Lord's will above our own. The discernment that comes to us during our daily spiritual pilgrimage helps us to lose our lives in order to find our true purpose in Christ. We may not totally understand how this process is evolving, but we trust that we will be given enough light for the next step on our journey.

When we die to ourselves in order to follow Jesus, the fruit we bear relates to the things that are eternal and belong to God's kingdom. During your spiritual pilgrimage, may you be given the discernment needed to die to self, lose your life in order to find it, and serve in order to become more of the person that God wants you to be!

Lord of life, help me to daily die to myself in order to bear the fruit of your kingdom! Amen.

SEPTEMBER 15

Jesus Christ Our Example

For to this you have been called, because Christ also suffered for you, leaving you an example, so that you should follow in his steps.

1 PETER 2:21

People who provide us with an exceptional example are important for all of us during our lifetime. Healthy role models in a family are very much needed to help children mature and develop into the persons that God created them to be. Sadly, there are countless children who don't have parents or others who can be an example for them. Children who are orphans because of death or war, or children who have been separated from their families, or who were raised in situations of abject poverty, or in the midst of addictions often struggle their entire life because they didn't have anyone to love them, protect them, and be an example for them.

My brothers and I were raised by my mother after she and my dad were divorced. My dad was minimally involved in our lives, and therefore my mom was our main life example or role model while we were growing up. She taught us many things *simply* by how she carried herself and raised her family. We didn't have a lot of material things, but we always knew that we were loved, and that by far is the most life-giving and sustaining quality.

In my teen years and into early adulthood, people from my home congregation and those with whom I worked and/or spent time at college became very important persons in my life, as I learned from them about how to live in this world. These men and women were from different backgrounds and had varied viewpoints and interests, but because I was always looking for knowledge and understanding, I was open to what they had to offer me by their words and how they lived.

Jesus is an example for all of us who are on this spiritual pilgrimage. By reflecting on what he said and how he lived, we learn about how to live as his disciple in our daily lives. May you see that Jesus can be a perfect role model for you and give you the wisdom and discernment that you need for today. By taking part in the spiritual practices of prayer, Bible study, and reflection you place your mind and soul in a better position to hear and see what Jesus is trying to show you!

God of all creation, may your Holy Spirit guide me to follow in the footsteps of Jesus and listen to his words and learn from his actions, so that I can become the person you want me to be! Amen.

SEPTEMBER 16

Remain True to Your Calling

> However that may be, let each of you lead the life that the Lord has assigned, to which God called you. This is my rule in all the churches.
>
> 1 CORINTHIANS 7:17

My late wife, Judy, entered a religious community right after she graduated from high school. The community, the Humility of Mary, was an order that taught her in school as she was growing up. The order, often called the "Blue Nuns" because of their blue habits, was a community that she was very comfortable with and thus when she decided to become a Catholic sister that was whom she joined. She was in the community for more than two years, but at some point during that time she decided to leave. She was always grateful for her time with that community, but she eventually felt that she was led to leave them.

After she left them, she continued to do ministry in a variety of ways that utilized her skills and gifts. At every church that we joined as we made corporate moves, she freely shared her time and talents. Among other things she was the director of the religious education program at a large Catholic parish. The point is that even though she left the "Blue Nuns" she continued listening to the Holy Spirit's guidance regarding her call to live as a disciple of Jesus.

On your spiritual pilgrimage, please be receptive to where the Holy Spirit may be calling you. Look for the discernment and guidance that may be coming to you through your spiritual practices, through people around you, through your retreat and worship times, or through ways that may be new and different. May you follow the Lord's call and rejoice in the life that God has given you!

Loving Lord, help me to listen to your voice coming to me in many different ways and then may I follow where it is leading me! Amen.

SEPTEMBER 17

Jesus Was Tempted and We Will Be Also

> And the Spirit immediately drove him out into wilderness. He was in the wilderness forty days, tempted by Satan; and he was with the wild beasts; and the angels waited on him.
>
> MARK 1:12–13

Being on this spiritual pilgrimage and taking part in prayer, Bible study, and reflection, and striving to be a faithful disciple of Jesus Christ doesn't mean that our lives will be perfect, devoid of all the ups and downs of life with which all creation must deal.

Jesus himself was sent to the wilderness and was tempted by the evil forces of the world. As fallible humans living in the midst of a world filled with all sort of forces, both good and bad, we, too, will probably have times when we have to go through the wilderness or desert periods in our lives.

Also, daily, maybe even hourly, there will come moments when we have to make decisions, where choices have to be made about our life or the lives of those around us.

If we attempt to keep our hearts and minds focused on God's kingdom and will in our lives as we follow the life and teachings of Jesus, the Holy Spirit will walk with us and help us discern our next step. Our lives may not be perfect, but we know that we are not walking alone, and are loved with a steadfast love!

God of all creation, help me to call upon you daily, so that in all the times of my life, whether they be on the mountaintop, or in the desert, or even when being tempted, your Holy Spirit will be comforting me, and giving me the discernment for whatever comes next! Amen.

SEPTEMBER 18

Jesus Our Help and Mentor

> Therefore he had to become like his brothers and sisters in every respect, so that he might be a merciful and faithful high priest in the service of God, to make a sacrifice of atonement for the sins of the people. Because he himself was tested by what he suffered, he is able to help those who are being tested.
>
> HEBREWS 2:17–18

After I graduated from college, I was fortune enough to receive a job in the insurance industry, which was like heaven to me after working full time for nearly nine years in a steel mill, while at the same time going to college part time. The insurance company moved my family and me to Denver, Colorado, for training to become a marketing representative. The training included a lot of class work, for I didn't know anything about the insurance business. Eventually, I was allowed to travel with a seasoned representative to learn things from a hands-on perspective.

That person had knowledge and experience about things that needed to be done, and issues that had to be addressed, and how to conduct oneself on those agency visits. I learned by listening and watching and thinking about how I would do things in the future. In time, I made the agency visits on my own and was later on moved to the Bay Area of Northern California where I was given my own territory of agencies whom I called upon. Had I not had the time with my mentor, I wouldn't have had the confidence nor the knowledge to be able to do what I needed to do.

This passage reminds us that Jesus became human just like us, was tested, and suffered just as we sometimes do. Because Jesus went through what he did, he is able to help us. Just as I was helped during my training by someone who had been through what I was going to be experiencing when I finished my training, Jesus experienced testing and suffering just as we may in our life. His spirit lives within us and will help us on our spiritual pilgrimage by giving us discernment, wisdom, and comfort, especially in our times of trial.

Because Jesus lived an earthly life as we do, he is able to be our help and mentor on our journey. May the spiritual practices of prayer, Bible study, and reflection bring you into a deeper awareness of Jesus' presence within you, and may his presence help you to live each day as his faithful disciple!

Living God, give me what I need today and may I look to Jesus as someone who was tested and suffered as we do, but who continued to walk as he was guided. May I do the same! Amen.

SEPTEMBER 19

God's Temple

> Do you not know that you are God's temple and that God's Spirit dwells in you? If anyone destroys God's temple, God will destroy that person. For God's temple is holy, and you are that temple.
>
> 1 CORINTHIANS 3:16–17

This is a very meaningful and humbling message to those of us on this spiritual pilgrimage, in that our body is the holy temple of God's Spirit who dwells within us. Think about that for a moment, both our body and all the bodies that form our faith communities are the vessels where God's Spirit lives! If we view our spiritual journey through this lens, we become more open to the discernment and guidance that may come through others along our spiritual walk. Our actions, thoughts, our very lives can be dramatically changed by the knowledge that we are God's temple. This also comforts us and allows us to feel more of God's love when we are going through the trying times of our life.

Often, we can become disheartened because of the challenges in our lives and in the lives of those around us. When our focus and attention are blinded by all of the negative things that are happening we can become weighed down and begin to doubt the promises of the Lord. But remember, the Lord's Spirit dwells within us! If we focus on God's presence within us, the many worries, concerns, and issues around us will become less distracting and we'll begin to daily deal with life differently.

May this passage encourage you to look at your life through the lens of knowing that you are God's holy temple, and may that give you the discernment and strength that you need to continue on your spiritual path!

Loving God, help me to understand that your Spirit dwells within me, and may that realization allow me to receive the discernment, wisdom, and support that come to me today! Amen.

SEPTEMBER 20

God Knows Everything about Us

> O Lord, you have searched me and known me. You know when I sit down and when I rise up; you discern my thoughts from far away. You search out my path and my lying down, and are acquainted with all my ways. Even before a word is on my tongue, O Lord, you know it completely. You hem me in, behind and before, and lay your hand upon me. Such knowledge is too wonderful for me; it is so high that I cannot attain it.
>
> Psalm 139:1–6

Living in our so-called modern society, with all of the creature comforts that we have with our sophisticated gadgets and a lifestyle that is the envy of many throughout the world, we can easily deceive ourselves into believing that it's possible to live a private life if we so choose. Even with the social media craze becoming more popular by the minute, there are nonetheless certain aspects of our lives that we want to keep to ourselves or share only with those who are closest to us.

However, this passage informs us that the Lord knows everything about the writer of this psalm, and this person is very excited about this and, in fact, goes to great lengths to outline all of the areas in which this true. The truth is that no matter how we may try to hide certain aspects of our lives from others, nothing can be kept from God. On our spiritual pilgrimage when we are trying to discern where God may be leading us and directing us, it might help us to remember that the Lord knows everything about us. When we can realize that God searches us, knows our thoughts, knows when we move, knows what we are going to speak before we say it, and is behind and before us, this should influence how we take part in this journey.

When we begin to fully understand that nothing happens in our lives, around us or in the world, without God knowing about it, that knowledge can help us to trust in the promises of God, because no matter what we are going through at the moment, the Lord will always be with us. As you take part in your spiritual practices and strive to become a lifelong disciple of Jesus Christ may you know that God is always aware of every aspect of your life today and for all time!

All-knowing Lord, help me to be open to the idea that you know all about me and care about every detail of my life. May that allow me to believe in and trust the guidance that will be coming my way! Amen.

SEPTEMBER 21

Do Everything for the Glory of God

> So, whether you eat or drink, or whatever you do, do everything for the glory of God.
>
> 1 CORINTHIANS 10:31

In this passage instructions are given regarding our actions so that others might not be hindered in their spiritual growth. St. Paul writes in verse 23 that "not all things build up" and encourages us to do everything for the glory of God.

As we strive for God's kingdom and attempt to hear and follow the discernment of the Holy Spirit, the way in which we live should reflect our focus. Through our daily actions, including how we carry ourselves, what we put into our bodies, and how much we allow issues around us to dictate our thinking, we are witnessing to those around us about whom and what are the most important aspect of our lives.

If we are, in fact, aware of that what we do publicly and privately can help or hinder others in their spiritual pilgrimage, we are more apt to pay attention to what we eat, drink, and say. How we behave may differ from one group to another. However, if we strive to do everything for the glory of God, then those around us will be impacted in a manner that brings them closer to becoming the person that God wants them to be, rather than being led in another direction. May your daily actions reflect the discernment that has been given to you by the Holy Spirit who always points to God's kingdom and will in your life versus your own agenda!

Lord of all glory, may everything that I eat or drink and all that I do bring glory to you, and in the process, help those around me with their spiritual journey! Amen.

SEPTEMBER 22

Put on the Whole Armor of God

> Finally, be strong in the Lord and in the strength of his power. Put on the whole armor of God, so that you may be able to stand against the wiles of the devil.
>
> EPHESIANS 6:10–11

One of the more challenging aspects of this spiritual pilgrimage is knowing how to obtain discernment and the guidance of the Holy Spirit on our daily journey. There are so many conflicting messages that can easily pull us away from where God may want us to go and from whom we are to be. These messages can come from many sources; our family and friends who are close to us, some of the many groups and communities of which we are a part, the media-crazed world that gives us constant information, as well as messages from the Holy Spirit understood in our own heart, soul, and mind.

One of the best ways to determine if the message is from God through the Holy Spirit is to ask ourselves if it honors the Lord, connects to the teachings of Jesus and allows us to follow the call that we have been given. We always have to discern whether the message is causing us to focus upon our own agenda, something that may be coming from the evil forces of the world, or is it from the Holy Spirit. Putting on the whole armor of God with our practices of prayer, Bible study, and reflection, and sincerely striving for God's kingdom in our lives positions us so we have a better chance of doing the Lord's will rather than our own.

This armor can't keep us from the pain and sorrow that come from being a frail human on this side of the kingdom. However, we can be assured that the Lord's strength will give us what we need to face today's perils. May you be open to wherever the Holy Spirit may be leading you, and may your armor be such that you know that God will be with you, no matter what you may be going through at the moment!

God of all strength and power, help me to put on your armor of discernment and protection that will allow me to stand against any challenges that may come my way today! Amen.

SEPTEMBER 23

Walk in the Truth

> I was overjoyed when some of your friends arrived and testified to your faithfulness to the truth, namely how you walk in the truth. I have no greater joy than this, to hear that my children are walking in the truth.
>
> 3 John 3–4

Walking in the truth seems to be a very important point in these two short verses, because the word truth is mentioned three times. Knowing and walking in the truth is an ongoing process for most of us, no matter our stage of life. When we're young, our awareness of truth generally comes from our parents, grandparents, relatives, guardians, mentors, teachers, and the various communities around us, such as churches, neighborhoods, or school groups. As we get older, we start to learn more about what truth is by our own life experiences and the interactions we have from a wide range of sources. One of the major challenges that we all face is filtering out what is truth coming from the mass media that gives us more information than anyone can use or understand.

At some point in our life we realize that some of what we hear around us may not be truth or even factual, and thus must be discarded. For some of us this can be difficult because many of the sources of information may come from people and institutions in which we've placed our trust and faith. Throughout history governments, political ideologies and in some cases even the church community have been the source of untruths, falsehoods, or wrongful acts. Furthermore, church leaders have, at times, allowed their human weaknesses to lead people and movements down the wrong path.

Discerning the truth for yourself on this spiritual pilgrimage shouldn't be taken lightly and is a daily and lifelong challenge. Through your spiritual practices of prayer, Bible study, and reflection together with regularly worshiping in a faith community where you can walk and grow together in truth with others, you will become a more discerning disciple of Jesus Christ. Take courage and do not let the loud voices around you drown out the quiet voice of the Holy Spirit offering you whatever discernment and truth you need for today and for your future!

Lord of all Truth, help me to listen to your truth coming to me through your Spirit and may this aid me in walking the path that you have for me today. Help me to share this truth with all those I meet! Amen.

SEPTEMBER 24

Jesus Walking with Us

> While they were talking and discussing, Jesus himself came and went with them.
>
> LUKE 24:15

Jesus joined two of his disciples walking along the road to Emmaus shortly after his resurrection. Jesus came up and walked with them and they didn't know who it was until after he ate with them. The disciples had a fairly lengthy and involved discussion about the recent events, of Jesus' crucifixion, death, and resurrection, but didn't recognize that Jesus himself was their traveling companion.

Does that ever happen today? Are we at times in the presence of something or someone holy, loving, or grace-filled and we didn't realize it? Sometimes like those disciples, we may be so hung up on the events going on around us or the problems that we are facing or the pain or sorrow that we're experiencing that we miss what is right in front of us.

Now to be fair to those two disciples, their world had been turned upside down and no doubt they were worried, confused, and unsure about the future, which makes it easier to understand how they missed that it was Jesus walking with them. We, too, should be open to the times that Jesus is present with us in the form of human or heavenly angels, or through the Holy Spirit's interaction in some situation in which we're involved, or some other way in which we receive spiritual discernment or guidance as we walk along on our journey. God's love and presence can be anywhere and everywhere even when we're not expecting it, maybe even as we are walking along, lost in our thoughts!

God of all compassion, help me to look for you wherever I may be, and may your love and comfort guide me on my pilgrimage! Amen.

SEPTEMBER 25

Growing in Grace and Knowledge

> But grow in the grace and knowledge of our Lord and Savior Jesus Christ.
>
> 2 PETER 3:18

How does a person grow in something, or learn about a new topic or subject, or how does one become good at doing a certain skill? Generally speaking, in order to develop in some area of life we need to become engaged in that field, to interact with or study about whatever it is that we want to acquire knowledge of. It's safe to say that knowledge and growth won't automatically come to us if all we do is think about it without putting some effort into attaining it. The development only comes when we take the first step, no matter how small that it is. Some action is required on our part.

Once we get started, we may be helped along the way and given insight and wisdom that we didn't expect. However, that usually won't happen unless we first open a book, or begin seeking what is needed. Likewise, growing in the grace and knowledge of Jesus Christ can only happen when we move toward Jesus in some manner. This grace and knowledge are always there, just like God's love and mercy are always there for us, but we have to be ready to receive it.

The Lord through the Holy Spirit wants to give us the discernment we need for our spiritual pilgrimage. Our role is to daily strive for God's kingdom and position our heart and soul to receive these love-filled gifts that allow us to become the persons that God wants each of us to be!

Loving Lord, help me to daily take the first step on this journey to be able to obtain the discernment, grace, and knowledge that you have for me! Amen.

SEPTEMBER 26

Perseverance

> Pray in the Spirit at all times in every prayer and supplication. To that end keep alert and always persevere in supplication for all the saints.
>
> EPHESIANS 6:18

One of the more challenging aspects that we have to learn about life in general and this spiritual pilgrimage in particular is that sometimes things don't come to us in the time frame that we would like. Often what we think should be an appropriate time of waiting for something to occur or for us to receive what we are anticipating maybe longer than expected. Most of us are not particularly patient, especially in this world of instant everything that has conditioned us to expect quick information at our finger tips. I generally hate to wait and that has caused some needless frustration on my part.

When it comes, however, to our spiritual journey and striving for God's kingdom on a daily basis, the waiting can take on an even greater role.

As many wise people have said in one way or another, our timing is not the same as God's timing. Guidance, discernment, and wisdom come to us on this walk, in God's time—the time in which the Lord knows is best for us.

Thus, perseverance in our spiritual practices, especially with our prayer life, is necessary. Seeking discernment from God is not the same as making a family or business plan for the next few years. Most of the aspects for that plan are mainly in our hands, on the time table we've devised, and on the environment around us. Direction from the Lord through the Holy Spirit depends less on our efforts and those around us and more on continuing to remain receptive to God's guidance, so that we can help in bringing about God's kingdom into our present time and space, and for us to become the people God wants us to be.

On your pilgrimage, may you be patient while at the same time continuing with your spiritual practices, persevering in doing what you are being led to do, and trusting that God's timing is far better than our own or that of the world around us!

Lord of life, help me to trust that you know what is best for me and for those that I love. Give me the perseverance to continue this journey in faith recognizing that no matter how long things may seem to take, you are with me wherever I happen to be! Amen.

SEPTEMBER 27

Learning Is Part of the Pilgrimage

> Make me to know your ways, O Lord; teach me your paths. Lead me in your truth, and teach me, for you are the God of my salvation; for you I wait all day long.
>
> Psalm 25:4–5

In 2000, after spending nearly twenty-eight years in the insurance industry, I left that field to enroll in Trinity Lutheran Seminary full time. I was guided to go while not fully knowing why. Initially that experience was a shock to my spiritual and mental makeup.

Throughout my life until that time I had always attended worship services wherever we lived. I took part in countless Bible studies, Sunday school activities as a teacher and a student, in small group activities, and of course did my own private study as part of my spiritual pilgrimage. However, that period at Trinity traumatized my system in many ways and especially as far as my knowledge of the Bible went. Even though I felt comfortable with my knowledge of certain things before going to the Trinity, my view of some aspects of Scripture was forever changed.

That first year at Trinity, and especially that first quarter, was one of the more trying times of my life. Besides the workload and the writing of paper after paper, it really caused me a lot of pain and discomfort, because what I was learning changed some of the long-held beliefs that I had about the Bible, its stories, and its historical background. That became a very stressful time for me, many things that I once held very sacred were drastically altered.

As you take part in your spiritual practices realize that you may be taught many different things along your journey, and there will always be something new to learn or a fresh way of understanding a long-held view. Such insights may indeed change you and could even cause you some discomfort. However, embrace what God may be doing in your life!

Lord of new life, teach me your ways and paths and lead me to your truth. Help me to embrace being changed in the process! Amen.

SEPTEMBER 28

Speak for Your Servant Is Listening

> Now the Lord came and stood there, calling as before, "Samuel! Samuel!" And Samuel said, "Speak, for your servant is listening."
>
> 1 SAMUEL 3:10

The story about how Samuel became a prophet of God is an interesting one, especially because he didn't at first recognize the Lord's voice. According to the beginning of this passage, the word of the Lord didn't happen very frequently in those days, nor was there widespread use of visions as a way to show God's direction. Three times in this passage Samuel hears God's voice and each time he thinks it is the voice of Eli. It was Eli who told him what to say the next time the voice came. On the fourth time Samuel said, "Speak, for your servant is listening." The Lord then told Samuel what was to happen to Israel. This first oracle was Samuel's introduction into becoming a prophet for God. The end of this passage notes that as Samuel grew the Lord was with him and all of Israel knew that he was a prophet for God.

Speak for your servant is listening is basically what we are saying when we pray the Lord's Prayer or take time to pray regularly, read the Bible, reflect on what the Spirit may be telling us, meditate and daily strive toward God's kingdom. We may not all be called to be prophets as Samuel was, but how we live on a daily basis can spread God's message of grace and love to those we meet. Just as the nation of Israel knew that Samuel was a prophet of God, people whom you meet every day will know that God is the Lord of your life.

Daily may you seek where and what the Lord, through the Holy Spirit, may be asking you to go and do, and may those around know that you are a servant of God!

Lord of all life, help me to be your servant, and guide me to become the person you want me to be, a lifelong disciple of Jesus Christ! Amen.

SEPTEMBER 29

We All Have Different Gifts

> For as in one body we have many members, and not all the members have the same function, so we who are many, are one body in Christ, and individually we are members one of another. We have gifts that differ according to the grace given to us.
>
> Romans 12:4–6

The teaching in this passage is also outlined in other passages in the Bible, that all of us are gifted and called to fulfill different roles in God's ministry and mission in this time and place, according to the grace given to us. Just as the human body has different parts that function and carry out their duties, so too does the body of Christ. We are all called and given different gifts to use in our various roles.

My two marriages are a good example of this. The written use of the English language is not one of my strongest suits. I have always been challenged in this area in my life, consequently the first college class I took was Communications 101, a basic English course, which I failed and had to retake.

My late wife, Judy, however, was really good in this area and helped me with my college papers and written correspondence afterward. Shirley is also very good in this and has been a big help with my seminary papers, sermons, and other publications. Judy and Shirley both used their talents to help me to fulfill the roles to which God has called me. In the same manner, I helped both of them and continue to help Shirley in areas that enhance her ministry. Shirley, Judy, and I helped each other in our mutual ministries and in life with gifts that the other didn't have.

Be open to where you are being called and listen for the discerning voice of the Holy Spirit, which daily offers guidance for what is needed in the body of Christ. God bestows skills and gifts to us to use in building up the body of Christ!

God of all creation, help me to accept my calling along this spiritual pilgrimage, and guide me to use my gifts for the building up of the body of Christ! Amen.

SEPTEMBER 30

Doers of God's Word

> But be doers of the word, and not merely hearers who deceive themselves.
>
> JAMES 1:22

Discernment on this spiritual pilgrimage can come from many different sources. We receive direction from our prayer life, from our friends and family members, from life events that happen all around us, and of course from the Holy Spirit leading and comforting us. There are many more ways in which we can be guided and indeed we each are given direction in ways that are specific to us.

Discernment often comes to us through the word of God; the Holy Bible is full of wisdom and insight that has stood the test of time. The desert mothers and fathers left us a wonderful example of how the Bible became an important part of their pilgrimage. They fed daily upon the Lord's word which increased their spiritual growth. That is why Bible study is such an important aspect of the spiritual practices.

This passage from James encourages its readers to be doers of the word, rather than merely hearers of it. Being doers of the word happens when we allow the Scriptures to become part of our life as it directs, comforts, and supports us on our daily walk.

As you start or enhance your spiritual practices may you become doers of the word of God and not just hearers of it!

Holy Spirit, help me to allow the word of God to become part of my life, and may that practice assist me in becoming a doer of the word, so that it is then reflected in my life and how I interact with those around me! Amen.

October

Hope

OCTOBER 1

Words of Comfort and Hope

> I lift up my eyes to the hills—from where will my help come? My help comes from the Lord, who made heaven and earth. He will not let your foot be moved; he who keeps you will not slumber. He who keeps Israel will neither slumber nor sleep. The Lord is your keeper; the Lord is your shade at your right hand. The sun shall not strike you by day, nor the moon by night. The Lord will keep you from all evil; he will keep your life. The Lord will keep your going out and your coming in from this time on and for evermore.
>
> Psalm 121

This psalm is frequently quoted and reminds us that God created heaven and earth and is our keeper now and forevermore. The Lord is worthy and deserving of our praise and trust. In our technologically sophisticated world, some may think that such trust is old-fashioned, even foolish. However, trusting in something that is here today and gone tomorrow, as are so many things in our throwaway culture, certainly isn't very wise or even practical.

Putting one's faith and hope in the Lord who made heaven and earth, and who was, who is, and who will be in the future, is to my way of thinking the only way to go. On your spiritual pilgrimage, may your eyes remain on the Creator of heaven and earth who is the source of the true and everlasting help!

God of all creation, who made the heaven and earth, help me to keep my eyes on you, my true and lasting helper! Amen.

OCTOBER 2

Waiting for the Lord

> I wait for the Lord, my soul waits, and in his word I hope. . . . For with the Lord there is steadfast love, and with him is great power to redeem.
>
> PSALM 130:5, 7B

Let me get this out there up front: *I have a hard time waiting!* There it is—I said it. I dislike waiting for people or for things to happen regardless of the reason. I have become a little better over the years as I continue to learn again and again that most of the waiting I do is out of my control, so why not just take a chill pill and get over it. However, that doesn't always work for me.

Additionally, I don't have enough space to cover all of the many times that I have prayed, begged, and cried out to God for any number of people and/or situations, only to end up waiting until the time was right or because what I wanted wasn't the best answer for me. Yes, I know waiting builds character and makes one strong, but I still have a hard time with it. I pray that the Holy Spirit will give you and me the patience that we need to wait for the Lord with hope!

Loving Lord, help me to trust your steadfast love and know that it is always with me, and help my heart and soul to indeed wait for you in hope! Amen.

OCTOBER 3

Life's Miracles

My late wife, Judy, couldn't talk, walk, or move her right side after her second surgery to remove a brain tumor. After several months of rehabilitation, she regained some functions, only to slowly lose them again, and then she passed away after a lengthy struggle. During that period, I began to increasingly reflect upon how the human body is created, grows, and functions. I eventually began to believe that many things couldn't be explained and were incomprehensible miracles of life.

Because of this I began to see the miracles present each and every day all around us throughout creation, such as: the changes of the seasons with all of their diversity of colors, plants, and animals; the beauty of a wonderful sunrise or sunset; and the birth and growth of children. My sense of awe regarding God's creation has been reinforced through my now blended family with its young children and the wonderful opportunity to see the world through their eyes.

There are so many miracles in life that can't be described in human terms—only experienced and enjoyed with a grateful and hope-filled heart!

God of new life, help me to see the daily miracles of life that you have created for all to delight in! Amen.

OCTOBER 4

Humans and Animals

> Your righteousness is like the mighty mountains, your judgments are like the great deep; you save humans and animals alike, O Lord.
>
> PSALM 36:6

This verse immediately makes me think of St. Francis of Assisi. Each year on October 4 many liturgical churches celebrate the Feast of St. Francis. The feast recognizes the life of St. Francis who is the Catholic Church's patron saint of animals and the environment. It has become a good day to have a blessing of the animals service.

My wife, Rev. Shirley Ross-Jones, began having a blessing of the animals service at the congregation she served in Louisville, Kentucky. She continues that practice at the church she is the pastor at in Alpena, Michigan. The service is generally held around October 4 to honor St. Francis and to bless the animals that are brought to the event. She also prays for the caretakers of the animals. It is a wonderful service for those who love their pets, and reminds them that God loves their animals just as the Lord loves humans.

This verse reminds us that God loves and cares for all of creation, humans, and animals alike. St. Francis is also remembered for his work and ministry with the poor and the lepers, besides his love for all of creation. May your spiritual pilgrimage open your heart and may it be filled with love for humans, animals, and the environment that God loves with an everlasting love!

Lord of the cosmos, may your Holy Spirit help me to see your presence in all of creation and inspire me to be a good steward of the gifts that are all around me! Amen.

OCTOBER 5

The Lord's Steadfast Love

> Your steadfast love, O Lord, endures forever.
>
> Psalm 138:8b

Feeling and seeing God's love when everything is going along smoothly is easy, but how about when we have pain, sorrow, or difficult times in our lives? Nowhere in the Bible that I know of does it tell us that our lives will be without challenges and totally perfect.

However, it is stated in many places that God will be with us and that the Lord's love lasts throughout eternity. When we meditate day and night on God's ways, and practice the steps of this spiritual pilgrimage, we will begin to see that *God's* steadfast love does indeed endure forever!

Loving Lord, give me the ability to trust and hope in your steadfast love, whether I am in the desert or on the mountaintop! Amen.

OCTOBER 6

Bless the Lord

> Bless the Lord, O my soul, and all that is within me, bless his holy name, Bless the Lord, O my soul, and do not forget all his benefits.
>
> Psalm 103:1–2

Blessing the Lord comes from our acknowledgment that everything we have is a gift from God. I love sunsets and sunrises and seeing them is a wonderful time to bless the Lord.

However, we can also bless the Lord anytime during the day for anything and everything, even the difficulties in our life, because God's love and presence are always with us. I would challenge each of you to find ways during this day to bless the Lord, even when you don't feel like it, or you have to look long and hard to do so. This blessing can allow you to see more of God's presence on your spiritual pilgrimage!

Lord of life, help me to bless you at all times and to enjoy the small daily happenings that are all around me! Amen.

OCTOBER 7

Love One Another

> Finally, all of you, have unity of spirit, sympathy, love for one another, a tender heart, and a humble mind.
>
> 1 PETER 3:8

There is a lot packed into this little verse. When I think of loving one another with a tender heart and a humble mind, I think of many people, but Vito often comes to mind first. Vito was my late wife's father and to some he might have appeared as somewhat gruff or tough.

However, after some initial challenges between us, he became a wonderful example of someone who loved with a tender heart and humble mind. His very life embodied this verse and even though he is now deceased, he continues to impact my life and the lives of many who knew him. May your spiritual practices allow you to be a person who embraces these traits!

God of love, help me to have a loving heart and to spread this love to those I meet today! Amen.

OCTOBER 8

Hope in the Lord

> Do not put your trust in princes, in mortals, in whom there is no help.... Happy are those whose help is the God of Jacob, whose hope is in the Lord their God.
>
> PSALM 146:3, 5

Each of us is expected to follow the rules and laws of the places in which we live, or suffer the consequences. Actions as simple as following the speed limit makes it safer and better for everyone. Good order is needed for things to flow on a daily basis.

However, this scripture is reminding us that we shouldn't put our complete trust in rulers or humans who are just as fallible as we are. Our complete trust and hope both for today and in the time to come should be in the Lord. May your spiritual pilgrimage allow you to daily trust more and more in the hope that is ours in God!

Holy Spirit, help me to place my trust and hope in the Lord rather than in humans! Amen.

OCTOBER 9

God Is Our Refuge and Strength

> God is our refuge and strength, a very present help in trouble. Therefore we will not fear, though the earth should change, though the mountains shake in the heart of the sea; though its waters roar and foam, though the mountains tremble with its tumult. There is a river whose streams make glad the city of God, the holy habitation of the Most High. God is in the midst of the city; it shall not be moved; God will help it when the morning dawns. The nations are in an uproar, the kingdoms totter; he utters his voice, the earth melts. The Lord of hosts is with us; the God of Jacob is our refuge. Come, behold the works of the Lord; see what desolations he has brought on the earth. He makes wars cease to the end of the earth; he breaks the bow, and shatters the spear; he burns the shields with fire. "Be still, and know that I am God! I am exalted among the nations, I am exalted in the earth." The Lord of hosts is with us; the God of Jacob is our refuge.
>
> Psalm 46

Please take a moment to read this psalm today and reflect on it. It speaks for itself. It gives us the assurance that no matter what comes our way the Lord is our refuge and strength. The earth may change, the mountains may shake, the waters roar and foam, etc., but God is always with us!

Help me, Lord, to not be afraid because of the floods and earthquakes of life, for you are my hope, my strength, and my help in times of trouble! Amen.

OCTOBER 10

New Birth

> Blessed be the God and Father of our Lord Jesus Christ! By his great mercy he has given us a new birth into a living hope through the resurrection of Jesus Christ from the dead.
>
> 1 Peter: 1:3

Our blended family has been fortunate enough to experience three new births in recent years. All three children were born healthy and continue to be so. Even though they live far away, it is so awesome to be a part of their lives and see them change and go through the many stages in their young lives. The joy we see in their lives increases the joy in our own lives.

Many spiritual writers throughout the centuries as well as the desert mothers/fathers have written about the fact that we have been given a new birth through the resurrection. Each day is new and we, too, are given new life daily as God's love grows within us.

We are constantly changing, growing into the living hope that is ours in Jesus, and that joy and hope alive in us can be seen and felt by others, increasing their hope as well. May you experience this new birth and new life on your spiritual walk!

God of creation, help me to see new birth in myself and in the wonderful life around me. May I share this new birth, joy, and hope with those in my life today! Amen.

OCTOBER 11

The Voice of God in a Great Storm

> May the Lord give strength to his people! May the Lord bless his people with peace!
>
> Psalm 29:11

The caption at the beginning of Psalm 29 is *The Voice of God in a Great Storm*. The psalm describes about how a thunderstorm moves over the land and causes chaos and impacts many aspects of life. In our current times, it seems that we can't go very long without reading or hearing about some part of the world that has been troubled by acts of nature or humans, be it wind, snow, rain, wildfires, violence, war, poverty, or disease, etc.

At times like these it is sometimes difficult to see or feel God's presence while we are in the middle of the event. Just living through to the next moment is all that we can do. However, this verse reminds us that in the midst of such times God's strength and peace are always with us. May you be able to feel this peace through whatever storms you encounter on your spiritual journey!

May God's peace and strength be with me even in the midst of the storms of my life and in the storms of the world! Amen.

OCTOBER 12

Complaining

> [The Lord said to Moses,] "I will be standing there in front of you on the rock at Horeb. Strike the rock, and water will come out of it, so that the people may drink." Moses did so, in the sight of the elders of Israel.
>
> EXODUS 17:6

In Exodus 16 and 17 the Israelites are very upset and begin complaining to Moses about not having any food and water. Even though God brought them from Egypt and Moses was leading them to the promised land they were still unhappy. Moses at one point mentions that they were ready to stone him. How would you have felt if you were Moses, for no matter how much had been done, it never seemed to be enough? Does this remind you of people you know today, or the attitude of our so-called modern society that constantly asks, what have you done for me lately?

In this journey, called our spiritual pilgrimage, we, too, may have times when we want to complain and whine to anyone who will listen to us. That is why having spiritual practices can give us the space and time to let it all hang out with God. These practices won't remove us from all of the challenges we face, but as this verse reminds us, God will be there with us!

Forgiving Lord, help me to be able to see you in front of me in all of life's situations! Amen.

OCTOBER 13

Hope That Does Not Disappoint

> And not only that, but we also boast in our sufferings, knowing that suffering produces endurance, and endurance produces character, and character produces hope, and hope does not disappoint us, because God's love has been poured into our hearts through the Holy Spirit that has been given to us.
>
> ROMANS 5:3–5

In our daily life, it is easy to become burdened with events happening around us and in the wider world. Because of modern communications systems, what occurs halfway around the globe becomes instant news for us. We can learn about many things so quickly and with such overwhelming detail that we may often feel as though we can't handle all of it. Many years ago, it would take days if not weeks to learn about what happened elsewhere. With the unceasing stream of news, we may be tempted to lose hope about the future of the world, and our own future as well.

However, in the Apostle Paul's letter to the Christians in Rome he wanted them, and also us, to know that hope is still there for us and for all of humankind. This hope doesn't come from any earthly source, but through the love of God. This hope doesn't disappoint us nor is it subject to the ups and downs of human life. When you hear of things in the world that pull you down, may your spiritual practices allow you to see the hope that is always there in God's love!

Loving Lord, give me the hope that is needed to daily walk in your light that overcomes the dark times of this earthly journey! Amen.

OCTOBER 14

Hope in the Steadfast Love of the Lord

> But this I call to mind, and therefore I have hope: The steadfast love of the Lord never ceases, his mercies never come to an end; they are new every morning; great is your faithfulness. "The Lord is my portion," says my soul, "therefore I will hope in him." The Lord is good to those who wait for him, to the soul that seeks him. It is good that one should wait quietly for the salvation of the Lord.
>
> LAMENTATIONS 3:21–26

Spiritual writers who want to express hope for those who are waiting for deliverance often quote the part of this passage about God's mercies being new every morning. Knowing that God's mercies are new every morning can be very reassuring to someone who is going through a difficult time where their faith is being tested.

When my late wife, Judy, went under hospice care we placed a hospital bed in our dining room where she lived out her remaining days. A monitor was placed in the dining room and also in my bedroom, which was upstairs, so I could hear her while I tried to sleep. Even if I didn't hear her at night my sleep was never that sound. When I woke up, my first thought was what I needed to do to care for her that day, and then about what was required for my job, and finally my thoughts would turn to the things necessary for maintaining the house.

After a few months of this, my emotional and physical energy started to wither. At some point, I started reading this passage during my prayer time, because it gave me hope about the future. As I started my day I needed to know that God's steadfast love did indeed come anew every morning. I would encourage you to embrace and meditate on this passage and other scriptures that remind you about and can give you hope about the steadfast love of God!

Lord of life, help me to wait quietly for your salvation and to hope in your mercies that never cease and are new every morning! Amen.

OCTOBER 15

Discipline Yourselves

> Therefore prepare your minds for action; discipline yourselves; set all your hope on the grace that Jesus Christ will bring you when he is revealed.
>
> 1 PETER 1:13

On this spiritual pilgrimage, we often refer to the spiritual practices of prayer, Bible study, and reflection. Making it a daily habit to take part in these routines is so important in becoming a lifelong disciple of Jesus Christ. Taking action, regardless of how small the effort maybe, brings us further along on our journey, and will gradually allow us to see more of God's vision for us.

This verse encourages us to prepare our minds for action as we discipline ourselves and as we set our hope on the grace that is ours because of Jesus Christ. This grace is a free gift from God through Jesus' life, death, and resurrection. However, our minds have to be engaged and alert as we take part in these spiritual practices, so that we become more receptive to the growth that is directed by the Holy Spirit. May your spiritual habits enable you to experience this hope in Jesus!

Gracious Lord, may my spiritual practices allow me to embrace the hope and grace freely given to me, and may this be shared with those I meet today! Amen.

OCTOBER 16

Hope Is Not Seen

> For in [by] hope we were saved. Now hope that is seen is not hope. For who hopes [awaits] for what is seen? But if we hope for what we do not see, we wait for it with patience.
>
> Romans 8:24–25

So much of this spiritual pilgrimage involves walking by faith and not being able to see very far ahead of our next step. This can be very frustrating for those of us who like to plan ahead and have some idea about what is coming next. However, many of the spiritual aspects of our life can't always be explained in a tangible or visible manner. God's saving grace can't be seen, only felt and experienced. Hoping in God's future kingdom takes a trusting heart.

Paul writes in this chapter to the believers in Rome about the future glory that is to be revealed. He wants them and us to know that if we hope for this future glory it is not something that will be able to be seen. For who hopes or waits for something already seen? Rather, we patiently wait with hope for things that aren't easily apparent, things unseen.

This is a very challenging aspect of the spiritual pilgrimage—to calmly hope for the future promises of God's kingdom. Our spiritual practices help us with our waiting even though the promises may not come any more quickly. May your spiritual journey help you to wait with patience for this promised hope!

Lord of grace, help me to wait in peace and contemplation for your promised hope and then share this hope with those I meet today! Amen.

OCTOBER 17

When I Cry to the Lord, My Hope Is That I Will Be Heard

> And now, O Lord, what do I wait for? My hope is in you. . . . Hear my prayer, O Lord, and give ear to my cry; do not hold your peace at my tears.
>
> Psalm 39:7, 12a

In today's so-called modern world we have countless ways of getting information and stories about what is going on everywhere. Because of all of the new and ever-improving electronic devices that humans now have, we can get up-to-the-minute news and world happenings at our fingertips. Several hundred years ago, events that happened around the world would have taken weeks if not months to reach us.

There are times when it seems that all of the world catastrophes receive the majority of the media's attention, and in much greater detail than we oftentimes need. Nonetheless, it comes anyway. One has to wonder with so much negative information coming at us, is it more than many can handle? Certainly, it's important to know what is going on elsewhere in the world and to care about and pray for those impacted by these happenings. But how much is too much, and at what point does it have a negative effect on those hearing the news?

As fallible humans in an imperfect world we need something beyond ourselves to help us cope each day with the influx of so much human suffering. The psalmist declares that hope is found in the Lord and trusts that our cries will be heard by God and we will be given peace. Being on this spiritual pilgrimage does not remove us from the hurt and pain that is all around us and throughout the world. However, daily walking the spiritual path can give us an inner peace together with the awareness that our ultimate hope is in God and not in anything of this world. May you have hope when you cry out about the trials of life, and know and believe that you will be heard!

Whenever the news in the world or around me weighs me down, Lord, hear my prayer and give me peace! Amen.

OCTOBER 18

A Lost Hope Is Now Reborn

Then he [the Lord] said to me, "Mortal [the prophet Ezekiel], these bones are the whole house of Israel." They say, "Our bones are dried up, and our hope is lost; we are cut off completely." "Therefore prophesy, and say to them, Thus says the Lord God: I am going to open your graves, and bring you up from your graves, O my people; and I will bring you back to the land of Israel. And you shall know that I am the Lord, when I open your graves, and bring you up from your graves, O my people. I will put my spirit within you, and you shall live, and I will place you on your soil; then you shall know that I, the Lord, have spoken and will act, says the Lord."

EZEKIEL 37:11–14

My late wife, Judy, and I had been married for more than twenty-eight years when she passed away. My grieving actually started before her death, for she was under hospice care for seven months before that. However, afterward I still felt somewhat like the Israelites, whose bones were dried up and whose hope was dim. I really struggled for a long time after her death, but in time started to feel better.

I learned how to live as a single person and went through some major life changes and eventually left my insurance career to enter Trinity Lutheran Seminary. There my life changed very drastically once again. The most major change was meeting, falling in love with, and then marrying Shirley Ross who had started at Trinity the same time as I did.

For me those years from the time that Judy was under hospice care, through seminary, and ending up in my marriage were somewhat like what is described in Ezekiel. The Israelites were down and out, however, God promised to give them a new spirit and a new hope. There was a new life for them in the future of which they weren't yet aware. After Judy's death, my life was like the pile of dried bones, but a few years later I was given a new and totally different life.

No matter where you are on this spiritual pilgrimage, may you look to the promises of our Lord, who can and will give you a new life, spirit, and hope. May you feel God's love on your journey and receive the gift of new life that awaits you!

Lord of hope, help me to look toward you and your promises of a new life, and may I joyfully share these promises with those I meet today! Amen.

OCTOBER 19

Humble Yourselves

> Humble yourselves therefore under the mighty hand of God, so that he may exalt you in due time. Cast all your anxiety on him, because he cares for you. Discipline yourselves, keep alert.
>
> 1 Peter 5:6–8a

One of the more challenging aspects of becoming a lifelong disciple of Jesus Christ is that of being humble. In the fast-paced, me-first, hard-charging, win-at-all-costs culture that we live in, humility is not often valued. Taking charge of situations and making tough decisions are expected qualities in today's corporate world. I worked in the insurance industry for more than twenty-seven years and realized early on that those qualities were needed in order for businesses to continually move toward their goals.

However, on this spiritual pilgrimage we are asked to put our faith in God, trusting that we'll be given the help we need to make the choices that have to be made. By casting all of our anxiety on God, we are saying that we believe that the Lord does indeed care for us and wants to walk with us on our journey. Of course, this doesn't mean that we will be free of the pains and sorrows that all humans experience nor will we have a life that is only filled with joy and happiness. It does mean that no matter what happens on our travels our hope and trust is in God who guides us and gives us strength.

Being humble is not a sign of weakness but rather an acknowledgment that everything that we have and everything we are come from the mighty hand of God; therefore, we trust in the Lord's promises rather than what humans can promise or provide.

Being disciplined and staying alert by maintaining the spiritual practices of prayer, Bible study, and reflection will increase your hope in God's promises and will enable you to humble yourselves under God's mighty hand!

Lord of life, may your Holy Spirit help me to cast all of my anxiety upon you, which will provide me with peace, and may I be able to share this peace with those I meet today! Amen.

OCTOBER 20

The Hope of Salvation

> For you are all children of light and children of the day; we are not of the night or of darkness. So then let us not fall asleep as others do, but let us keep awake and be sober.... But since we belong to the day, let us be sober, and put on the breastplate of faith and love, and for a helmet the hope of salvation. For God has destined us not for wrath but for obtaining salvation through our Lord Jesus Christ.
>
> 1 Thessalonians 5:5–6, 8–9

This passage outlines upon what the hope of Christ's disciples is established—it is based on the salvation obtained through the life, death, resurrection, and ascension of our Lord Jesus Christ. This hope allows us to faithfully live today and tomorrow and gives us the trust to love those around us and to love God and all of God's creation.

In a number of places the Apostle Paul writes about light, day and night, and darkness in describing how the disciples are supposed to live on a daily basis. He also talks a lot about being awake or being alert. He wanted his audience to be awake and sober regarding the way in which we live on a daily basis rather than being asleep as if it were nighttime. Our spiritual practices help us to be awake and alert.

When Paul writes, "for a helmet the hope of salvation," he wants us to know that we have received salvation as a gift through Jesus Christ. This gift of salvation directly impacts how we think and live and guides our daily actions. May this hope keep you awake and alert to where God may be leading you!

Lord of hope, through your Holy Spirit help me to have hope for today and for the time to come, and may this impact how I witness to those around me! Amen.

OCTOBER 21

Hold on to Hope

> Let us hold fast to the confession of our hope without wavering, for he who has promised is faithful.
>
> HEBREWS 10:23

The passage from which this verse is taken is encouraging those reading it to persist in their journey, and to hold on to the faith, hope, and love that are theirs in Jesus Christ their Lord. Because of Jesus' sacrifice we can have hope in the promises of God in the midst of our faith walk. Maintaining hope, however, in the middle of challenging times can be difficult for even the most faithful followers. This can be even more of a struggle when we're in the middle of difficult circumstances for an extended period of time.

I once found myself in a very uncomfortable situation at a time in my life shortly I'd accepted a position in Buffalo, New York, with a regional insurance company. After I had been with the company for less than six months I knew that it was a company that I couldn't work for and a city that I couldn't live in, for the long term. Talk about being in a tough situation! I had to convince my family to think about moving again shortly after we got there and I had to find another job in a different city, as there were none for me in Buffalo at that time.

I had always prayed in the mornings and at various times during the day, but because of the situation that I was in, my prayer life took on a brand new aspect. I had many moments of doubt, but I continued trying to believe that things would work out. Because I wanted out so badly, I began going to an open church during my lunchtime to pray in general, and in particular about getting a new job. I did my part in trying to make that happen by floating resumes and searching for positions that might interest me, but I intentionally increased my prayer time so that I would be open to God's help and guidance whenever it came.

Praying at noontime became a practice that has continued for me in one form or another since then. Praying gave me hope and helped me to trust in God's promises that the Lord would be with me no matter what. It took almost a year, but I found another position in a different city and remained in that until I went to seminary. The additional prayer time provided me with hope and strength especially when things seemed hopeless.

We don't always get what we are praying for but that doesn't mean that the Lord doesn't love us or has abandoned us. This long wait was a time of spiritual growth for me, and even if the job hadn't come about, I would still have been a different person because of what I had been through and how my prayer life had changed. May your spiritual practices help you to experience the hope that comes from the promises of God!

God of faith, hope, and love, help me to see that you are with me in all stages of my life, and may that assurance give me the courage to share that faith, hope, and love with those around me! Amen.

OCTOBER 22

Hope That Gives Us Great Boldness

> Since, then, we have such a hope, we act with great boldness.
>
> 2 Corinthians 3:12

In this second letter to the church at Corinth, the Apostle Paul is encouraging his readers to speak out and act with great boldness, for their hope is in Jesus Christ. He reminds them in verse 4 from this passage to have "the confidence that we have through Christ toward God." Thus, having the hope and courage to be bold on our spiritual pilgrimage comes not from our own abilities but through our relationship with God through Jesus Christ.

On this journey the Spirit may nudge us to speak out or act with boldness regarding something in which we are involved. If we depend solely upon our own wisdom, strength, or effort, we'll be limited by our own abilities. However, when our hope and courage are in God the Holy Spirit will give us what is needed to accomplish what we have been asked to do. Our responsibility is to begin taking the steps that are shown to us. We may not know where it will finally take us, or how long the journey may be, but the hope and courage that we receive will be sufficient for us to complete it!

Holy Spirit, help me to understand that my hope on this pilgrimage is in Jesus Christ and that hope will allow me to speak and act with great boldness! Amen.

OCTOBER 23

God Working in Us

> I pray that you may have the power to comprehend, with all the saints, what is the breadth and length and height and depth, and to know the love of Christ that surpasses knowledge, so that you may be filled with all the fullness of God. Now to him who by the power at work within us is able to accomplish abundantly far more than all we can ask or imagine, to him be glory in the church and in Christ Jesus to all generations, forever and ever. Amen.
>
> EPHESIANS 3:18–21

This passage was written to help the reader understand how God is at work in them and how the love of God through Jesus Christ surpasses all knowledge. God's love is not limited by any human measurement or boundary. Verse 20 gives us hope on our spiritual pilgrimage that because God is at work within us, we are able to accomplish abundantly far more than all we could ever ask or even begin to think about or imagine.

You may have some challenges in your life that seem overwhelming at the moment and you aren't able to see any way around or through them. Allow this passage to give you hope that God is at work within you and in your situation. Lean on your spiritual practices to give you the hope and encouragement to continue each day on your walk.

One of the most trying times in my life was when I started taking college courses part time while working full time in the steel mill. I wasn't fully prepared for that challenge and therefore I failed my first class. That was a very important turning point in my life. I had a full-time job in the mill making a good wage and didn't need a college degree to continue working that job. Thus, it would have been easy to stop at that point. However, I was guided to take another class rather than dropping out, but promptly got a D in the second course! I retook the course I had failed and got a C that time, and seven *long* years later earned my degree that opened the door for me in my business career.

When I took the first course the instructor stated that half of our class would not finish all of the required course work for a degree. Because I failed that course, I could very well have been in the half that never finished. However, through a number of factors, including trusting in God's promises, I was able to do far more than I could ever have imagined when I first started.

On your spiritual pilgrimage, continue to be open to the many ways in which the Lord may be using you to bring about God's kingdom here on earth as you become the person you were created to be—a faithful, lifelong disciple of Jesus Christ. Be encouraged that the Holy Spirit who dwells within you will empower you to do far more than you could ever imagine in bringing about God's kingdom into this present time!

Holy Spirit, give me the hope and encouragement so that I might be able to accomplish abundantly far more than all I might ask or imagine, and may this be a witness of your love to those I meet today! Amen.

OCTOBER 24

Called to a Life of Hope

> So that, with the eyes of your heart enlightened, you may know what is the hope to which he has called you.
>
> EPHESIANS 1:18

This short passage is very powerful in that it offers us hope in our daily walk as a disciple of Jesus Christ. Verse 17 tells us that as we come to know Jesus we will receive the spirit of wisdom and revelation and then our heart is enlightened and we will know the hope to which we are called.

Having hope in which to live as we travel on our spiritual pilgrimage is *so* important as we attempt to keep our focus on God's kingdom for the present time and for the time to come. All of us are called by God through the Holy Spirit to fulfill some role for God's ministry and mission. In that calling we have been gifted with the tools and skills to carry out whatever has been asked of us.

However, with that calling we haven't been promised that we will not have demanding challenges to overcome or that everything will be a walk along a sun-filled sandy beach. There will be times of stress as well as times of joy and thus having hope along our journey is so essential. We are not meant to go it alone or without the support, comfort, and guidance of the Holy Spirit. On your spiritual pilgrimage, may you embrace the hope and support that are available as you take part in your spiritual practices and as you walk together with others in your faith community!

God of all life, help me to receive your hope today, and may this hope give me what is needed to fulfill my calling for you! Amen.

OCTOBER 25

Hope Even When We Are Cast Down

> Why are you cast down, O my soul, and why are you disquieted within me? Hope in God; for I shall again praise him, my help and my God.
>
> Psalm 43:5

This passage outlines how the writer wants to be able to once again praise God on the holy hill of the Lord, which more than likely was meant to be the temple in Jerusalem. Even though the person feels cast down, they want to continue to have hope in God so that at the altar of the temple they will be able to praise the Lord with a harp with exceeding joy.

As we take part in this spiritual pilgrimage God makes no guarantees that our life will be without problems and stress free. There will be times when we, too, like the psalmist, feel cast down, hurt, or depressed. At such times, it seems impossible to gather the strength to be able to worship and praise God with a joyful attitude.

There have certainly been periods in my life when it was very difficult to praise God, times such as when: I was expelled from college for having too low of a grade point average; again, after my late wife's (Judy) second operation to remove a brain tumor when she couldn't walk, talk, or move her right side; and again, at the death of my mother. These are a few of the times in my life when I felt cast down and God's hope and love seemed far away.

However, during those times I felt the prayers of family and friends helping me make it through the day until I was able to find the strength to hold onto the hope that is ours in God. During your journey, may your prayers and the prayers of those around you give you the confidence to trust and believe in God's hope and love that are always with you, even when they seem far away!

Loving Lord, help me to have faith in you no matter what I may be going through at this time, and may your love be reflected in my life as I come to praise you today! Amen.

OCTOBER 26

The Hope That Is in You

> But in your hearts sanctify Christ as Lord. Always be ready to make your defense to anyone who demands from you an accounting for the hope that is in you.
>
> 1 PETER 3:15

Attempting to live with hope regarding the future may go against the thinking of many in this world who can only see the pain, violence, and injustice that are constantly reported by the news media. We should, of course, be aware of what is going on around us and in the wider world, so that prayers and compassion can be directed to those who are impacted by the destructive forces of nature and humans. When our love is focused on those who are hurting we can then take steps to do our part in helping those in need.

However, one of the more important aspects of this spiritual pilgrimage is the attitude of hope that is in us because of our relationship with God through Jesus Christ. Such hope enables us to know and trust that the future of the world isn't in human hands but in divine hands. Through our daily words and actions, we can be witnesses to those around us that hope in God is so different from any worldly hope that is based upon human effort. On your journey, may your hope be in the Lord who loves you, your family, those all around, and indeed all of creation. May that love give you the hope and courage that are needed for today!

God of all hope, help me to trust you about what is happening in my life and in the life of the entire world around me. Help me to be a reflection of that hope and trust to all I meet today! Amen.

OCTOBER 27

Hope in God's Good Gifts

> If you then, who are evil, know how to give good gifts to your children, how much more will the heavenly Father give the Holy Spirit to those who ask him!
>
> LUKE 11:13

Jesus is talking in this passage about the need for persistent prayer. He also emphasizes the importance of asking, searching, and knocking, and further tells us that if we are capable of responding to the needs of our children, how much more our heavenly Father will give us what we need. This is cause for hope for those of us on this spiritual pilgrimage, that God not only loves us but knows what we need. Because of the Holy Spirit we are not alone and will be given the daily guidance for the next step on this journey.

When we ask, God listens. Our hope is increased when we are aware that God is love and can't help but love us, all humankind, as well as all of creation. As you take part in the spiritual practices of prayer, Bible study, and reflection, allow passages like this one to encourage you on your pilgrimage. The Lord only wants to give us good gifts, but that doesn't mean that we'll always receive everything that we ask for or want. Just like a loving parent who only wants the best for their child and may withhold certain things because they may cause more harm than good, God knows what is best for us in any given moment in time.

When our hope is based on trusting that God knows what is best for us we are able to live in faith about the future and in our relationship with our Lord. May your hope be based on God's love versus the fleeting things of this world that are here today and gone tomorrow!

Lord, may my hope be in you, and you alone, for you know what I need for today and in the future! Amen.

OCTOBER 28

No More Tears

> They will hunger no more, and thirst no more; the sun will not strike them, nor any scorching heat; for the Lamb at the center of the throne will be their shepherd, and he will guide them to springs of the water of life, and God will wipe away every tear from their eyes.
>
> REVELATION 7:16–17

In our modern society, tears or crying are sometimes viewed as a sign of weakness. Some people cry easily while others hold in their emotions. I know that for most of my adult life I generally didn't cry except for major things, such as the loss of a loved one. That all changed for me, however, after I went through my late wife's battles with cancer and her time under hospice care.

Judy had two operations to remove brain tumors, but eventually the tumor came back, and there wasn't anything else we could do, so hospice was brought in to help care for her. We cared for her at home until she passed away. That entire experience caused more changes in my emotional and mental state than I care to think about and therefore I now cry more often than before that period. It doesn't necessarily have to be anything profoundly sad to cause me to tear up. I simply feel things more deeply than before and this causes me to become more emotional than I used to be. Whenever I feel anguished about something that is happening to someone in my family, a close friend, or even something happening in another part of the world, I can easily tear up.

That's who I am now. However, this passage gives hope to everyone who trusts in the promises of the Lord that all of humankind's tears will be one day wiped away as we gather around the throne of God. On your spiritual pilgrimage, may you rejoice in the hope that the future is in the Lord's hands and not in our hands or the hands of any other human!

Lord of all hope, help me to trust in your promises that all of our tears and pain will ultimately be taken away, and may that awareness influence how I live today and interact with those around me! Amen.

OCTOBER 29

Hope in God's Steadfast Love

> His delight is not in the strength of the horse, nor his pleasure in the speed of a runner; but the Lord takes pleasure in those who fear him, in those who hope in his steadfast love.
>
> PSALM 147:10–11

The Lord takes pleasure in those who fear (that is, those who worship and obey the Lord) and hope in God's steadfast love. When we worship, and obey something or someone we do so because we have hope in them. There are countless things that we can worship and put our hopes in as we live in this fast-paced society. We can worship other humans, be they sport stars, world leaders, or powerful individuals; we can also worship material things, like cars, homes, money, or a certain lifestyle; we can also worship certain institutions, like a world religion, a new world order, or some movement. The list is endless, and it can change over time.

When we worship, and obey the Lord, however, our hope is in God's steadfast love, which has always been, is now, and will be forevermore. All of the other things or people that we can worship will come and go and will only last for a certain time period. God's steadfast love may not be as visible as other things that are on constant display in our media-crazed world, but this love never goes away and is always with us.

On your spiritual pilgrimage, may your spiritual practices allow you to experience this hope through God's steadfast love and realize that this love is walking with you every step of the journey!

Lord of all love, when I worship and obey you, help me to have the hope needed for today, a hope that comes from your steadfast and overflowing love! Amen.

OCTOBER 30

Hope in the Gospel Message

> For we have heard of your faith in Christ Jesus and of the love that you have for all the saints, because of the hope laid up for you in heaven. You have heard of this hope before in the word of the truth, the gospel that has come to you.
>
> COLOSSIANS 1:4–6

We learn about hope from any number of people, places, and circumstances. While very young, if we are fortunate enough to have parents or guardians who are providing loving care for us, we learn about hope when our needs and cares are supplied. When we cry because we are wet, hungry, or sick and receive what is essential, we begin to have hope that we will be taken care of the next time something is needed. As we grow older, hope is reinforced by our extended family, grandparents, friends, and others outside of our family, such as teachers.

At some point we realize that everything that we want or need isn't always furnished, and we learn to become more selective with those in whom we place our hope, understanding that they may, at times, disappoint us. Hoping in others can be challenging and frustrating for some of us who are, by nature, trusting and open.

The hope of the faith community in this passage was grounded in the gospel message of Jesus Christ. Their hope, faith, and love sprang from the gospel's infallible word of truth rather than from parents, grandparents, friends, and anything else in this world that might fail them. We sometimes have a tendency to put our hope in things or people we see every day, but those are only temporary.

On this spiritual pilgrimage, may you trust in the gospel message of Jesus Christ, believing that you'll be given the hope you'll need in this life and in the time to come. God's promise of salvation will never fail us!

Graceful God, help me to have the hope needed to trust and believe that your message of grace is all that I need to get through today and all of the days to come! Amen.

OCTOBER 31

Scriptures Give Us Hope

> For whatever was written in former days was written for our instruction, so that by steadfastness and by encouragement of the scriptures we might have hope.
>
> ROMANS 15:4

After finishing high school I went to work in a steel mill in my hometown, Youngstown, Ohio. During that time, I started to read positive-thinking books in order to help with my low self-esteem. I read a number of them and began to use some of the methods and ideas that they expressed. There were a number of good life lessons in those books which were important to learn. They helped me, and gave me a confidence that I didn't previously have. I will always be grateful for what they taught me and how they influenced my life.

However, over the years, Scripture began to take on a much more important role in my life and spiritual journey. Those books could only help me so much; I needed something deeper. The wisdom and insight gained from the study of the Bible far exceeded what I had been able to gain from reading positive-thinking books.

I would encourage you to daily seek God's word in order to gain insight and wisdom on your spiritual walk. Scripture is meant to encourage us and give us hope about the future and the promises of our Lord!

God of all creation, may your word take root in my life and change how I view the physical and spiritual aspects of life, and may this focus be reflected in how I live on a daily basis! Amen.

November

Faith Equals Trust

NOVEMBER 1

Trust

> Then Job answered the Lord: "I know that you can do all things, and that no purpose of yours can be thwarted."
>
> JOB 42:1–2

Most of us know the story of Job, a righteous person, who endured tremendous suffering. He lost his family, possessions, and health and hit rock bottom. However, as the story weaves through countless chapters, Job is humbled and, in time, able to profess his total trust in the Lord.

Most of us, thankfully never have to go through what Job had to endure. But we all have life tragedies and events in life that cause us distress. May this story help you to trust in the Lord who is always faithful!

Almighty God, may I daily trust in your strength rather than on my own human shortcomings! Amen.

NOVEMBER 2

The Lord's Help

> Unless the Lord builds the house, those who build it labor in vain.
> Unless the Lord guards the city, the guard keeps watch in vain.
>
> PSALM 127:1

My late wife, Judy, did a cross stitch with the first half of this verse on it and framed it. She did it many years ago, and even after several moves and my remarriage it still hangs in our home.

When Judy and I were first married, we had many of the same challenges that young couples have today with a few extra thrown in. We knew that we had to keep God at the center of our marriage, as much as possible, in order to make it.

Having this verse on our walls helped to remind us that without keeping the Lord always before us, we would be laboring in vain. We were fortunate and thankful to have been married for more than twenty-eight years when she died!

Protecting Lord, help me to trust in your grace and in all my efforts help me to always allow you to do the building in and through me! Amen.

NOVEMBER 3

By Faith

> By faith Abraham, when put to the test, offered up Isaac.
>
> HEBREWS 11:17

Read Hebrews 11:7–28 for the writer's many examples of faith. This passage records the faith of Noah, Abraham, Isaac, Jacob, Joseph, and Moses. Many of these verses begin with the words *by faith*. As you reflect on this passage, think about the times in your life when you were called/asked to walk by faith and not by sight.

Our spiritual pilgrimage requires courage and strength. However, these qualities come from our relationship with God through Jesus Christ and is developed over time as we daily strive for God's kingdom!

Faithful Lord, increase my faith so that when the challenges of life come I will have the courage and strength that are needed for the next step! Amen.

NOVEMBER 4

God's Faithfulness

> What if some were unfaithful? Will their faithlessness nullify the faithfulness of God? By no means! . . . Let God be proved true.
>
> ROMANS 3:3–4a

This verse is somewhat of a tongue twister, talking about one's faithlessness versus God's faithfulness. As fallible humans, we have times when we doubt, become discouraged, or take misguided steps. It happens to all of us no matter how strong our faith seems to be or how well our spiritual pilgrimage appears to be going at a given moment.

That doesn't mean, however, that we are any less loved. God *is* love and can't help but love us. In our moments of distress the Lord is always there waiting for us to turn our focus upon God's will in our lives, versus our own desires. During your daily challenges and joys may you see God's love in all of life's situations.

Loving Lord, help me to daily believe that no matter how unfaithful I might be as a fallible human, you are still faithful to me! Amen.

NOVEMBER 5

Trust in the Lord

> Trust in the Lord with all your heart, and do not rely on your own insight. In all your ways acknowledge him, and he will make straight your paths.
>
> Proverbs 3:5–6

These are several of my favorite Bible verses that have helped me over the years. I have memorized Bible verses for decades to help me cope with the challenges of my life. While traveling in my marketing job (before going to seminary) I would write a verse on an old business card and then place it on my car dash. This helped me in attempting to keep a positive outlook as I went from one agency visit to another. I chose specific verses to help me maintain a positive attitude and a peacefulness within myself regardless of what happen during those agency visits.

Later in my career I wrote Bible verses on a white board in my office for my support, but they also helped others who saw them. Thus, memorizing and silently reciting Bible verses is very much who I am and helps me to keep my focus on God's kingdom on my spiritual pilgrimage. You might want to try something similar to assist you on your journey.

God, please give me the faith to trust in you with all my heart and not lean on my limited insight and understanding! Amen.

NOVEMBER 6

God's Spirit of Faith

> For God did not give us a spirit of cowardice, but rather a spirit of power and of love and of self-discipline.
>
> 2 Timothy 1:7

God doesn't want us to live a life of dread and fear, but rather one that allows us to become the persons that God created us to be. The writer of this letter wants Timothy, the reader, to not be afraid, for the Lord's Spirit will be with him. Neither Timothy nor we should allow the issues of life to keep us down indefinitely; God's Spirit of love is more powerful than our fear.

As fallible humans, we sometimes experience nervous, stressful, or fearful moments. But, God's Spirit can help us overcome our fears. Prayer, reflection, Bible study, and frequent worship can help move us into a position where we are more open to following the Holy Spirit's guidance in our lives as we're given a spirit of power and of love!

Lord, give me the spirit of power and love to help me overcome my fears! Amen.

NOVEMBER 7

New Adventure

> Our steps are made firm by the Lord, when he delights in our way; though we stumble, we shall not fall headlong, for the Lord holds us by the hand.
>
> Psalm 37:23–24

When Shirley and I were married, Psalm 37 was one of the readings that we chose for the worship service. This psalm holds a lot of meaning for both of us, and we knew that we wanted and needed the Lord to be at the center of our new adventure.

We both started Trinity Lutheran Seminary at the same time but had never met prior to orientation. We eventually discovered that we had many things in common: both of our spouses had died; we each had a daughter and son and both our daughters and sons were almost identical in age; we were both huge Notre Dame football fans; and each of us had been on our spiritual pilgrimage for a number of years.

We married about a month before Shirley was to begin her year of internship which meant that she would be learning how to be a pastor while I would be learning what life was going to be like as a pastor's spouse. We also had no idea where we would be living once she completed her final year of seminary work, received a call to a congregation, and then began her life as an ordained pastor!

We were also starting over in a new marriage after being single, following our long and very happy marriages with our late spouses. Thus, we knew that to begin this new adventure the Lord had to uphold us when we stumbled, for we surely would have challenges to face.

May these verses give you courage and strength whenever you face a new stage in your life!

O God, may I have the trust necessary to take the steps as guided by the Holy Spirit and the faith to believe that even if I stumble you will always pick me back up! Amen.

NOVEMBER 8

Unafraid

> They are not afraid of evil tidings; their hearts are firm, secure in the Lord. Their hearts are steady, they will not be afraid.
>
> PSALM 112:7–8A

One of the most difficult decisions that my family had to make was the one to put my late wife, Judy, under hospice care. She'd had two operations to remove tumors from her brain and had already received the maximum amount of radiation allowed. Chemotherapy would have a lot of side effects and, at best, only slow the growth of the newest tumor, not eliminate it. She had already endured several years of hospital visits, a nursing home stay, endless treatments and doctor appointments, and now she was facing another tumor growing inside of her.

The decision we made was extremely difficult. On the one hand, we loved her and didn't want to see her suffer any more than she had to. But by going under hospice care we were saying that we wouldn't try anything else to prolong her life. Our thought was to just keep her comfortable. We weren't afraid of making the choice that we felt had to be made, but it was still gut wrenching.

As you take part in your spiritual pilgrimage may your heart be steady and secure in the Lord when making tough life decisions!

Loving God, please allow me to have trust in you about all the decisions in my life and help me to be unafraid of whatever comes my way! Amen.

NOVEMBER 9

Faith to Believe in the Unseen

> Now faith is the assurance of things hoped for, the conviction of things not seen. Indeed, by faith our ancestors received approval. By faith we understand that the worlds were prepared by the word of God, so that what is seen was made from things that are not visible.
>
> HEBREWS 11:1–3

Believing in and hoping for something that we can't see requires us to trust in someone/something who is greater than we are. In my late teen years, my faith allowed me to take a step in hope while not knowing the outcome.

My hometown was Youngstown, Ohio, and after high school I got a job in one of the steel mills in town. After working for several months, I was talking with my mother and telling her that I wanted to do something more with my life. She suggested taking college courses; her suggestion, however, was a bit overwhelming to me and required a lot of faith for me to even think about doing that back then. I hadn't been a good student; I suffered from low self-esteem, and didn't have a lot of confidence; *in addition*, I didn't have any idea what I needed to do to begin college.

But with her encouragement and a little faith, I enrolled and took the first course, which I promptly failed because I wasn't ready for college work. After failing that course I could have stopped there. I was making good money in the mill and wouldn't have had to worry about taking any more courses as a few of my coworkers did. However, in faith I signed up for another course and got a D in that. Then I tried one more time at the course that I had failed and got a C in it. About seven years later, while going to school part time and working full time in the steel mill, I earned my bachelor's degree. If I hadn't taken the first course and then continued the struggle, my life would have been so very different.

Many of us may have had times in our lives when taking unknown steps was difficult to do, but we had faith to believe in something that we couldn't see. Trusting in the promises of God can be challenging because most of the time we aren't able to see beyond the next step, let alone further down the road. Our spiritual practices, however, help to increase our faith so that we're able to take steps without being able to see very far down the path.

May your spiritual pilgrimage allow you to have faith in the assurance of things hoped for, without the conviction of things seen!

God of the past, present, and future, help me to have the faith needed to trust in your promises, and may this faith give me the courage to take the next step in this journey and, in the process, be able to share this faith with those I meet today! Amen.

NOVEMBER 10

Our Faith and Hope Are Set on God

> Through him [Jesus Christ] you have come to trust in God, who raised him from the dead and gave him glory, so that your faith and hope are set on God.
>
> 1 Peter 1:21

Because of Jesus' life, death, resurrection, and ascension we have all of our sins forgiven, are in a right relationship with God, and have the gift of eternal life now and in the time to come. Through Jesus Christ we have come to trust in God and have our faith and hope set on God; it is through him that all these things have come to pass.

During his life on earth Jesus showed the way to God and the Lord will also provide people for us who will show or lead us to the right path as well. My mother's family moved from Virginia to Ohio and joined Jerusalem Baptist Church on the east side of Youngstown. My grandmother made sure that all of her children went to church every Sunday and my mother did the same thing for my three brothers and me. We were in Sunday school and church every Sunday, unless something really drastic had happened. That practice of attending church has stayed with me my entire life.

Over the years, I have moved many times to a number of different states and cities and have attended a cross section of churches. In all the moves, my family has always tried to find a Christian community of which we could become a part. Thus, through my grandmother and then through my mother I started and have continued the habit of attending worship no matter where I lived. Because of their faithful examples, I have a faith and hope set on God.

You may have had someone in your life who has helped you develop a trust in God; remember to offer thanks for those very special people who have helped you. As you continue with your spiritual practices be receptive to the Holy Spirit who is equipping and leading you to bring others to trust and hope in God!

Wonderful Lord, deepen my trust and hope in you so that I may be a witness to those whom I meet today! Amen.

NOVEMBER 11

God Has Not Left Us Alone

So Jesus said, "When you have lifted up the Son of Man, then you will realize that I am he, and that I do nothing on my own, but I speak these things as the Father instructed me, And the one who sent me is with me; he has not left me alone, for I always do what is pleasing to him." As he was saying these things, many believed in him.

JOHN 8:28–30

In this passage from the eighth chapter of John, Jesus is declaring that he is the promised Messiah as well as foretelling the disciples of his coming death. He is trying to prepare his followers for what Jesus and they would soon be facing, but some of them continued to have trouble understanding exactly what he was saying. In time, they understood, but at that moment they were confused.

Jesus was telling the disciples that his faith and trust were in God his Father who had given him the words that he'd been speaking to them. He also made it clear to them that he did nothing on his own and that the Lord who had sent him was always with him. He was revealing to his disciples and us the relationship he had with his Father.

It is important for those on this spiritual pilgrimage to remember what Jesus taught, so that we can, too, can be assured that God will always be with us. Our spiritual practices open us to the guidance of the Holy Spirit and help us to live and speak in the ways in which we'd led; we do that knowing that God will always be with us and that we'll never be alone!

Loving Lord, give me your guidance and help me to see your presence each day as you walk beside me. May I then share your loving presence with those I meet today! Amen.

NOVEMBER 12

Peace from Trusting in the Lord

Those of steadfast mind you keep in peace—in peace because they trust in you. Trust in the Lord forever, for in the Lord God you have an everlasting rock.

ISAIAH 26:3–4

Peace is a word that has many different meanings depending upon the situation or context in which it is used. In periods of conflict within and between countries, peace could be achieved when the warring parties come together and resolve the issues that divided them. From a family standpoint, peace could be attained if family members decide to forgive old hurts. A greeting of peace can also be a wish for the well-being of others at a worship service or in written correspondence.

However, true peace, a peace in which you can put your trust, comes from a relationship with a higher power. This passage talks about a peace that comes about when we trust that God is our everlasting rock. Isaiah tells us that when we are steadfast, when our daily focus and trust are on the Lord, we will be kept in peace.

Of course, we know that even with this inner peace our lives will still be confronted with the challenges, pains, and sorrows common to all life. However, the peace that comes from having a relationship with our Lord gives us the strength to navigate through those times. May your spiritual practices help you to experience this inner peace and may you experience God as your everlasting rock!

Lord of new life, help me to trust you with a steadfast mind so that I may have this inner peace and be able to share it with those I meet today! Amen.

NOVEMBER 13

A Faith That Conquers the World

> ... for whatever is born of God conquers the world. And this is the victory that conquers the world, our faith. Who is it that conquers the world but the one who believes that Jesus is the Son of God?
>
> 1 JOHN 5:4–5

A faith that conquers the world doesn't come from our own efforts, wisdom, or plans. This faith comes because we believe that Jesus Christ is the Son of God. Accepting that our faith comes as a gift from God though Jesus goes against what our culture teaches about the importance of one's individualism and one's own accomplishments. In the eyes of the world putting our faith in Jesus could indicate to some that we are weak, timid, and/or irresponsible and lacking in character and leadership ability.

However, expressing faith in Jesus as the Son of God takes courage and strength of character, for it goes against the messages hyped by society. As we take part in the spiritual practices of prayer, Bible study, and reflection we are renewed and strengthen for our journey. The spiritual pilgrimage is not always easy and free of barriers. However, God's love will be with us, even when the way is dark, narrow, or unclear. May your faith in Jesus allow you to overcome the things of the world that prevent you from becoming the person that God wants you to be!

God of all faith and believing, give me the courage and strength of character to continue on my spiritual walk, so that the worldly obstacles in my life can be overcome in Jesus' name! Amen.

NOVEMBER 14

Faith to Trust in the Promise of God

> No distrust made him [Abraham] waver concerning the promise of God, but he grew strong in his faith as he gave glory to God, being fully convinced that God was able to do what he had promised. Therefore his faith "was reckoned to him as righteousness."
>
> ROMANS 4:20–22

The story of Abraham and the faith he showed in God's promises is recorded in several places in the Bible. Abraham believed that God would do what was promised, even when things around him seemed to suggest otherwise. On our spiritual pilgrimage, we are often called upon to trust in something that others can't see or understand. You or people you know may have, at some point in life, been in a situation similar to that of Abraham.

That happened to me after my first wife's death. I slowly began to think about attending Trinity Lutheran Seminary. I had spent more than twenty-seven years in the insurance industry and wasn't in a position to take early retirement, but was given some really clear direction to go. The odd thing for me was that I knew that I was being led in the direction of seminary, but I wasn't sure why. I very strongly believed that in order to become an ordained pastor a person should have received a call from God in some form or fashion, and I had not received that call. However, as time went by, it became clearer and clearer that I should go anyway.

After I enrolled and started taking classes, people would ask me why I was there and I would reply that I'd been guided by God to come, but I didn't know why. Over time people began telling me that I would make a great pastor; however, I definitely didn't feel called to be one.

Attending Trinity required faith to trust in God's promises because I truly didn't know why I was to go. However, later on it became clear why I went when I met and married Shirley Ross, earned a master of theological studies degree, and began my current ministry.

On your spiritual pilgrimage, may you, like Abraham, have the faith to trust in the promises of God, so that when you are called to act you can do so knowing that God will be with you!

Saving Lord, help me to have the faith required to trust in your promises, and may that faith and trust allow me to follow the guidance of the Holy Spirit today and every day! Amen.

NOVEMBER 15

The Lord Is the Stronghold of My Life

> The Lord is my light and my salvation; whom should I fear? The Lord is the stronghold of my life; of whom shall I be afraid?
>
> PSALM 27:1

Throughout the Bible there are numerous passages encouraging us to trust in God's faithfulness. In this verse the psalmist is declaring that the Lord is the stronghold of their life and because of that, there is nothing to fear. We all have had times in our lives when we lacked the faith to trust God in the midst of difficult or even frightening situations. But what was true for the author of this verse is true for us today—if the Lord is our refuge, our strong fortress, of whom or what then should we fear?

Being able to trust is something that I, personally, have had challenges with at various times in my life. At one point in my professional career, one of the insurance companies I worked for took all of their management staff to an outward-bound experience with a company called Pecos River Learning Centers. Pecos River worked with organizations to help train their employees to trust one another and work together as a team while doing various tasks.

I was worried about it before I went and even tried to talk my boss out of making me go, which didn't work! Those few days took me *way out* of my comfort zone. One of the activities was to climb up a tall pole, which was at least twenty feet high, and then jump off the pole and hit a bell some distance away, with nothing underneath you! In order to accomplish this scary feat I had to trust that my teammates would hold me up securely with ropes attached to my body.

I am deathly afraid of heights and told my teammates this the day before we were scheduled to do it. I let them know that I didn't want to take part in this. However, because we had already participated in some other team-building events prior to that I came to trust in my teammates. I was able to climb the pole and jumped off it in faith. Someone took a picture of me jumping off; I still have that photo on my desk. It was a wonderful experience for me and one I will always remember and for which I am very grateful.

On your spiritual pilgrimage trust that God is indeed your light and stronghold; therefore, you have nothing to fear as you travel through life with all of its valleys and mountains!

Lord of all creation, help me to trust that, regardless of wherever and whatever you ask me to go or do for your kingdom's sake, you'll always be with me and will hold me in your loving arms! Amen.

NOVEMBER 16

Entrusted

> But I am not ashamed, for I know the one in whom I have put my trust, and I am sure that he is able to guard until that day what I have entrusted to him. Hold to the standard of sound teaching that you have heard from me, in faith and love that are in Christ Jesus. Guard the good treasure entrusted to you, with the help of the Holy Spirit living in us.
>
> 2 Timothy 1:12b–14

The author of this letter is writing to encourage the reader to have faith and also reminding them of the sound teaching that has been entrusted to them. When we entrust people with things that are valuable we expect that they will carefully guard what we've given them. This holds true whether we are talking about material or spiritual things. For some of us the spiritual things of life are of even greater significance.

What is being entrusted here is sound teaching about Christ Jesus, who abolished death and gave life to humankind (v. 10). The writer of this letter had faithfully proclaimed the good news of the gospel and the reader is being asked to continue witnessing to its message.

When we can put our trust in the promises of God that are ours through Jesus Christ, we become stewards of the gift of the gospel that has been entrusted to us. On your spiritual pilgrimage trust in the promises made and pray that Holy Spirit will guard the treasure entrusted to you. May your spiritual practices give you the direction and courage to become bold disciples of Jesus Christ!

Lord of life, help me to embrace this sound teaching of the gospel message that you have entrusted to me, and may I be able to share this teaching with those I meet today! Amen.

NOVEMBER 17

Faith to Forget What Is Behind

> Beloved, I do not consider that I have made it my own; but this one thing I do: forgetting what lies behind and straining forward to what lies ahead, I press on toward the goal for the prize of the heavenly call of God in Christ Jesus.
>
> PHILIPPIANS 3:13–14

These verses have been of great help to me on my spiritual pilgrimage. One thing that the verses encourage us to do is to focus on one thing at a time. This may sound rather basic, but it is an important aspect of the spiritual journey. When we focus on too many things at once, very often nothing is done well. Multitasking may work with some things in life, but while on this spiritual walk focusing on God's kingdom and God's will in our lives should come before everything else.

St. Paul is urging us to forget what lies behind and strain forward to what lies ahead in order to press toward the heavenly call of God in Christ Jesus. Forgetting what is behind is not easy to do for we sometimes have a need to relive or rehash past events and in the process, keep them in the forefront of our minds and souls.

However, this passage encourages us to forget what has happened in the past in order to focus on what is to come. This is where faith comes in. We have to trust that the past is in God's hands as in the present and the future. Learning from the past is an important aspect of maturing as a human being. However, once we've learned from the past we need to let it go in order to receive what is coming. It is extremely difficult, if not impossible, to hold onto the past while at the same time attempting to reach out toward the future.

May your spiritual practices give you the trust to let go of what lies behind in order to strive toward God's heavenly call!

Lord of all creation, help me to trust your promises to be with me on this pilgrimage and give me the courage to let go of the past in order to strain toward your promised future! Amen.

NOVEMBER 18

Deliverance

> I sought the Lord, and he answered me, and delivered me from all my fears. . . . This poor soul cried, and was heard by the Lord, and was saved from every trouble. The angel of the Lord encamps around those who fear him, and delivers them.
>
> PSALM 34:4, 6–7

Over the years, I have memorized Bible verses as a way to help me on my spiritual pilgrimage. Generally, I try to learn them and reflect on them during my jogging times as a way to keep my mind on God's will in my life. This passage is one of those that I've used over and over because of the support and reassurance that it gives me. It reminds me that the Lord will hear me, will deliver and save me, and that I am surrounded by the angel of the Lord.

I would encourage you to mediate on these verses to help you trust in the promises of God that you will be heard and delivered. Try to envision the angel of the Lord protecting and comforting you. Think of how parents so unfailingly surround their baby with constant love and security.

In the same way when we call upon God we will be heard and surrounded with the Lord's steadfast love and grace. May scriptures such as these verses help you to trust in the fact that God hears you and loves you with an ever-present love!

Loving Lord, help me to call out to you knowing that you always hear me and will have your holy angels surrounding and comforting me! Amen.

NOVEMBER 19

My Heart Trusts in the Lord

> The Lord is my strength and my shield; in him my heart trusts; so I am helped, and my heart exults, and with my song I give thanks to him.
>
> PSALM 28:7

Being able to trust others is developed very slowly over time as those persons demonstrate that they are deserving of our trust. As adults, we're somewhat wary of being hurt; whereas most children are by nature trusting, especially when they've been nurtured in a loving and caring environment. When a child is young and has been cared for and loved by those around them, their trust in most cases is deeply rooted. But as one gets older there are more and more occasions when we're disappointed, betrayed, or otherwise hurt by those we've trusted. When that happens our willingness to become vulnerable and trust again can take a lone time to rebuild.

The psalmist knows the importance of placing one's trust in God. Maybe they've had experiences when it felt as if all was lost or times when someone they've trusted let them down; however, they learned that the Lord was their strength and shield at all times. At the very core of the psalmist's inner being trust in God abounds.

Because of that trust the psalmist's heart exulted and sang songs of praise to the Lord. Trusting in the promises of the Lord gives us reason to also sing songs of thanks in which we can acknowledge the saving grace of God to those around us. On your spiritual pilgrimage, may you be able to trust that the Lord will be your strength and shield and in the process, may this allow you to sing songs of praise!

Lord of all life, help my heart to trust that you will be with me, protect me, and guide me, and may this knowledge give me the courage to sing songs of thanks and praise to you! Amen.

NOVEMBER 20

Faith through God's Grace

> For the promise that he would inherit the world did not come to Abraham or his descendants through the law but through the righteousness of faith. If it is the adherents of the law who are to be the heirs, faith is null and the promise is void. For the law brings wrath; but where there is no law, neither is there violation. For this reason, it depends on faith, in order that the promise may rest on grace and be guaranteed to all his descendants, not only to the adherents of the law but also to those who share the faith of Abraham.
>
> ROMANS 4:13–16

Abraham, who is often referred to as the father of many nations, is held up as one who believed the promises of God. In this situation, the promises were based on faith and not on anything that Abraham or his descendants did or didn't do as it pertained to the law. God's grace is both hard and easy to comprehend. It is difficult because we live in a society that is focused on one's own achievements as a measuring stick to determine if one's life is a success or not. On the other hand, grace seems to be less challenging because *all* we have to do is have the faith to believe that because of Christ's righteousness we are reconciled to God and have the gift of eternal life now and throughout eternity.

Having faith in the Lord because of God's grace can be tough to do because of the environment in which we live. Our culture is constantly giving us messages about the importance of working harder and smarter, obtaining material wealth, achieving powerful worldly positions, dressing for success, and having the latest technological gizmo that emphasizes one's station in life. The implication in all these subliminal messages is that unless we're up with all the latest trends we may not be considered a significant person in the world's eyes.

Please don't get me wrong, these aspects of life in and of themselves aren't the issue, but rather the importance we give to them and how we allow them to influence us can be a barrier to our spiritual pilgrimage. When the things of the world become the primary focus of our lives, causing our relationship with the Lord to take fourth or fifth place in importance, then it becomes much harder to trust in God's promises rather than the promises of the world.

Having faith to trust in the promises of God's grace is a lifetime journey. Because we all have faults and shortcomings, there will be good and not so good days of believing and trusting. Beginning and/or maintaining your spiritual practices will not keep you from the low and painful periods of your life; however, they will encourage and help you to lean on the faith you have in the promises of the Lord. God's grace will always be with you no matter what you may be going through at the moment!

Grace-filled God, help me to trust in your faithful promises that are based on your grace and love and not on any of my human shortcomings! Amen.

NOVEMBER 21

Christ Dwelling in Our Hearts through Faith

> I pray that, according to the riches of his glory, he may grant that you may be strengthened in your inner being with power through his Spirit, and that Christ may dwell in your hearts through faith, as you are being rooted and grounded in love.
>
> Ephesians 3:16–17

One of the more challenging aspects about this spiritual pilgrimage is that it doesn't take us out of the pain and sorrow of life that can overtake and sometimes overwhelm us. Even if we strive for God's kingdom on a daily basis and continue our spiritual practices of prayer, Bible study, and reflection we are still fallible humans living in an imperfect world. We will still experience death, illnesses, tragic events, and times of doubt and uncertainty.

Knowing that we are loved by God and loved and supported by those around us doesn't always take away the pain of life; however, experiencing such love does help us make it through another day. This passage is in the form of a prayer, for the writer is praying that the readers may be strengthened in their inner being with the power of the Holy Spirit, and that Christ may dwell in their hearts through faith as they are rooted and grounded in love.

This prayer is about our inner being: our heart, the place deep within us that can experience the love of God and receive the power of the Holy Spirit—the place where Christ dwells in faith. Becoming aware of Christ's presence and the Holy Spirit's power in our inner being gives us the faith to trust in the promises that God will be with us no matter what may come our way!

Gracious Lord, help me to be aware of Christ's presence through the Holy Spirit dwelling within my heart and strengthening my inner being. May this awareness deepen my faith so that I may face whatever may come my way. For you, O Lord, have been with me, are with me now, and will be with me in the future! Amen.

NOVEMBER 22

Faithful Service

> Jesus . . . was faithful to the one who appointed him, just as Moses also "was faithful in all God's house." . . . Now Moses was faithful in all God's house as a servant, to testify to the things that would be spoken later. Christ, however, was faithful over God's house as a son, and we are his house if we hold firm the confidence and the pride that belong to hope.
>
> HEBREWS 3:1–2, 5–6

Being faithful in today's world can mean many things to different people. A person may be described as being faithful to their friend, marriage, family, employer, or country, but that faithfulness can take various forms. The meaning and understanding of faithfulness can change from generation to generation or from culture to culture.

I worked for a number of different companies before I went to seminary. Moving from one insurance company to another had both positive and negative aspects to it. I left each company for different reasons, but chief among those reasons was the fact that I could no longer support the company's actions and policies. In my mind, if I couldn't faithfully work with a belief in what I was doing and didn't feel that I could represent the company's policies to the agencies that I was responsible for, then it was time for me move on. I didn't leave at the drop of a hat and generally tried to work through any issues, because I knew that there are no perfect companies. So, I would pray and reflect on the situation and if things didn't appear as if they might change, I would eventually leave for another position with a different organization.

Being faithful as Christ was to God's house is an entirely different kind of faithfulness. Such faith is based on the steadfast love of God through Jesus Christ, which is more permanently rooted than any faith that we may have in the companies that we work for or the world's institutions that we encounter in our lifetime. God's grace, love, and mercy enable us to be faithful disciples of Jesus when earthly structures and organizations will, at some point, cause us to lose faith in them. May your faithfulness to the Lord be grounded in God's love which never fails us!

Loving Lord, help me to trust in your promises that you will never leave me, and may these promises give me the faith to serve your purpose today! Amen.

NOVEMBER 23

Not Tested Beyond Our Ability

> No testing has overtaken you that is not common to everyone. God is faithful, and he will not let you be tested beyond your strength, but with the testing he will also provide the way out so that you may be able to endure it.
>
> 1 CORINTHIANS 10:13

This is a very encouraging verse, which promises that God is faithful and will not let us be tested beyond our ability to handle whatever it is that is coming our way. Also, God will provide a means to help us through it. Depending upon what you are currently facing in your life, this statement might indeed be helpful and encouraging *or* you may feel doubt and even anger rising within you as you read this verse.

Any number of things could cause you to be skeptical of the promise in this passage. You might be dealing with the recent death of a loved one, or you may have lost your job or are struggling greatly to make ends meet with the job you do have, or you may have been impacted by some weather-related catastrophe that will take you years from which to recover, or you may be dealing with ongoing family challenges that never seem to cease, the list could go on and on.

One of the times in my life when I may have questioned the promise of this verse was when my late wife, Judy, went under hospice care and we kept her at home. For more than three months I managed her care in the best way that I could, along with hospice, and things seemed to be going along okay, but then one day I hit a brick wall and couldn't do any more. I was physically and emotionally exhausted and in my despair reached out to my parish nurse, telling her of how overwhelmed I was. She arranged help for me, and a number of women from my church, and then also from Judy's church, along with a few friends, began a rotating schedule of care for the remaining three months of her life. With their assistance, I was able to regroup and find the energy to continue caring for Judy at home rather than in a facility.

On your life journey, you, too, may have times when everything *around* you and *in* you doubts if things could possibly get any worse and you are at the end of your rope. There is hope, however, even in the darkest times, because God is faithful. Help, strength, and guidance will come your way, although it may not be as quickly as you'd like. God knows what you need, so just be open to whatever is provided for you in the form of friends, family, and offers of help.

Sometimes when we are stressed and under profound pressure, we may not have the time or energy to continue with our spiritual practices. Do what you can, at least pray the Lord's Prayer, or have some of your favorite scriptures or mantra sayings be repeated during the day. Rest in the knowledge that others are lifting you up in prayer as well. Continue your spiritual practices when you're able to do so.

No matter what you may be going through trust in God's faithfulness and everlasting for you!

Faithful Lord, help me to believe that no matter what I may be going through at the moment, your steadfast love is always with me, walking with me, and carrying me when I don't have the strength to walk by myself! Amen.

NOVEMBER 24

Have No Fear

> It is the Lord who goes before you. He will be with you; he will not fail you or forsake you. Do not fear or be dismayed.
>
> DEUTERONOMY 31:8

Moses spoke these words to Joshua as the nation of Israel was preparing to enter the promised land. They were words that would give them the faith to trust that the Lord would be with them in this new place. Part of the challenge of being on this spiritual pilgrimage is that we also may be asked to go to a new place, or be guided to step out in faith to enter a different phase in our lives, or be asked to take a risk. Verses such as this one can give us the courage to move forward.

When I was a young man, I was led to take a risk and step out in faith. My late wife, Judy, and I met while we were students at Youngstown State University in Youngstown, Ohio. I grew up in Youngstown and Judy was from a town less than sixty miles away. Neither of us had ever lived anywhere else but that part of the country. When I finished my college degree my hope was to find a job in the area because both of our families were there. However, I was offered a job with a national insurance company and that position required that we move far away.

Thank goodness Judy was willing to take the risk to move away from our families. I am not sure that, had I not been married to her, I would have been willing to move away by myself. Judy had an open and trusting inner spirit which was beneficial to me at that time, as well as countless times later on.

The company moved us to Denver, Colorado, which was a great place to train for the new job, but a huge step for both of us, because we would be so far from our family and friends. The move worked out very well for us and in hindsight it doesn't seem like a really big deal, but at that point in our lives it was a tremendous step with many unknowns!

Please be receptive to what God through the Holy Spirit may be asking you to do next on this journey; it may involve risk, it may take you out of your comfort zone, and it may take you to places you have never been before. The important thing to remember is that the Lord will go before you, you will not be alone nor will God fail or forsake you. May you have the faith to trust in these unfailing promises of God to be with you!

Lord of life, help me to trust in your words of comfort knowing that no matter what I may be asked to do, you will always go before me and be with me every step of the way! Amen.

NOVEMBER 25

Faith Based on the Power of God

> My speech and proclamation were not with plausible words of wisdom, but with a demonstration of the Spirit and of power, so that your faith might rest not on human wisdom but on the power of God.
>
> 1 CORINTHIANS 2:4–5

Throughout history people have often been judged on outward appearances and external qualities. How someone dresses or speaks, together with their level of confidence or lack of it may determine how they are initially viewed. No matter how hard we may try not to judge, our first impressions are largely decided upon the outward appearance, reputation, or words of the person whom we're meeting for the first time. In a consumer-driven society that spends large amounts of money and time on makeup, clothes, and physical fitness, we often fail to get below the surface to the real essence of a person when trying to decide on their credibility.

The Apostle Paul was, according to tradition, a small and not particularly attractive man, which may have prompted him to write the words of this particular passage. He wanted his audience to understand that his power and authority didn't rest in him but rather was a demonstration of the Spirit at work within him. Paul's consistent message was always about the crucified and resurrected Lord Jesus Christ.

He said that he came to them in weakness and fear and thus relied on the power of God, so that their faith rested not on human wisdom but solely on the Lord. Paul wasn't interested in giving them grand words with an awe-inspiring performance, nor coming with beautiful clothes. He wanted his message to solely be on God's power and what Jesus had done for all of humankind.

On our spiritual pilgrimage, it is easy to be swayed by messages that bombard us all the time, words coming from many different places and sources. In attempting to discern what is really important on our journey, we need to ask ourselves, "Is this message based on someone's opinion or does it reflect God's wisdom and the life and teachings of Jesus Christ?" May that be the criteria that you use when hearing a message or sermon, as well as when you're reading and/or reflecting upon something that someone has written!

Gracious Lord, may your Holy Spirit walk with me today and help me to know what comes from you as opposed to what comes from the many other voices that I hear! Amen.

NOVEMBER 26

Who Will Roll Away the Stone for Us?

> When the sabbath was over, Mary Magdalene, and Mary the mother of James and Salome bought spices, so that they might go and anoint him. And very early on the first day of the week, when the sun had risen, they went to the tomb. They had been saying to one another, "Who will roll away the stone for us from the entrance to the tomb?" When they looked up, they saw that the stone, which was very large, had already been rolled back.
>
> Mark 16:1–4

The actions of these three women demonstrated a tremendous amount of faith; for even though they didn't know how they were going to remove the stone from Jesus' tomb to anoint his body, they went to the tomb anyway! They didn't know how things would turn out, but they stepped out in faith because that is what they were led to do. We have the advantage of reading this story two thousand years later and knowing what happened. They didn't know what lay ahead as they set out very early that morning for the tomb where Jesus had been laid, but they walked by faith.

Think about the emotions those women must have been experiencing that morning. They had been at the foot of the cross and saw their beloved friend and savior have an agonizing death. Their grief and sorrow must have been overwhelming; however, they got up before dawn to do what they felt they needed to do.

Their faith is a wonderful example for us today. Hopefully we will be given the faith to trust the Holy Spirit's guidance when we're asked to take a stand, go out on a limb, become involved in a new project, or leave behind an old habit in order to go in a new direction.

On our spiritual pilgrimage, when we step out in faith, we are trusting that we are in God's hands, and that whatever stones we may encounter will be removed. Like these women, we, too, may not be able to see any further than the very next step.

May we trust and take that step, knowing that the Lord will be with us, and the Holy Spirit will direct us. On your journey, may your spiritual practices help you to listen and receive the guidance that will be coming!

God of the future, help me to have the faith to trust in the wisdom, direction, and comfort that the Holy Spirit has for me, and may my life reflect the faith that these women had! Amen.

NOVEMBER 27

Spiritual Eyes

> So we do not lose heart. Even though our outer nature is wasting away, our inner nature is being renewed day by day. For this slight momentary affliction is preparing us for an eternal weight of glory beyond all measure, because we look not at what can be seen but at what cannot be seen; for what can be seen is temporary, but what cannot be seen is eternal.
>
> 2 CORINTHIANS 4:16–18

The Apostle Paul is encouraging his audience to not lose heart, but to remain true to their calling. Even as our bodies are deteriorating, our spiritual or inner nature is growing and being renewed on a daily basis. This passage also states that the things of this life that we can see are temporary and are only with us for a short while. The things of our spiritual life, however, cannot be seen but will remain for all of time.

I have been fortunate enough to have been given really good vision. Currently I only need glasses for reading, while most of the other times I can see well without them. I know that many people need glasses or contacts to function. My late wife, Judy, had to start wearing glasses before she was ten years old, and without a good pair of glasses she encountered numerous vision problems. When Shirley and I were married in 2002 she was already wearing glasses and wears them throughout the day. Thus, I am very thankful for the gift of good sight that I've been given.

Being able to see is a wonderful gift and my heart goes out to anyone who is without sight, or has impaired vision, and has had to make many adjustments in life. However, according to Paul, our spiritual vision is even more important than our physical vision. If we are spiritually blind, we are unable to see that the things of this world are temporary and will, in time, pass away. If our spiritual focus is on what is temporary, we can soon begin to believe that this present world is all there is; that there isn't anything else out there for us. This view could become a stumbling block that prevents us from looking beyond the hurts and sorrows of this life.

On the other hand, when we are able to trust in the promises of God and in the eternal things that we cannot see, we are much more open to the hope that is ours and that gives us the strength to continue walking our spiritual path. May your spiritual practices give you the vision and insight to look at the eternal and not the temporary!

God of all sight, may your Holy Spirit give my spiritual eyes the ability to see beyond what is here today and look forward to what is to come as it relates to God's kingdom for today, tomorrow, and into eternity! Amen.

NOVEMBER 28

Nothing Can Separate Us from the Love of God

> For I am convinced that neither death, nor life, nor angels, nor rulers, nor things present, not things to come, nor powers, not height, nor depth, nor anything else in all creation, will be able to separate us from the love of God in Christ Jesus our Lord.
>
> Romans 8:38–39

Think for a moment about the times in your life when you've thought that all was lost, or you couldn't see the end of a very long and trying situation, or someone's death caused you to become depressed and you wondered where God was in all of it. You may have had a time when you or a loved one had an illness that was life threatening, where everything seemed uncertain and without much, if any, hope for a positive outcome. All of us at one time or another may have been in these, or similar, positions.

Just reading or hearing about the tragic events occurring around the world could cause us to question whether God really cares about all of this human suffering. Tragic and horrifying world everts often pain me, because I don't understand why humans have a need to impose pain, suffering, and even death upon other humans for no apparent reason. Sometimes things feel completely out of control and hopeless to me and so I pray for all concerned, the victims, and the ones responsible for the violence, placing it all in God's hands where our only hope lies.

Reflecting on my own life, I've certainly had painful times, as we all do along our pilgrimage. The situations that have caused me the most anguish have revolved around my family. Looking back over my difficult times, such as earning my undergrad degree, dealing with challenges in my professional life, moving from one place to the other, or struggling financially at various times in my life, don't seem to be as dreadful now as it did when I going through them.

However, after my late wife's illness and death I came to realize that for me the most important things in this earthly life were love, family, friends, and relationships. Of course, my spiritual pilgrimage and my relationship with God are the foundation of my life, but right after that is my family. As time went by my focus changed and the material things that once were so important became less and less essential. The events of life have changed me, but losing Judy caused the most drastic change of all.

God's love was there for me through all of the stressful times of my life, it was just that often I couldn't see it or feel it because the pain or sorrow was so overwhelming. Sometimes I was able to see it in and through others who helped, encouraged, and supported me. But at other times, I just had to keep on walking in faith before I would once again become aware of the Lord's presence with me. Feeling God's love throughout whatever was happening in my life caused me to look at life differently.

This is a very powerful passage that is often quoted and used to encourage and comfort those who are struggling with difficult and overwhelming situations. May it support you and may you have the faith to trust that nothing, absolutely nothing, in this world can separate you from the love of God in Christ Jesus our Lord. God's love will always, always be with you regardless of where you are or what is happening on this journey!

Lord of love, help me to look for your comfort, support, and guidance no matter what I may be going through at the moment. May I daily remember that absolutely nothing in this world can ever separate me from your love! Amen.

NOVEMBER 29

Walking by Faith and Not by Sight

> So we are always confident; even though we know that while we are at home in the body we are away from the Lord—for we walk by faith, not by sight.
>
> 2 CORINTHIANS 5:6–7

Think for a moment about all of the times that you couldn't clearly see what was going to happen next in your life, and with uncertainty you stepped out in faith and went where you thought you should go. Such situations are a real test of your faith and trust in God. None of us like to fail, come up short, do something that ends up making us look foolish, or make a mistake that is costly or from which it takes a long time to recovery. In my own life, I have had my fair share of all of these outcomes. But as most of the wisdom writers have noted, "this too will pass."

On our spiritual pilgrimage, so much of our walk only becomes clear one step at a time. Sometimes even our next step may be clouded over, causing anxiety and uncertainty. Throughout my life, I have tried to listen to the Holy Spirit's guidance; but over and over again I had to step out in faith without fully knowing what the outcome would be. My journey has taken me to many different places, both geographically and spiritually. Since I left Youngstown, Ohio, my hometown, I have lived in eight different cities in six states. My spiritual practices have changed many different times over the years and have caused my focus on this life and on God's kingdom to change and evolve as well.

My history is shared with you only to show that in life and on this pilgrimage our steps may take us to places and situations that are totally new and unknown to us and that will more than likely create change in us and cause us to be stretched. All of this may make us feel uncomfortable at times and we may even experience some pain with these changes. As the Apostle Paul noted, this walk is done by faith and not by sight. May your spiritual practices of prayer, Bible study, and reflection give you the faith to trust in the guidance that the Spirit gives to you. May you have the courage to heed the discernment and wisdom that you've received, and when called to do so, step out in faith even when you can only see what is right in front of you and no further!

Loving Lord, help me to walk by faith and not by sight, keeping my focus on your kingdom and will in my life. May my steps be a witness to those around me that my faith and hope are in you! Amen.

NOVEMBER 30

Saved through Faith

> For by grace you have been saved through faith, and this not your own doing; it is the gift of God—not the results of works, so that no one can boast.
>
> EPHESIANS 2:8–9

One of the more challenging aspects of this spiritual pilgrimage to understand is that we have been saved from our sins and granted eternal life now and in the life to come because of Jesus' sacrifice on the cross, which is a free gift of God's grace and not dependent upon our own efforts. It is a gift of grace and not based on anything we have done, so that none of us can boast because of having received this gift through our own good works. Our good works come from hearts filled with joy and gratitude for what God in Christ has done for us.

Equally difficult to comprehend is the concept that it requires faith to believe in the Lord's grace and love. The good news, however, is that even our faith is a gift from God, as is our free will, which means that we can accept or reject this gift of grace. That's what so amazing about grace; grace means that there is *nothing* we can do to make God love us more and *nothing* we can do to be loved less! Our part is to be an open and willing spirit thankfully receiving this gift of grace through the faith given that God has also given to us

On your journey, may you be ready to receive this gift of grace, knowing that you are loved and cared for by God who has given you the faith needed to become a lifelong disciple of Jesus Christ!

Grace-filled Lord, help me to daily receive the faith that you have for me, so that I might accept your gift of grace which has saved me. May I reflect your infinite grace and love to all those I meet today! Amen.

December

Discipleship

DECEMBER 1

Called

> There is one body and one Spirit, just as you were called to the one hope of your calling, one Lord, one faith, one baptism, one God and Father of all, who is above all and through all and in all.
>
> EPHESIANS 4:4–6

We are all called on this spiritual pilgrimage to fulfill one or more roles in bringing God's kingdom into this time and into the lives of those around us, as well as our own individual lives. This call can take shape in any number of ways, be it large or small, public or private.

All of us are called to something; however, often it can be challenging to find what the exact call is, and even more difficult to try to carry out the call. That is why being involved with the spiritual practices of prayer, Bible study, and reflection are so helpful, to help discern our call and the steps in carrying it out!

Holy Spirit guide and support me in uncovering my daily call as a disciple of Jesus Christ! Amen.

DECEMBER 2

God Disciplines Us

> Know then in your heart that as a parent disciplines a child so the Lord your God disciplines you. Therefore keep the commandments of the Lord your God, by walking in his ways and by fearing him.
>
> DEUTERONOMY 8:5–6

I have often said that having a good marriage is one of the hardest things humans ever do. That being said, I believe that being a good parent is probably the second most demanding of our lifetime. I, of course, know that there are countless people who have never been married and/or who have never been parents, but who have certainly fulfilled difficult and challenging roles in their lives. But from my standpoint, becoming a caring, loving spouse and a nurturing, encouraging parent are right up there when it comes to the aspects of life that can be both very difficult and rewarding at the same time, often even in the same day.

This passage informs us that just as a parent disciplines a child, so God also disciplines us. A loving parent should always have the best interest at heart when dealing with their child. They want to help their children develop into healthy, productive, and compassionate adults. The role of a parent is also about preparing their offspring to be aware of things in life that could be harmful to them and/or others. It starts with the simple things of life like not running out into a busy street and progresses to the more complex issues of how to treat others on a daily basis.

According to these verses, the Lord also disciplines us and helps us grow into a deeper more mature relationship with God and with others. But, we must first be willing to allow this to happen. This passage instructs us as to how this is accomplished. If we faithfully attempt to keep the word of God in our hearts and try to walk in the Lord's ways we are in fact opening ourselves to God's discipline and discernment in our lives. Keeping our spiritual practices as a priority in our daily lives certainly helps us to walk in God's ways.

On your spiritual walk, be receptive to this discipline, discernment, and direction, that the Lord continually provides, for God loves you with the abiding love of a parent and only wants the best for you now, and in the time to come!

Heavenly Parent, help me receive what you are trying to teach me, and may this allow me to become the person you want me to be today! Amen.

DECEMBER 3

The Parable of the Rich Fool

> And he [Jesus] said to them, "Take care! Be on your guard against all kinds of greed; for one's life does not consist in the abundance of possessions."
>
> LUKE 12:15

The parable of the rich fool is told in Luke 12:13–21. Jesus uses this parable to illustrate that the purpose of life is not about obtaining possessions, but rather in being rich toward God. Read this passage to get Jesus' full message.

Each day on our spiritual pilgrimage we have to make choices, both large and small ones, regarding our focus and our attitude. We, of course, have a responsibility to provide for our families and to be good stewards of the gifts given to us. Jesus isn't saying that having the necessities of life is wrong. What he is saying is that the man was foolish because his actions denied God and those around him.

First of all, he didn't consider that his abundant harvest was a gift from God and instead began to think of his possessions as his source of security, totally apart from God, which is idolatry. Second, he failed to accept the responsibility that came with the gift of great wealth: that of generously sharing it with others, in other words, he was greedy. His focus was only on laying up all his grain and goods so that he could relax, eat, drink, and be merry for years to come. He was as poor spiritually as he was materially wealthy. In telling this parable Jesus wants us to not leave the Lord out of our daily focus and future planning, and that life isn't just about obtaining material possessions!

God of infinite love and mercy, help me to recognize that my life is not the sum total of what I acquire but the sum total of my relationship with you! Amen.

DECEMBER 4

Daily Discipline

> ... therefore be serious and discipline yourselves for the sake of your prayers.
>
> 1 PETER 4:7B

The ministry I feel called to is that of assisting Christian communities and church bodies with their spiritual pilgrimages. Any positive movement from these groups can come about with prayer, Bible study, and reflection. This is done to allow us to become the persons that God wants us to be, lifelong-learning disciples of Jesus Christ.

Many desert mothers and fathers have shown that this takes discipline, and a willing and open heart and spirit. This is something that is done is daily, and is ongoing on our earthy walk. May you find the time and space to embark on or enhance your spiritual practices!

Heavenly God, give me the daily discipline to become a lifelong disciple of Jesus Christ! Amen.

DECEMBER 5

God Wants to Dwell with Us

> I [God] dwell . . . with those who are contrite and humble in spirit.
>
> ISAIAH 57:15B

When we think of dwelling with someone we often think of people who are close to us, those who love us and want to be around us. Of course, there are other situations where we dwell with people who share a common goal or task, such as those in the military or in a college dorm. They may not love us or want to around us, but they do so for the sake of the common goal.

The act of dwelling referred to in this verse is of the nature of a relationship based upon love and wanting to be around someone. There are countless passages in the Bible that reference where God wants to dwell with humankind and, in fact, loves being with us. Our part is to be contrite and humble in heart and spirit so that we are able to receive this gift!

Living Lord, allow my spiritual pilgrimage to prepare my heart and spirit to receive your indwelling in my life! Amen.

DECEMBER 6

A Vision for the Appointed Time

> Then the Lord answered me and said: Write the vision; make it plain on tablets, so that a runner may read it. For there is still a vision for

the appointed time; it speaks of the end and does not lie. If it seems to tarry, wait for it; it will surely come, it will not delay.

HABAKKUK 2:2–3

I generally hate to wait! Sometimes I can deal with it, but most of the time I want to get moving, get on with the task, and get it done! Of course, our society doesn't help with the issue of impatience because we live in a world of instant gratification. When we (and I include myself in this) can't have what we want when we want it, we wonder why!

However, spiritual writers and the Scriptures tell us that walking this spiritual journey comes without a calendar, clock, or stop clock. We are told to wait for God's vision, even when we can't see what we are waiting for! In my own walk that has been one of the more challenging aspects of this spiritual process.

When you have moments of doubt that things are not going fast enough, try to remember that God's time frame isn't ours and the vision comes at the Lord's appointed time!

Eternal God, daily give me the patience to wait for your timing on my spiritual pilgrimage and may my waiting periods also be a time of spiritual growth! Amen.

DECEMBER 7

The Lord Surrounds Us

As the mountains surround Jerusalem, so the Lord surrounds his people, from this time on and forevermore.

PSALM 125:2

In our society, there are many ways to surround ourselves so that we feel protected. Having a well-built home with a security system, a car that has all of the latest safety features, being employed in a building that requires badges or other devices to gain entrance, etc., are some of the ways that help us to feel protected.

Trusting that the Lord always surrounds us can certainly help to bring us peace of mind and/or a sense of security. There is a song, "Jesus Be a Fence Around Me," that I love and has been recorded by many artists. The words ask that Jesus will be a fence surrounding us every day. This fence is with us as we travel, as we fight our battles, guiding our footsteps, helping us when we fall, and during our hour of weakness. On your spiritual pilgrimage, may you feel God's fence surrounding you every day!

My hope is in you, O Lord, to surround me and protect me for today and for all times! Amen.

DECEMBER 8

Rejoice and Pray

> Rejoice in the Lord always; again I will say, Rejoice. Let your gentleness be known to everyone. The Lord is near. Do not worry about anything, but in everything by prayer and supplication with thanksgiving let your requests be made known to God. And the peace of God, which surpasses all understanding, will guard your hearts and your minds in Christ Jesus.
>
> PHILIPPIANS 4:4–7

This is the Advent season, and some faith traditions hold extra midweek services as a way to prepare for celebrating the Christmas event of Jesus' birth. Another way that we can prepare our hearts for Christmas is to rejoice that God loved humankind *so* much that God came to earth in a vulnerable baby to live among us. Jesus embodied the Lord's grace, love, and mercy, and when we begin to understand the depth of that love for us, we worry less, faithfully pray each day trusting God for all our needs, and experience Christ's peace within our hearts.

Rejoicing and being involved in prayer doesn't make us immune from the trials and challenges of this life. However, they just may allow us to experience the peace given to us freely and which the world can't take away. May this Advent season be one of rejoicing and of prayer!

As I prepare for the birth of Jesus Christ, wonderful Lord, help me to daily rejoice and pray for the peace that the world cannot give or take away! Amen.

DECEMBER 9

Discipleship and Learning

> When Jesus saw the crowds, he went up the mountain; and after he sat down, his disciples came to him. Then he began to speak, and taught them....
>
> MATTHEW 5:1–2

This passage is commonly known as the beginning section of the Beatitudes, in which Jesus gave all of the "Blessed are you" statements. However, what sometimes gets lost in this passage is the fact that Jesus apparently left the crowds and only spoke these words to his disciples. Thus, he is giving those close to him the wonderful words that Matthew records in chapters 5–7.

The other lesson that comes from these verses is that discipleship involves constant learning. Jesus always seems to be teaching, both by words and through his actions. The word *disciple* means above all else—*learner or pupil*. We will always be learning about God's kingdom and our call/role in that kingdom. Striving for God's kingdom and being a disciple on this spiritual pilgrimage is a lifelong learning process!

As I take part in my spiritual practices, may I be prepared to always be in a learning mode, for this is my calling as well! Amen.

DECEMBER 10

Children of Light

> For once you were darkness, but now in the Lord you are light. Live as children of light—for the fruit of the light is found in all that is good and right and true. Try to find out what is pleasing to the Lord.
>
> EPHESIANS 5:8–10

The writer of Ephesians is encouraging the followers in Ephesus to live differently than they once did. As children of the Lord they are to leave the former ways of darkness and become children of the light. When they do so, their lives will demonstrate that which is good, right, and true, and they will be more open to discovering what is pleasing to God.

From the writings of the desert mothers and fathers, as well as those of our contemporary times, taking part in the spiritual practices would be one way to learn how to live as children of the light, versus walking in the darkness, while at the same time learning what is pleasing to God. This is a daily challenge for all of us because of the many barriers that confront us in our fast-paced and modern culture. May your spiritual pilgrimage give you the courage and wisdom to live as a child of the light while at the same time finding out what is pleasing to the Lord!

God of light, guide me to be a child of the light while surrounding me with your steadfast and overflowing love! Amen.

DECEMBER 11

Making Disciples

> Now the eleven disciples went to Galilee, to the mountain to which Jesus had directed them. When they saw him, they worshiped him; but some doubted. And Jesus came and said to them. "All authority in heaven and on earth has been given to me. Go therefore and make disciples of all nations, baptizing them in the name of the Father and of the Son and of the Holy Spirit, and teaching them to obey everything that I have commanded you, And remember, I am with you always, to the end of the age."
>
> MATTHEW 28:16–20

This passage is commonly referred to as the Great Commission. This was the final time that Jesus was with his closest followers before his ascension, as recorded in Acts 1. The message or task put forth by Jesus seems to be fairly straightforward—to make disciples of all nations.

The other great commandment that Jesus gave us was to love God and love our neighbor as ourselves. Without such love, anything we do falls short, for we are seeking our own glory rather than the Lord's glory, and are not striving for God's kingdom, but rather our own agenda.

Jesus' commission still is of real importance to us today, so if during our spiritual journey, we become a more faithful, loving disciple of Jesus, we can then, in fact, become a more steadfast participant in this divine commission.

When those we meet are able to see and feel the love of Jesus radiating through our lives in what we do and say, and can feel a genuine love of Jesus in our hearts, they may come to love God as we do. With the Holy Spirit leading us, we don't have to worry about the results or what comes from our actions, the results belong to God. Our role is to be open to where the Spirit is guiding us on our journey.

As you take part in the spiritual practices of prayer, Bible study, and reflection, may you become better equipped to share this love with those around you, and in the process help in making disciples of those who are willing to follow the path to become a lifelong, loving disciple of Jesus Christ!

God of the great commission, help me to become a more faithful, loving disciple of Jesus Christ, and in the process, be able to reflect his love to those I meet today! Amen.

DECEMBER 12

Abounding in Hope

> May the God of hope fill you with all joy and peace in believing, so that you may abound in hope by the power of the Holy Spirit.
>
> ROMANS 15:13

As we come to the midpoint of the Advent season, the frantic pace of Christmas shopping, decorating, and partying is about now reaching a frenzied level. However, for the Christian church, Advent is a time to prepare our hearts and spirits for the coming of Christ into the stillness of our souls. Advent is a time set aside to reflect on this wonderful gift of love given to humankind by God who is love.

The Advent season is a time of preparation and hope. However, living in hope can be challenging, because it is so easy to become discouraged by the things happening around us, such as the storms of nature, politics, or economics, as well as the storms in daily life. But the hope of God is *always* there, even when clouds of worry and discouragement hide God's presence. By focusing on the Lord's word and love we're given the strength and guidance to navigate through these storms. May you be filled with hope despite whatever you may be facing you at the moment!

During this Advent season, may my prayer life open me to the hope that I have from God through the Lord Jesus Christ! Amen.

DECEMBER 13

Being Purified

> But who can endure the day of his [the Lord of hosts] coming, and who can stand when he appears? For he is like a refiner's fire and like fullers' soap; he will sit as a refiner and purifier of silver, and he will

> purify the descendants of Levi and refine them like gold and silver, until they present offerings to the Lord in righteousness.
>
> MALACHI 3:2–3

This passage from Malachi reminds us that part of this spiritual pilgrimage includes being purified and refined by God, both outwardly and inwardly.

My mother and father were divorced when I was fairly young, and my mother raised her four sons as a single mom. Now that I am a parent and grandparent I marvel at how she did it! However, we made it through, and my brothers and I all became productive adults. Hearing the words "a refiner's fire" makes me think of the times that my mother tried to purify us, so that we would be better people.

My mother believed that when one of us was badly out of line, a spanking was required. This is something not condoned in our society today, but my mother felt she needed to do that at certain times to keep us out of trouble and to help us grow into responsible young men.

On your spiritual journey, may you be open to the Lord working through the Holy Spirit to purify you to become the person that God wants you to be. This will probably require change and even some discomfort for you, but God knows what is needed to purify and to refine you!

Lord of Hosts, help me to be receptive to your refiner's fire and fullers' soap as you purify me, so that I become the person you created me to be, a lifelong disciple of Jesus Christ! Amen.

DECEMBER 14

Faith Community

> And let us consider how to provoke one another to love and good deeds, not neglecting to meet together, as is the habit of some, but encouraging one another, and all the more as you see the Day approaching.
>
> HEBREWS 10:24–25

This passage is often quoted to encourage people to worship regularly with a faith community. From my own personal experience, being connected to and involved with a worshipping community has been an important part of my spiritual pilgrimage. Over the years, the faith communities I have attended have been a great source of spiritual support and help to me. I realize that there are no perfect faith communities, just as there are no perfect people. All of the communities had aspects that I didn't always like but the good far outweighed the bad. My family and I have been formed and blessed by faith communities diverse in geography, culture, and theology.

Jerusalem Baptist Church in Youngstown, Ohio, was the cradle where my faith formation began. While attending Youngstown State University, I became involved in its Campus Christian Fellowship. Being a part of this organization and others on campus enabled me to participate in an environment whereby people from different faiths, backgrounds, and cultures could come together in unity.

Following my marriage to my late wife, Judy, St. Elizabeth Ann Seton Catholic Church in Pickerington, Ohio, was the faith community that nurtured my family for a number of years. As I moved around the country professionally, my family and I were also involved in several other Catholic churches. I later joined Epiphany Lutheran Church (ELCA), also in Pickerington, where I once again became involved in various ministries.

Other faith communities were Bethany Lutheran Church in Louisville, Kentucky, where I was their worship leader and spiritual consultant, as well as Christ Lutheran Church, also in Louisville, where I served as director of small group ministries. The two churches that Shirley has served as pastor has also contributed to my walk, St. Paul Lutheran Church in Louisville and St. Paul Lutheran Church in Alpena, Michigan.

On one's spiritual pilgrimage it is vitally important to be part of a faith-filled community. If you are a part of one that nurtures you in your journey, that is a wonderful support. However, some of you may have even been hurt by a community and are struggling with joining another. Keep searching because God is alive and present in Christ's church!

Holy Spirit, help me to embrace the spiritual aspects of community life that can assist me in becoming a lifelong disciple of Jesus Christ, and may that support and love be something that I can share with others! Amen.

DECEMBER 15

Written on Our Hearts

> . . . and I [the Lord] will write it [the law] on their hearts; and I will be their God, and they shall be my people.
>
> JEREMIAH 31:33B

In this passage, Jeremiah writes about the fact of how the Lord will make a new covenant with God's people, which will be written upon their hearts. What is written on one's heart is something that will last and becomes part of one's entire being. Through prayer, Bible study, and reflection God's word becomes part of our spiritual essence. Another way that God's word is written on our hearts is by memorizing Bible verses that hold value for us.

Each week I memorize and focus on a different Bible verse. Memorizing Bible verses is something that I have done most of my life and it helps me cope with the challenges of life. Memorizing Bible verses has also helped keep my mind and heart on God's kingdom each day of my spiritual pilgrimage; may it do the same for you!

May your word, O Lord, dwell in my heart and may it help me know that you are my God and that I am your child! Amen.

DECEMBER 16

Here Is Your God

Strengthen the weak hands, and make firm the feeble knees. Say to those who are of a fearful heart, "Be strong, do not fear! Here is you God."

ISAIAH 35:3–4A

This passage from Isaiah is used during the Advent season in some faith traditions. Advent is a time of waiting and preparing anew for the birth of the Christ within us and who is still to come. Some of the imageries expressed in this passage paints a picture of God at work in our lives.

Verse 3 talks about the hands and knees being made stronger. We use our hands and knees to pray and to seek God's will in our lives. When our limbs are faithfully engaged in prayer, we become more aware of the Lord's presence in our lives. Then God can strengthen our fearful hearts and make us strong. Isaiah wanted the Israelites to know that the Lord was with them, "Here is your God." God is also walking with us even when we can't see or feel the Lord's presence, God is here. May you sense this presence in your lives on your Advent journey!

Loving Lord, allow me to wait and watch anew for Jesus' birth in my heart as I use my hands, knees, and entire body during my worship and prayer times! Amen.

DECEMBER 17

God Walking Among Us

> If you follow my statues and keep my commandments and observe them faithfully, . . . I will place my dwelling in your midst, and I shall not abhor you. And I will walk among you, and will be your God, and you shall be my people.
>
> LEVITICUS 26:3, 11–12

God walking with us and among us is a very meaningful image, especially when we are going through trying times in our lives. Such a time for me was when my late wife, Judy, was placed under hospice care. After two operations to remove brain tumors, radiation treatments, countless doctor and hospital visits, exams and procedures, our family decided that nothing more could be done and thus we called in hospice.

We set up a hospital bed in our dining room and tried to make her comfortable there. The hospice staff was very helpful to us. During that time, I tried to continue to work from my home while also caring for Judy when the hospice staff wasn't available. That was my routine for more than three months until one day I hit a wall and couldn't do it anymore, I was emotionally and physically exhausted. I called my church parish nurse and assistant pastor for help.

The parish nurse arranged for some women of the church to come by and help with Judy's care. Help also came from women at Judy's church and a few other friends who provided support. Without their help, I don't know how I would have made it. During that time, we never put Judy in a nursing home and she died peacefully at home. These women were like angels to me because of what they did. As angels, they were God's agents to me as they walked with me during that time. They expressed God's love to Judy, my family, and me.

When we attempt to strive for God's kingdom and will in our lives our spirit becomes more willing to see how the Lord comes to dwell and walk with us. During your spiritual pilgrimage, may you look for ways that God may be walking with you and among you at all times of your life!

Lord of my journey, help me to see you and feel you around me, and may your presence give me the courage to share this gift with those I meet today! Amen.

DECEMBER 18

Growing in the Knowledge of God

> For this reason, since the day we heard it, we have not ceased praying for you and asking that you may be filled with the knowledge of God's will in all spiritual wisdom and understanding, so that you may lead lives worthy of the Lord, fully pleasing to him, as you bear fruit in every good work and as you grow in the knowledge of God.
>
> COLOSSIANS 1:9–10

As this passage notes, we are to grow in God's will in all spiritual wisdom and understanding. Our knowledge about the Lord's will in our life and about God's kingdom will change and evolve over time. Being a lifelong disciple of Jesus Christ carries with it the responsibility to always be looking for ways to grow in our faith and in the knowledge of God.

I entered Trinity Lutheran Seminary because I believed God was leading me to do that. I didn't, however, know why I was going, only that I was meant to go. One thing I was very certain of was that I wasn't called to be an ordained pastor.

Throughout my adult life, I had always believed that I knew the Bible fairly well and was firm in many of my faith beliefs. However, the first quarter at Trinity was one of the most challenging and demanding times of my life. The remaining quarters had their stresses as well, but that first quarter was off the charts.

A number of things that I understood to be true about the Bible were challenged or radically altered during that period. Some of the classes and the discussions caused me to seriously reflect on and reevaluate a number of my long-held faith beliefs. Throughout the two-year program, I encountered many new ideas that helped me to grow in my knowledge of God and my understanding of the world. I received a master of theological studies degree marking the end of my formal theological education; however, many years later I'm still reading, reflecting, learning, and being challenged as my faith continues to grow, deepen, and change.

Each day in our spiritual pilgrimage we receive wisdom and new understanding from the Holy Spirit regarding God's will for our life. We should always endeavor to grow in the knowledge of God's will by being open to new insights and revelations even when they challenge what we once thought to be truth.

Lord of wisdom and understanding, help me to embrace the Holy Spirit who is moving me along on this spiritual journey and in the process changing me! Amen.

DECEMBER 19

Advent Anxiety

> It is these worldly people, devoid of the Spirit, who are causing divisions. But you, beloved, build yourselves up on your most holy faith; pray in the Holy Spirit; keep yourselves in the love of God; look forward to the mercy of our Lord Jesus Christ that leads to eternal life.
>
> JUDE 19–21

Only a few more days until Christmas. So much of the society is focused on the material aspects of the celebration of Christmas. We have endured our fair share of ads trying to convince us that until we buy the latest new thing our life will be less than perfect. We know that this isn't true, however, the daily message of buy, buy, buy can weigh us down or put us off our spiritual center.

During this Advent season continue with your spiritual practices of prayer, Bible study, and reflection to keep you focused on where the Holy Spirit may be leading you. What we buy today only satisfies for the short term, but God's love will last for eternity. May there be little or no division in your life about what is really important at this time of the year and all of the days of your life!

Loving Lord, during this Advent season may I keep my mind on what is important for me today and for the time to come! Amen.

DECEMBER 20

Our Cross / Our Calling

> He [Jesus] called the crowd with his disciples, and said to them, "If any want to become my followers, let them deny themselves and take up their cross and follow me."
>
> MARK 8:34

These words of Jesus are also recorded in Matthew and Luke' gospels emphasizing their importance to Jesus' followers then and now. Many who followed Jesus did so because of his miracles, but they failed to grasp the deeper meaning and purpose of his ministry.

He told them that to follow him they had to deny themselves and then take up their cross. Jesus knew that he would be killed because of his teaching and his identity as God's Son. He was telling those who wanted to follow him to take up their cross—not someone's cross or Jesus' cross—but their cross.

The idea of taking up one's cross means that all of us, no matter what our age, skin color, sex, place of birth, education, or social status, are called to fulfill a specific role in bringing God's kingdom into this time and place. Your cross or calling is different from mine or that of your family members, neighbors, coworkers, or members of your church family. As you take part in your spiritual pilgrimage ask the Holy Spirit to reveal to you, what cross Jesus is asking you to willingly pick up and to carry. Be aware that the cross that we're carrying can and probably will change as we move along on our path!

Lord of life, today guide me to pick up my cross and embrace your call in my life! Amen.

DECEMBER 21

Bearing Fruit

> [Jesus said] I am the true vine, and my Father is the vinegrower. He removes every branch in me that bears no fruit. Every branch that bears fruit he prunes to make it bear more fruit. You have already been cleansed by the word that I have spoken to you.
>
> JOHN 15:1–3

I don't claim to know much about farming or growing gardens; however, I have known many people who were really good at it. One such person was my late wife's father, Vito, who knew a lot about growing things. He had a huge area on his property in Ashtabula, Ohio, where he generally put in a very large garden, until his health slowed him down.

Every morning, before the sun got too hot, he would go into his garden to weed, clear out debris, prune, and water his garden. He knew that in order to have a good harvest much work was needed and he willingly and lovingly did that. He loved seeing things grow and of course grew more than he could ever use, so he gave away a lot of his produce. Whenever our family visited him during the summer, we always went home well supplied with wonderful fruits and vegetables from his garden.

Vito and countless other gardeners and farmers have always known that pruning is necessary for growth and for having a great garden. Jesus understood that the branches in the vineyard (i.e., his followers) also required pruning in order to grow and mature and therefore had been cleansed (pruned) by his words.

As followers of Jesus we are like branches in need of pruning in order to bear more fruit. The removal of the unfruitful branches and the pruning or cleansing may at times be painful; however, it is a necessary step in order for us to bear the fruit of God's kingdom. We may not fully understand this process when it is happening, but often as we look back on those times in our lives, we're able to understand why the removal or pruning was necessary.

As you take part in the spiritual practices of prayer, Bible study, and reflection may you be open to allowing God's word and the Holy Spirit to remove, prune, and cleanse those parts of your inner being that will allow you to become the person that God wants you to be!

Lord of all creation, help me to be a willing branch ready to be pruned so that your fruit can grow in me, and may that growth be shared with those I meet today! Amen.

DECEMBER 22

The Cost of Discipleship

> Then Jesus told his disciples, ... "For those who want to save their life will lose it, and those who lose their life for my sake will find it. For what will it profit them if they gain the whole world but forfeit their life? Or what will they give in return for their life?"
>
> MATTHEW 16:24A, 25–26

This message may confuse some who are living in this fast-paced, me-first society. Many in our current culture are not able to understand nor do they even care to think about losing their life for something they can't control and which may not increase their importance in the eyes of the world. However, the gospel writers must have thought that this message was important enough that it is expressed in all four Gospels.

Jesus wanted his disciples and us to know the cost of following him and striving to become his lifelong disciple. The passage from Matthew comes immediately after Jesus tells Peter that he was setting his mind on human things rather than divine things. Therefore, losing one's life for Jesus' sake means putting God's will and kingdom *first* in our lives rather than upon those things on which we and the world are so focused.

Giving up of one's life wasn't and isn't for the faint of heart, but what we must remember is that when we lose our life for Jesus' sake we actually find it. We will be more alive and living the life for which God created us with a deep sense of purpose and great joy. On your spiritual pilgrimage, may you be willing to risk losing your life for Jesus' sake and for God's kingdom here and now!

Holy Spirit, give me the courage and wisdom to be able to lose my life for Jesus' sake, and with this new life allow me to be a witness to others of Jesus' saving, life-giving grace! Amen.

DECEMBER 23

Joseph and Change

> When Joseph awoke from sleep, he did as the angel of the Lord commanded him; he took her as his wife.
>
> MATTHEW 1:24

Christmas is nearly here! The Advent season is almost over. All those last-minute Christmas chores are being hastily completed. However, for a moment, let's think about how important Joseph's act of faith was to the birth of Jesus. Joseph had planned to quietly dismiss Mary, as was his right in the culture at that time. However, he changed his mind and contrary to his own beliefs, did as the angel of the Lord had commanded.

Just as the angel of God came to Joseph causing him to change what he had thought of doing, so, too, God through the Holy Spirit speaks to us through prayer, Scripture, a spiritual book, or in any number of ways. On this spiritual pilgrimage, hopefully we, also, are open and willing to change direction as was Joseph. The Spirit's message may cause us to move in a new direction modifying our plans and following those that God has shown us!

On my Advent/spiritual pilgrimage may I be willing to follow the Holy Spirit and like Joseph be willing to be changed for the sake of God's kingdom! Amen.

DECEMBER 24

Christmas Eve

> When they saw this, they made known what had been told them about this child; and all who heard it were amazed at what the shepherds told them. But Mary treasured all these words and pondered them in her heart. The shepherds returned, glorifying and praising God for all they had heard and seen, as it had been told them.
>
> LUKE 2:17–20

It's always amazing how the Christmas story touches our hearts anew every year. The birth of God's Son is a mystery and an awesome gift all wrapped up in swaddling clothes. Because God became incarnate in a Jewish baby born to Mary more than two thousand years ago, the *world* was forever changed! We are also profoundly changed because of Jesus' birth, and like the shepherds we also praise the Lord for this gift of pure love. We, too, like the shepherds, are compelled by God's amazing love to let others know what we have heard, seen, and experienced in our own lives because of this gift.

Jesus' birth certainly impacts our spiritual pilgrimage—how we live in the world, what we believe, and how we worship. Just as the birth of Jesus changed the world and daily changes us, we like the shepherds and angels need to proclaim the good news of Christ's birth to others through what we say and do each day. As this Advent season comes to a close, may the celebration of Jesus' birth be a reason to glorify and praise God in all times and places!

Lord of life, help me to be a reflection of this fantastic gift of love from you, and may this gift impact how I live today and every day! Amen.

DECEMBER 25

Christmas Day

> And the Word became flesh and lived among us, and we have seen his glory, and the glory as of a father's only son, full of grace and truth.
>
> JOHN 1:14

Remarkably Christmas Day marks the end of the Christmas season for the majority of people in our culture. By Christmas night the post-Christmas blues are setting in—all of the shopping, parties, baking, gift—wrapping, overeating, etc., are drastically winding down or abruptly ending. Hopefully you have had or will take the opportunity to reflect on what the Word becoming flesh and living among us truly means for humankind and for you and your loved ones.

As the beginning of John's gospel tells us, this Word was with God in the beginning of creation and all things came into being through him. In him was life, and the life was the light of all people, which means you and me and everyone around us now, in the past, and in the future as well!

With this knowledge, we can go forward with the faith and trust that Jesus' life is light for us today and forever. May this day and what it means to the world give you the courage to continue on your spiritual pilgrimage so that Jesus' light is reflected in all that you do!

Thank you, O Lord, for Jesus, the Word made flesh on that long-ago Christmas, and living among us today. May his presence fill me with joy, so that I willingly share my life and love with others! Amen.

DECEMBER 26

Jesus Presented to the Lord

> After eight days had passed, it was time to circumcise the child; and he was called Jesus, the name given by the angel before he was conceived in the womb. When the time came for their purification according to the law of Moses, they brought him up to Jerusalem to present him to the Lord.
>
> LUKE 2:21–22A

The day after Christmas, when many take a collective deep breath and hopefully quietly reflect on the wondrous gift that has been given to us by the God of creation. Possibly you may do just that before starting up again with all of the harried aspects of our modern society. It's a wonderful day in which to contemplate the words in Luke. Joseph and Mary named their newborn son Jesus, as they were guided to do. They also took him to the temple to present him to the Lord to be circumcised according to Jewish practice.

We may not be able to present anyone in a temple. However, our children, grandchildren, nieces, nephews, stepchildren, foster children, children in our lives, or any children who are hurting or struggling near or far away, etc., can be prayed for and we can present their needs to the Lord.

During this Christmas season, may it be a time to continue to reflect on the miracle of Jesus' birth and all that means in our lives. Consider also holding up in prayer, presenting to the Lord, those children near or far who are in need of someone's love, care, concern, and prayers!

God of new birth, please hear my prayers for children everywhere, and may your love surround them this day! Amen.

DECEMBER 27

Bonding Time

When I was working in the business world, I was generally able to take time off between Christmas and the New Year. This period became a special bonding period for my immediate family when our children were young and we lived in Denver and then northern California. Our extended families were back in northeast Ohio and so we often spent those Christmas holidays alone, away from parents, grandparents, siblings, and cousins.

We usually received some board games as Christmas gifts and during the Christmas break we played games for hours and thoroughly enjoyed being together. I look back on that time as a blessing and a very special gift for we grew closer as a family and had a lot of fun together. May this be a time of reconnecting, bonding, and fun for you, your family, and close friends!

God, help me to look for times and ways to bond with family and friends during the holidays and throughout the year! Amen.

DECEMBER 28

Discipleship and Stewardship

> Do not store up for yourselves treasures on earth, where moth and rust consume and where thieves break in and steal; but store up for yourselves treasures in heaven, where neither moth nor rust consumes and where thieves do not break in and steal. For where your treasure it, there your heart will be also.
>
> Matthew 6:19–21

These verses are taken from the passage that is commonly referred to as the Sermon on the Mount. This part of Matthew's gospel takes place on a mountain where Jesus went to escape the crowds and speak to his disciples. He was teaching those who were closest to him and who had made a commitment to follow him. These messages weren't for everyone, but rather for those who wanted to become his faithful disciple.

What Jesus told them was contrary to the thinking of that time, and in fact of all time. He encouraged them to put their trust in the things of God and God's kingdom, rather than trusting in the things of the world such as their possessions and properties (for us today our savings accounts, stock or retirement funds), for where their treasure is, so would their heart be also.

Jesus pointed out that being a follower of his required that one look at treasures from a stewardship standpoint instead of an ownership basis. Disciples understand that earthly possessions are gifts to be wisely used for bringing about God's kingdom here and now, rather than being hoarded, stored, and subject to rust, moths, and thieves. Thus, if one's heart is focused on heavenly matters the use of material possessions will be much different than if the heart is centered on storing up treasures here on earth.

May your spiritual pilgrimage allow you to become faithful stewards of all of the gifts that have been given to you on your journey to become a lifelong disciple of Jesus Christ!

God of all creation, help me to see that everything that I have is a gift from you, and help me to be a good steward of this treasure as I strive to be your faithful disciple today and always! Amen.

DECEMBER 29

Strengthened and Encouraged

> There they [Paul and Barnabas] strengthened the souls of the disciples and encouraged them to continue in the faith, saying, "It is through many persecutions that we must enter the kingdom of God."
>
> Acts 14:22

Paul and Barnabas traveled from city to city proclaiming the good news of Jesus Christ and many became his disciples. When they returned to Antioch they spoke encouraging words to Jesus' followers. They wanted the disciples to be strengthened in their souls and encouraged in their faith.

Think about the times when you have been strengthened and encouraged by people around you, as well as times when you were able to do the same for others. This has happened many times in my life, and one of the most memorable was after my late wife's second surgery to remove a brain tumor. After this operation, she couldn't talk, walk, or move her right side. She spent twelve weeks in two different hospitals and a nursing home recovering from the effects of the surgery, receiving radiation, and relearning basic life functions again.

Needless to say, that was a very trying time for my family and me. During those weeks, I was with her for some period of every day. Needless to say, I eventually grew extremely tired and became emotionally exhausted. Even though it was very demanding, we were certainly strengthened and encouraged by the many people who prayed for us, visited us, called us, sent us cards, brought meals to us, and were there to support us and help us in any way that they could.

That experience certainly changed me and caused me to see so many things in life differently. I know that I am now much more empathetic to others struggling with all kinds of difficulties and tragedies. I will always remember with gratitude those who helped us and became God's hands and feet of love for us. Without such love and compassion that time would have been even more challenging and lonely. May we all strive like Paul and Barnabas and others to strengthen the souls and offer encouragement to those who are experiencing challenges in life, so that they can feel God's love through us!

God of all love, strengthen and encourage me on this spiritual pilgrimage and in the process, allow me to be a support for others whom I meet today! Amen.

DECEMBER 30

Living a Worthy Life

> Only, live your life in a manner worthy of the gospel of Christ, so that, whether I come and see you or am absent and hear from you, I will know that you are standing firm in one spirit, striving side by side with one mind for the faith of the gospel.
>
> PHILIPPIANS 1:27

As we come to the end of another year many of us reflect on what has transpired over the past twelve months. This can be a positive or less than positive review depending upon how we see the year. More than likely, there were probably both highs and lows that may have impacted us in many different ways. Looking back over the events, appointments, celebrations, etc., written on the past year's calendar or looking at photos from the year are but two ways to reminisce and reflect upon the last twelve months. Consider carving out a time to discuss and share the meaningful events of the year with loved ones and family members.

Something else that is often done at this time is to look forward to the coming year with all of its possibilities and concerns. Of course, trying to predict what the new year will be like is impossible for us to do. Instead, we should take it one day at a time, giving thanks for each new day and God's presence with us; however, not worrying about or anticipating what the future might hold can be very difficult to do.

This passage from Philippians encourages us to live life in a manner that is worthy of the gospel of Jesus Christ. Again, this can be hard to do because of the many competing forces around us. Read verses 21–30 of this passage for more clarification regarding St. Paul's thinking and circumstances. Living a worthy life takes effort each day as we try to the best of our ability to keep our hearts and minds focused on God's will in our lives while striving for God's kingdom.

Be encouraged to continue on your spiritual pilgrimage in the upcoming year striving, with the help of the Holy Spirit, to live a life that is worthy of your calling.

Lord of all creation, help me to live a worthy life in this upcoming new year, and may that life be a witness to others of your infinite grace, love, and mercy! Amen.

DECEMBER 31

Beginnings and Endings

> For everything there is a season, and a time for every matter under heaven: a time to be born, and a time to die, a time to plant, and a time to pluck up what is planted.
>
> ECCLESIASTES 3:1–2

When my late wife, Judy, and I were married we had Scripture verses read from the book of Ecclesiastes. We felt that this passage had a special meaning for us as we started our married life. We were from very different cultural backgrounds as well as religious ones; she was raised in the Catholic faith and I was bought up in the American Baptist tradition. We had a few challenges as we began our life together, but we both shared a strong faith in God and the spiritual aspects of our lives helped us to overcome the issues that confronted us.

As the writer of Ecclesiastes tells us, life holds many seasons of beginnings and endings. When Judy's cancerous brain tumors ended her life, we had been married for more than twenty-eight years. The end of her life and, thus, the ending of our marriage was a lot more difficult than the beginning of our life together. Through our time together our faith in God and each other became stronger over the years. On your spiritual pilgrimage, may you be open to new beginnings and endings and be willing to follow where the Holy Spirit may be guiding you!

Eternal Lord, give me the courage to embrace the new beginnings and endings in my life throughout this spiritual pilgrimage as a disciple of the Lord Jesus Christ! Amen.

Some final words from Jesus about becoming his disciple!

Do not store up for yourselves treasures on earth, where moth and rust consume and where thieves break in and steal; but store up for yourselves treasures in heaven, where neither moth nor rust consumes and where thieves do not break in and steal. For where your treasure is, there your heart will be also.

The eye is the lamp of the body. So, if your eye is healthy, your whole body will be full of light; but if your eye is unhealthy, your whole body will be full of darkness. If then the light in you is darkness, how great is the darkness!

No one can serve two masters; for a slave will either hate the one and love the other, or be devoted to the one and despise the other. You cannot serve God and wealth.

Therefore I tell you, do not worry about your life, what you will eat or what you will drink, or about your body, what you will wear. Is not life more than food, and the body more than clothing? Look at the birds of the air; they neither sow nor reap nor gather into barns, and yet your heavenly Father feeds them. Are you not of more value than they? And can any of you by worrying add a single hour to your span of life? And why do you worry about clothing? Consider the lilies of the field, how they grow; they neither toil nor spin, yet I tell you, even Solomon in all his glory was not clothed like one of these. But if God so clothes the grass of the field, which is alive today and tomorrow is thrown into the oven, will he not much more cloth you-you of little faith? Therefore do not worry, saying, "What will we eat?" or "What will we drink?" or "What will we wear?" For it is the Gentiles who strive for all these things; and indeed your heavenly Father knows that you need all these things. But strive first for the kingdom of God and his righteousness, and all these things will be given to you as well.

So do not worry about tomorrow, for tomorrow will bring worries of its own. Today's trouble is enough for today.

MATTHEW 6:19–34

www.ingramcontent.com/pod-product-compliance
Lightning Source LLC
Chambersburg PA
CBHW071230230426
43668CB00011B/1377